D1164657

**CALGARY PUBLIC LIBRARY
OCTOBER 2013**

*"Oh how I wish that I had been raised a Christian in such a company as this! There is obvious delight in each one's sharing. The words, photographs, and recipes all speak with loving purpose—to celebrate life with each other around a simple table! Pass this book around; the celebration must continue!"*
— GRAHAM KERR, AUTHOR OF TWENTY-NINE BOOKS ON FOOD AND LIFESTYLE, AND FORMER HOST OF *THE GALLOPING GOURMET* TELEVISION SHOW

*"I loved, loved, loved this cookbook. In addition to delicious recipes, it includes cooking tips and inspiring notes to honor the significant moments of life: from a baby's birth to the passing of loved ones, and everything in between."*
— SUZANNE WOODS FISHER, AUTHOR OF *AMISH PEACE: SIMPLE WISDOM FOR A COMPLICATED WORLD*

*"Mennonite Girls Can Cook Celebrations is the perfect resource for meals and more as you plan for occasions in life that turn into memories you'll cherish for years to come. The seemingly endless recipes and helpful ideas flow from the pages to your kitchen."*
— BETH WARDEN, HOST OF *TODAY'S FAMILY WITH BETH WARDEN* SYNDICATED RADIO SHOW

"Food has the ability to build community, and Mennonite Girls Can Cook Celebrations is the proof! Along with their thoughtful reflections, these delicious recipes invite us to slow down and celebrate the joy of breaking bread together."
— NANCY SLEETH, AUTHOR OF *ALMOST AMISH: ONE WOMAN'S QUEST FOR A SLOWER, SIMPLER, MORE SUSTAINABLE LIFE* AND COFOUNDER OF BLESSED EARTH

"The girls from Mennonite Girls Can Cook live by a simple motto: 'Serve to bless, not to impress.' But if their acclaimed first cookbook is any indication, their eagerly anticipated follow-up book will both bless and impress everyone, even those eating gluten-free."
— JEANINE FRIESEN, EDITOR OF *THEBAKINGBEAUTIES.COM* AND AUTHOR OF *THE EVERYTHING GUIDE TO LIVING GLUTEN-FREE*

"The best celebrations are centered around feasts served on beautifully decorated tables. Thanks to the Mennonite Girls, we discover myriad reasons to celebrate. They not only share their secrets of feast-making, but offer nourishing food for the soul as well."
— LELA GILBERT, AUTHOR OF *SATURDAY PEOPLE, SUNDAY PEOPLE: ISRAEL THROUGH THE EYES OF A CHRISTIAN SOJOURNER*

"I see Mennonite Girls Can Cook Celebrations as a catalyst to help people embrace life and commemorate the relationships that we hold dear to our hearts. Congratulations on this second book!"
— CHEF DEZ, FOOD COLUMNIST, CULINARY INSTRUCTOR, AND COOKBOOK AUTHOR

# MENNONITE GIRLS CAN COOK

## Celebrations

BIRTH ❧ CHILDHOOD ❧ MARRIAGE ❧ FAMILY ❧ OUTDOORS
COMMUNITY ❧ HOSPITALITY ❧ MILESTONES ❧ HOLIDAYS ❧ LIFE

*Lovella Schellenberg*

*Anneliese Friesen*

*Betty Reimer*

*Bev Klassen*

*Charlotte Penner*

*Ellen Bayles*

*Judy Wiebe*

*Julie Klassen*

*Kathy McLellan*

*Marg Bartel*

**Library and Archives Canada Cataloguing in Publication**

Mennonite girls can cook celebrations / Lovella Schellenberg ... [et al.].

Includes index.
ISBN 978-0-8361-9675-7

1. Mennonite cooking. 2. Cooking, Canadian. 3. Cookbooks. I. Schellenberg, Lovella, 1959-

TX715.6.M463 2013          641.5′66          C2013-900310-X

MENNONITE GIRLS CAN COOK CELEBRATIONS
Copyright © 2013 by Herald Press, Waterloo, Ont. N2l 6H7
Published simultaneously in the United States of America by Herald Press, Harrisonburg, Va. 22802. All rights reserved.
Library of Congress Control Number: 2013930418
Canadian Entry Number: C2011-900519-0
International Standard Book Number: 978-0-8361-9675-7
Printed in Canada
Cover photo by Beatriz Photography
Design and layout by Reuben V. Graham

17 16 15 14 13     10 9 8 7 6 5 4 3 2 1

To order or request information please call 1-800-245-7894 in the US or 1-800-631-6535 in Canada. Or visit www.heraldpress.com.

**Herald Press**
A division of Mennonite Publishing Network
Mennonite Church USA and
Mennonite Church Canada

**Herald Press**
Waterloo, Ontario
Harrisonburg, Virginia

*Dedicated to the generations to follow.*
*May our homes always reflect reasons*
*to celebrate the love of God through hospitality*
*to our families, friends, and strangers*
*who may be angels in disguise.*

# CONTENTS

# PREFACE

## WHAT HAPPENS WHEN MENNONITE GIRLS COOK

While we were writing our first cookbook, *Mennonite Girls Can Cook*, which celebrates recipes from our heritage, we had no idea that there would be such an outpouring of appreciation from readers. As the book made its way to your kitchens and coffee tables, you as readers and cooks began sharing the emotions you experienced as you remembered the recipes that your *Omas* and mothers had made in their simple kitchens—kitchens which had doors open wide to welcome family and friends. A vibrant and fulfilling ministry is evidently occurring around kitchen tables all over the world. Lives are changed when homes are opened and people feel special and valued.

One of the most exciting aspects of our first cookbook was being able to contribute our author royalties to the Good Shepherd Shelter in Ukraine, the land of our ancestors. At the time of this writing, a greenhouse has been built to provide fresh garden produce for the children who live in the shelter and for at-risk children in the surrounding community. The royalties from *Mennonite Girls Can Cook* will continue to benefit these children, and the royalties from the cookbook that you hold in your hands, *Mennonite Girls Can Cook Celebrations*, will help to provide clean water for people in Africa.

It was the responses from many of you that inspired us to create this cookbook, which celebrates the beauty of memories we create when we honor the significant events in life and bless those around us. Indeed, we began to realize as we worked on that first volume that our conversations were often filled with stories of celebrations and the special foods that accompany them. All ten of us as authors share an appreciation for the moments in life that shape who we become. Some occasions are planned and anticipated for months, and others are unexpected and bring great sorrow. Regardless of whether we experience joy or sadness at these junctures, unique bonding occurs when families and friends commemorate events that humanity has experienced through the ages.

*Unique bonding occurs when families and friends commemorate events.*

## FROM BIRTH TO DEATH

As authors, we were privileged to be born into families in which our births were celebrated. In many families, preparations begin months before a child makes its appearance, and no home is ever the same from that moment on. On the day a child is born, there are congratulations and well-wishes, and parties often celebrate the birth. Each year on the anniversary of the arrival, we plan parties to celebrate another year. For some blessed people, these anniversaries are multiplied many times so that years down the road milestone birthday parties are still being held.

Our sovereign God knows not only how many hairs we have on our heads but how many days we are given to live on this earth. On the day that someone passes from this earth, loved ones make arrangements to celebrate the life he or she lived. Though there is grieving and sadness over the loss of life, families draw closer as they recount stories about the loved one who is no longer with them.

*We choose to make memories, because we recognize that we have but one life to live.*

Between birth and death, we choose to make memories, because we recognize that we have but one life to live. What we fill our days with matters. The ten of us who authored this book have over five hundred years of memories that influence what we have written. During the months of writing and recipe testing, we shared the joys and sorrows that have marked our own lives and celebrations. As in the previous book, you will find devotionals in sections titled "Bread for the Journey." You will also find some of our personal stories, in which we reflect on the major themes of this book.

Another way to connect with us personally is to visit our blog, www.mennonite girlscancook.ca. There you will also find new recipes, updates about our giving projects, and discussions of cooking, hospitality, and faith.

## CELEBRATING FAITH

It is the small efforts that we make on behalf of others that will be remembered after we are gone. Time that we spend blessing others stores up treasures in heaven, for we never know whose lives will be affected for eternity. Our hope is that we will inspire you to experience joy the way God designed us to. He created the relationships between families and created the beauty of nature that we can enjoy. True celebrations grow out of thankfulness and remind us to glorify God for the gift of life and for the promises in his Word. Some of our celebrations are incredibly precious. Anniversaries, birthdays, family times, accomplishments, lifelong friendships, times to rest and rejuvenate, births, and even deaths: these passages deserve to be honored. So much more, then, do the most important events in human history—the birth, death, and resurrection of Jesus—deserve to be told and retold through our celebrations.

The ten of us celebrate life through our faith. We invite you to open the pages of this book and be drawn into the hope that the best is still to come. ☙

*—Lovella Schellenberg*
ABBOTSFORD, BRITISH COLUMBIA

10

11

# ACKNOWLEDGMENTS

*B*eing part of the creation of a book is a privilege and a unique journey in itself. The ten of us will carry the memories surrounding the plans and activities of July 11, 2012, for the rest of our lives, and we are grateful to the many people who contributed to that event and to this entire cookbook project.

As we gathered for a celebration high tea in Bev and Harv's backyard in British Columbia on that July day, our purpose was twofold. Amy Gingerich from Herald Press came with the contract for this cookbook in hand, which we signed and then celebrated together. We also gathered to have photographs of our group taken for this volume.

Preparing to celebrate this new cookbook was not unlike arranging details for a wedding. Anneliese and I (Lovella) spent time with Jan Martens from Fragrant Memories Floral Design discussing flowers for the celebration table. I watched my rose bushes the week before, willing the blooms and buds to cooperate for Jan to add into the floral design.

Bev had invited us to use their beautifully landscaped backyard for our high tea. Ahead of time we met in Bev's dining room, wondering if we should trust the weather report and have our high tea outside or, in consideration of typical West Coast weather, go with the safer plan of having our high tea inside. Bev's husband, Harv, told us not to worry. He and his men would move the massive antique table and chairs outside early enough to set and decorate it, and, if necessary, they would put up a tent to protect us from the elements.

Ellen is our tablescape expert, and we left the planning of that in her capable hands. Car loaded with as many totes as it would allow, she traveled from northern Washington to make our table beautiful. She spent hours layering the table with ruffled curtains and Bev's tablecloths and also provided tiered serving dishes for the food as well as plates and glassware that she had been collecting in her travels for months. Royal Albert "Sweet Violet" china that I had collected since my first year in high school graced the table, and we all stood back in wonder when we saw the full effect on that beautiful sunny morning.

As we did for our first book, *Mennonite Girls Can Cook*, we called on Beatriz Photography to visually capture the essence of our friendship. Bea photographed us and the celebration high tea table for several hours. We exercised great restraint by setting our own cameras aside while we smiled, swatted mosquitoes, knelt on our aging knees, climbed trees like kids, and did our best to look like we were interacting without actually talking, a near impossibility for us. We piled into a few cars and drove the country roads to a dairy farm owned by Judy's friends, Tom and Laury Degroot, and had our photo taken on their porch. As we had for the first cookbook, we posed with a car from another era, this time a 1958 Edsel belonging to Walt Esau.

13

Earlier in April, Anneliese, Ellen, Judy, and I had attended the West Coast Mennonite Central Committee relief sale in Fresno, California, doing cooking demonstrations and signing copies of our first book. We spent our evenings planning the theme, categories, and the framework for this sequel, *Mennonite Girls Can Cook Celebrations*, and we found inspiration for a color theme. Late in spring, Anneliese, Kathy, and I combed fabric stores near and far looking for a variety of fabrics that would give us each a unique but matching apron. Julie then spent days sewing hostess aprons like the ones that were popular gifts to young women in the 1960s when they served for friends at their wedding receptions. Julie expertly sewed and personalized each of the sheer cotton aprons, and each is a memento of this book that we will cherish forever.

When the day of the celebration high tea finally arrived, we used the rare opportunity of being together to each bring to the table the food we submitted to the "Celebrating Marriage" section of this cookbook. Later in the afternoon, Marg and John hosted us and our husbands in their backyard, where we enjoyed an outdoor Mongolian grill meal prepared by some of their friends. After numerous hours of phone conversations and many emails, it was also a delight and privilege to spend time with several of the Herald Press staff, including Publisher Russ Eanes and Director of Media Amy Gingerich, who, along with Designer Reuben Graham, have supported us in numerous ways throughout our work on these two cookbooks. We are grateful also to Kay Dusheck of Ridge Road Indexing in Iowa, who donated her indexing services for our first cookbook and who again skillfully created the index at the back of this book.

Everyone contributed to making our time together in July a blessing. Charlotte and Betty once again made the trek across the mountains to join us, and Kathy, who has an especially creative eye for making food beautiful, created a finale fitting the occasion: a summer fruit trifle that we now share with you, in a recipe you will find within these pages. The whole day was a wonderful time of sharing and we rejoiced together in the opportunity to use our resources once more in this way. We feel immense gratitude for all those who have made these cookbooks possible: our families, our friends, our church communities, and you, our readers, who have given purpose and joy to our work.

On that July day, just as Bea was finishing the photography and was about to leave us to enjoy our high tea, we joined together around the table to sing the doxology. This hymn of praise felt exactly right, for it is God who brought us together. We reserve our deepest gratitude for him. ✎

*—Lovella, for all the authors*

# CELEBRATING *Birth*

The miracle of a new life is the perfect reason to gather around the table for a brunch celebration. From appetizers to baked goodies, we have some of our favorite brunch recipes for you.

## CELEBRATE WITH

*Behold, children are a heritage from the Lord.*
PSALM 127:3 (ESV)

# ANNELIESE REFLECTS *on* BIRTH

## EXPECTANT WITH ANTICIPATION

It's been a while since we were told
That in the New Year
There'd be a new child to hold.
My heart leaped for joy—
Tears welled at this wonderful news.

Now the waiting has changed meaning
From an expectant view into infinity
To a watch, expecting any time.
And the anytime anticipation
Makes every moment a possibility.

He has assembled the furniture.
The car seat is buckled in tight.
Maybe he even read instructions,
Because this time it had to be right.
I see a twinkle in his eyes.

She's wondering how life will change.
I watch as she sits up straighter,
Shifting in her seat to get comfortable.
In spite of her breathing getting harder,
Her hands caress her rounded tummy.

I recall—I can almost feel those silent sighs,
Leaving a life of just the two of us
And waiting for this mystery, this miracle
That wove our lives together.
A part of him and a part of me, forever.

Two lives joined to create another,
Hidden from sight by all—yet
Fearfully and wonderfully made.
Each step ordained by a Master Weaver,
Each day before it comes to be.

So we wait in wonder in this process.
We remember and cannot help but give praise
As we watch our children become parents.
How precious are his thoughts and ways—
How vast the sum of them! ∽

—*Anneliese*
(INTERWOVEN WITH WORDS
FROM PSALM 139:13-17)

# SPARKLING RHUBARB SORBET

## SERVES 6–8

➤ 3 cups / 750 ml white sugar
➤ 5 cups / 1.25 L water

➤ 10 cups / 2.4 L diced red rhubarb

1. In a large saucepan, bring sugar and water to a boil over high heat. Stir to dissolve sugar.
2. Add rhubarb to the saucepan and return to a boil. Lower heat and simmer about 10 minutes or until rhubarb is tender and falling apart. Remove from heat and allow to cool 10 minutes.
3. Place a fine sieve over a large bowl. Ladle the rhubarb sauce into the sieve, catching the juice in the bowl. Use a wooden spoon to gently press out any remaining juice.
4. Pour the juice into a large glass pan or bowl and place in the freezer. Stir every hour until frozen. Break the frozen juice into pieces and pulse in a food processor until smooth. This may need to be done in batches unless the food processor bowl is large.
5. Alternatively, freeze the juice in an ice cream maker according to the manufacturer's instructions.
6. To serve as a drink, scoop it into pretty glasses and top with your favorite clear sparkling beverage; the sorbet will melt slowly as you sip your drink. Or serve the sorbet with vanilla ice cream for a refreshing dessert.

*TIPS*

- If your rhubarb does not have red stalks, add a few drops of red food coloring to give the sorbet a pink hue.
- The sorbet can be stored in a plastic container for up to a month.
- Allow 3–4 hours for the freezing process, depending on the temperature of the freezer and the depth of the dish.

*—Lovella*

The rhubarb growing in my garden came from the family farm where I grew up. When my husband and I got married, my dad dug up a bit of the root and we planted it in our first garden. Now part of it has come with us to our farm.

Rhubarb sorbet has become a favorite in our home in the spring. The ways to serve it seem endless, as any carbonated beverage creates a new flavor combination.

# HONEY GINGER FRUIT SKEWERS

## SERVES 12

- 24 watermelon balls
- 24 honeydew melon balls
- 24 fresh pineapple chunks
- 1½ cup / 375 ml blueberries
- ½ cup / 125 ml pineapple juice
- ¼ cup / 60 ml orange juice

- ¼ cup / 60 ml liquid honey
- ¼ teaspoon / 1 ml ground ginger
- 24 (4-inch / 10-cm) wooden skewers
- 12 tiny parfait glasses
- Fresh mint leaves for garnish

1. Place watermelon, honeydew, and pineapple in the bottom of a pan.
2. Whisk together pineapple juice, orange juice, honey, and ginger in a small bowl. Drizzle the juice marinade over the fruit. Cover and refrigerate for 1–2 hours.
3. Remove fruit from refrigerator and thread onto skewers, interspersing with blueberries.
4. Place 2 skewers in each parfait glass and drizzle with a small amount of the juice marinade.
5. Garnish with fresh mint leaves if desired.

Pretty as a picture, these fruit skewers are the perfect beginning for a gathering of friends around the table. When we authors met for high tea at Bev's, a tiny parfait glass with fruit skewers was nestled in the center of each place setting. Fruit adds variety and color to a table of dainties and sandwiches. Threading it onto skewers makes it finger food.

*—Judy*

# CHILLED ASPARAGUS BOUQUET *with* CHIVE DIP

## SERVES 10–12

- 20–25 fresh asparagus spears
- Fresh chive stems
  (with blossoms, if in season)

- Small chunks of ice, enough
  to fill serving container
- Cold water and ice cubes
- Boiling water

## CHIVE DIP

- 1 cup / 250 ml mayonnaise
- 1 teaspoon / 5 ml rice vinegar
- 2 tablespoons / 30 ml
  white vinegar
- 1 teaspoon / 5 ml dry mustard
- ½ teaspoon / 2 ml sugar

- 3 tablespoons / 45 ml fresh chives,
  finely chopped
- ½ tablespoon / 7 ml
  fresh parsley, finely chopped
- ¼ teaspoon / 1 ml dried dill weed
- 1 teaspoon / 5 ml lemon zest
- ¼ teaspoon / 1 ml salt

1. Combine all ingredients for chive dip in a small bowl. Mix well, cover, and refrigerate.
2. Wash asparagus and cut off the bottom 2 inches / 5 cm of each stem. Place spears in a 9 x 13-inch / 22 x 33-cm glass pan.
3. Cover the bottom of a second 9 x 13-inch / 22 x 33-cm pan with ice and cover with cold water to create an ice bath. Set aside.
4. Bring a kettle of water to a boil and pour boiling water over asparagus spears, letting them sit for no longer than 2 minutes.
5. Drain and immediately immerse hot asparagus in the ice bath.
6. Allow asparagus to completely cool in the ice bath. This will take 2–3 minutes.
7. Drain well.
8. Place cool, dry asparagus on a clean tray. Cover and refrigerate, up to several hours, until ready to arrange the bouquet. The asparagus spears should be cold and crisp.
9. To arrange the bouquet, fill a glass container with small chunks of ice. Poke chilled asparagus spears into the ice, creating a bouquet. Add fresh chive stems, with blossoms, if possible.
10. Serve immediately with well-chilled chive dip.

*—Kathy*

Chilled asparagus spears become a lovely edible centerpiece for a special occasion.

# RED PEPPER JELLY TARTS

## YIELDS 36 MINI-TARTS

- 1¼ cup / 310 ml flour
- 2 tablespoons / 30 ml fresh parsley, minced
- ½ teaspoon / 2 ml salt
- ½ cup / 125 ml cold butter, cubed
- 1 cup / 250 ml sharp cheddar cheese, finely grated
- 2–3 tablespoons / 30–45 ml ice water (approximately)
- 8 ounces / 250 g cream cheese or Camembert cheese
- ⅓ cup / 75 ml hot red pepper jelly

1. Preheat oven to 350° F / 175° C.
2. Combine flour, parsley, and salt in a bowl.
3. Using a pastry blender or 2 knives, cut butter into mixture to make fine crumbs. Stir in cheddar cheese.
4. Add water, 1 tablespoon / 15 ml at a time, stirring with fork, until the dough holds together.
5. Press dough into a disk and wrap in plastic wrap. Refrigerate for at least 30 minutes.
6. Remove dough from refrigerator and divide into 36 little balls.
7. Press each ball into the bottom and up the sides of a mini-tart pan.
8. Divide cream cheese into 36 equal portions and place 1 portion into each shell.
9. Bake for 10–15 minutes.
10. Take tarts out of the oven and top with red pepper jelly.
11. Bake for an additional 10 minutes, until the crust is golden brown.

*—Charlotte*

The first time I made these tarts, I served them to our Bible study group, which is fairly large. After tasting one tart, I quickly realized that I should have tripled the recipe! Layered in a two-bite treat, the cream cheese and red pepper are a good combination of flavors. It is hard to stop at just one or two.

25

# BROCCOLI CHEESE SOUFFLÉ ROLL

## SERVES 6

- ⅓ cup / 75 ml butter
- ½ cup / 125 ml onion, finely diced
- ½ cup / 125 ml flour
- 1 teaspoon / 5 ml dry mustard
- ¼ teaspoon / 1 ml cayenne pepper
- 1 teaspoon / 5 ml salt
- 4½ cups / 1.1 L milk
- 8 ounces / 225 g sharp cheddar cheese, grated
- 6 eggs

1. Line an 11 x 17-inch / 28 x 43-cm baking sheet with parchment paper, letting the 2 short ends extend beyond the pan for easier removal of the soufflé. Spray the parchment paper and pan sides with cooking spray.
2. Preheat oven to 350° F / 175° C.
3. Melt butter in a saucepan. Add onion and sauté until translucent.
4. Add dry ingredients and stir over medium heat until mixture is dry and crumbly.
5. Using a whisk, add milk in small amounts until mixture becomes a smooth, thick paste. Add remaining milk and whisk over medium heat until the mixture bubbles. Add cheese and stir until smooth.
6. Measure 2 cups / 500 ml sauce for the soufflé batter. Set aside remaining sauce for broccoli filling and serving sauce.
7. Separate eggs, placing egg whites in one large bowl and egg yolks in another.
8. Beat egg whites with a mixer until stiff.
9. To make the soufflé batter, whisk a small amount of the cheese sauce into the egg yolks at a time, in order to gently warm the eggs and prevent them from scrambling. Continue adding a little at a time until you have added the entire 2 cups / 500 ml.
10. Add 1 cup / 250 ml beaten egg whites to the soufflé batter and stir gently to lighten batter. Fold in remaining egg whites.
11. Spread batter evenly in the pan and bake until golden brown, about 25 minutes.
12. Remove the soufflé from the oven and cover with a clean tea towel. Lay another baking sheet on top and flip over to turn out the soufflé. Remove the top pan and carefully remove the parchment paper from the soufflé. Lower the oven temperature to 325° F / 160° C.
13. Carefully spread the broccoli filling (below) onto the hot soufflé and roll up. Place on an oven-proof serving plate.
14. Return to the oven to keep warm for up to 30 minutes. Slice and serve with sauce.

## BROCCOLI FILLING

- 1 pound / 500 g broccoli
- 1⅓ cup / 325 ml cheese sauce (set aside from soufflé in step 6)

1. Cut broccoli into small pieces; steam until tender crisp.
2. Add cheese sauce to broccoli and set aside.

## SERVING SAUCE

> Remaining cheese sauce (set aside from soufflé in step 6)

> ½ cup / 125 ml milk

1. Stir milk into remaining cheese sauce over low heat until heated through.
2. Drizzle over the soufflé roll to serve.

*TIPS*

- For a light, fluffy soufflé, avoid beating egg whites too long. Too much beating results in curdled-looking egg whites that lose their glossiness.
- To make the soufflé a day ahead, cover with plastic wrap and refrigerate after step 12. To reheat, remove plastic wrap and heat in a 325° F / 160° C oven for 30 minutes.

I first sampled a broccoli cheese soufflé roll at a cousin's luncheon almost twenty years ago. My cousin Caroline served the light, fluffy roll with a crisp green salad. It was a delicious lunch, and our conversation around the table as daughters of sisters on my mom's side was a special time. Caroline's mother, Mary, was my mom's dearest friend. It is with that tender relationship in mind that I share this recipe.

*—Lovella*

# QUICHE *with* CHEDDAR PASTRY
## SERVES 6

## PASTRY

- 2 cups / 500 ml flour
- ½ teaspoon / 2 ml salt
- 1 tablespoon / 15 ml sugar

- 1 cup / 250 ml sharp cheddar cheese, grated
- ⅔ cup / 150 ml cold shortening, grated
- 6 tablespoons / 90 ml ice water

1. Preheat oven to 375° F / 190° C.
2. Stir flour, salt, and sugar together in a mixing bowl.
3. Grate cheese and cold shortening into flour mixture. Stir to coat well with flour mixture.
4. Stir in ice water, 1 tablespoon / 15 ml at a time, until pastry comes together into a smooth ball. Flatten into a disc.
5. Lightly flour pastry mat or counter. Roll out pastry to fit a 9-inch / 22-cm pie plate.
6. Roll pastry around rolling pin. Lay rolling pin on top of pie plate and unroll to drape pastry over pie plate.
7. Press pastry into pie plate, cut off excess dough, and flute edges.
8. Bake empty shell for 10 minutes. Remove from oven and allow to cool. While shell bakes, start on the filling.

## FILLING

- 8 strips bacon
- 5 large eggs
- 1½ cup / 375 ml half and half (light cream)
- ¼ teaspoon / 1 ml dried tarragon
- ½ teaspoon / 2 ml white pepper
- ½ teaspoon / 2 ml salt

- ¼ cup / 60 ml green onions, finely chopped
- 1 cup / 250 ml fresh spinach, finely chopped
- ¾ cup / 175 ml cheddar cheese, grated
- ½ cup / 125 ml Swiss cheese, grated
- Pancetta-style bacon for garnish (optional)

1. Fry bacon until crisp. Place on a paper towel to absorb extra fat. Chop bacon into small pieces and set aside.
2. Beat together eggs, half and half, and spices until frothy.
3. Stir in green onions and spinach.
4. Place crumbled bacon on the bottom of the partially baked pastry shell. Top with cheddar cheese and then Swiss cheese.
5. Pour egg mixture over all.
6. Bake quiche in preheated 375° F / 190° C oven for 40 minutes. To check for doneness, insert a knife into the center. Knife will come out clean when done.

Quiche makes a lovely entrée for a brunch. Serve with fresh fruit.

*—Kathy*

# HAM *and* CHEESE PINWHEELS

## YIELDS 5 DOZEN PINWHEELS

### REFRIGERATOR YEAST DOUGH

- 6 cups / 1.4 L flour (approximately)
- ½ cup / 125 ml sugar
- 2 teaspoons / 10 ml salt
- 2 tablespoons / 30 ml instant yeast
- ½ cup / 125 ml margarine or butter, softened
- 2 eggs, beaten
- 2 cups / 500 ml warm milk or water

1. Place 4 cups / 1 L flour into a large mixing bowl. Add sugar, salt, yeast, and margarine.
2. Add beaten eggs to mixture.
3. Add milk or water (or half milk and half water) and mix until dough is sticky. Add remaining flour until dough forms a medium-soft ball.
4. Knead by hand for about 5 minutes, or use a mixer with a dough hook attachment for several minutes, until dough is smooth and elastic.
5. Place dough in a greased bowl. Cover bowl and refrigerate for several hours or overnight.

### HAM AND CHEESE PINWHEELS

- 15 ham slices (approximately)
- 1 pound / 500 g cheddar cheese, sliced
- 2 tablespoons / 30 ml milk
- 2–4 tablespoons / 30–60 ml poppy seeds or sesame seeds

1. Before taking dough out of the refrigerator, prepare ham and cheese. Cut each slice of ham into 2-inch / 5-cm squares and the cheese into 1½-inch / 4-cm squares. Each pinwheel will require 1 square of sliced ham and 2 squares of cheese.
2. Divide dough into 4 equal portions.
3. Roll each portion into a 12–14-inch / 30–35-cm square.
4. Using a pizza cutter, cut each portion into 16 3-inch / 7.5-cm squares.
5. From each corner of each square, make a 1-inch / 2.5-cm diagonal cut toward the center. Do not cut through the center. See photo A.
6. Place a square of cheddar cheese in the uncut center portion of each square of dough. Top each with a square of ham and then top ham with another square of cheese. See photo B.

These pinwheels take a bit of time to make, but they freeze well. They make a hearty snack for game night. To make a quick packed lunch, pop a few frozen pinwheels in a sandwich bag in the morning and they'll be ready to eat at noon.

The refrigerator yeast dough is also great for crescent or cloverleaf rolls. Mix it before you go to bed and bake them fresh in the morning.

7. Pull the right point of each triangular-cut section toward the middle to form a pinwheel. The trick is to use the same corner on each triangular section of the square. Secure the points in the center with a toothpick. See photo C.
8. Place pinwheels on parchment-lined baking sheets and let rise, covered with plastic, in a warm place until doubled in bulk.
9. Just before baking, brush each pinwheel with milk and sprinkle with poppy or sesame seeds. See photos D and E.
10. Bake in a preheated 375° F / 190° C. oven for 10 minutes or until nicely browned.
11. Place on racks, remove toothpicks, and allow to cool. Some of the cheese will have formed puddles, which you may remove before serving, if you like.

*TIPS*

- Use ham that has been sliced slightly thicker than the usual deli slices and cheese slices that are approximately ¼-inch / ½-cm thick.
- Whole wheat flour can be substituted for up to a third of the flour in this recipe.

*—Bev*

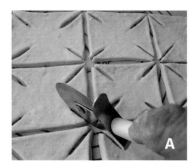
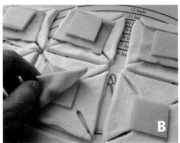

31

# STICKY BANANA PECAN ROLLS

## YIELDS 12 MEDIUM ROLLS

### SYRUP

- ¼ cup / 60 ml butter
- ½ cup / 125 ml brown sugar
- 2 tablespoons / 30 ml corn syrup
- 36–48 pecan halves

### PASTRY

- 2 cups / 500 ml flour
- 2 tablespoons / 30 ml sugar
- ½ teaspoon / 2 ml salt
- 3 teaspoons / 15 ml baking powder
- ½ teaspoon / 2 ml baking soda
- 6 tablespoons / 90 ml butter, room temperature
- 2 large bananas, mashed
- ½ cup / 125 ml buttermilk
- Extra flour for shaping and rolling

### FILLING

- 2 tablespoons / 30 ml butter, melted
- ¼ cup / 60 ml brown sugar

1. Line bottom of oven with aluminum foil or place a baking sheet on the lower rack to catch gooey drippings. Preheat oven to 400° F / 205° C.
2. To make the syrup, melt butter, brown sugar, and corn syrup in a small saucepan, stirring until smooth.
3. Remove syrup from heat and divide into 12 cups of a medium muffin tin, about 1 tablespoon / 15 ml per serving. Add 3 to 4 pecan halves to each cup.
4. Mix dry ingredients in a bowl, cutting in butter.
5. Add bananas and buttermilk, stirring until dry ingredients are well incorporated. Dust with extra flour until not too sticky to handle.
6. Transfer dough to a floured surface and knead gently for about 10 seconds, shaping it into a rectangle. Roll out to about 15 x 10 inches / 40 x 25 cm.
7. Spread with melted butter and brown sugar. Roll up, beginning at long end.
8. Cut into 12 equal slices and place on top of syrup and pecans in muffin tins.
9. Bake 15–18 minutes, until nicely browned on top. Immediately invert pan onto a baking sheet or serving tray, and allow to rest a few minutes before lifting off pan. Serve warm.

*—Anneliese*

A blend of a scone, a banana muffin, and brown-sugary gooeyness! How can you go wrong?

I first had these cookies in 1974, when my mother made them for her first grandchild's baby shower. They melt in your mouth, and you'll want more than one.

# WALNUT MERINGUE CRESCENTS

## YIELDS 40–48 CRESCENTS

- 2 cups / 500 ml flour, sifted
- 1 teaspoon / 5 ml baking powder
- ¼ teaspoon / 1 ml salt
- ¾ cup / 175 ml butter, chilled
- 1½ teaspoons / 7 ml active dry yeast
- 2 tablespoons / 30 ml warm water
- 2 eggs, separated

- ¼ cup / 60 ml sour cream
- ½ teaspoon / 2 ml vanilla extract
- ½ cup / 125 ml sugar
- ½ cup / 125 ml walnuts, finely ground
- ½ teaspoon / 2 ml almond extract
- Icing sugar

1. Sift flour, baking powder, and salt together into mixing bowl.
2. Cut in butter.
3. Dissolve yeast in warm water.
4. Stir egg yolks (reserve the egg whites), sour cream, and vanilla into the yeast mixture.
5. Mix wet ingredients into the flour mixture.
6. Form dough into a ball, wrap in plastic wrap, and refrigerate for 1 hour.
7. After the hour, preheat oven to 400° F / 205° C.
8. To make the meringue, beat reserved egg whites until foamy. Gradually add sugar and beat until stiff. Fold in walnuts and almond extract.

## ASSEMBLING CRESCENTS

1. Divide refrigerated dough into 4 equal portions.
2. Sprinkle counter with icing sugar. Place dough on counter and roll each portion into a 7–8-inch / 18–20-cm circle.
3. Cut each circle into 10–12 wedges.
4. Spread 1 heaping teaspoonful / 5 ml of the meringue on each wedge.
5. Roll, beginning at the wide end.
6. Bake on lightly greased baking sheet for 10–12 minutes or until golden brown.
7. Remove from oven and sprinkle lightly with icing sugar. When cooled completely or just before serving, sprinkle with more icing sugar.

*TIP*
- Using a pizza cutter to cut the rolled dough into wedges works well.

*—Ellen*

35

# CITRUS *and* CRANBERRY MINI-MUFFINS

## YIELDS 3 DOZEN MINI-MUFFINS

- 2¼ cups / 560 ml white flour
- ½ cup / 125 ml whole wheat flour
- 2 tablespoons / 30 ml baking powder
- ½ teaspoon / 2 ml salt
- 1 cup / 250 ml sugar
- Zest of 1 lemon
- ½ cup / 125 ml pecans, toasted and chopped
- 2 cups / 500 ml cranberries, coarsely chopped
- 2 eggs
- 1 cup / 250 ml buttermilk
- ½ cup / 125 ml butter, melted
- 1 cup / 250 ml icing sugar
- Juice of 1 lemon

Cranberries and pecans pair beautifully with a hint of lemon in this tender little muffin. Have the dry ingredients mixed ahead of time and combine with your wet ingredients to have muffins ready to bake in minutes. This will give your home a welcoming aroma when guests walk in the door.

1. Preheat oven to 400° F / 205° C.
2. Combine flours, baking powder, salt, and sugar in a medium bowl.
3. Stir in lemon zest, pecans, and cranberries. Make a well in the center of mixture.
4. In another bowl beat eggs and buttermilk. Add melted butter and mix well.
5. Pour wet mixture into the well of dry ingredients, mixing until dry ingredients are just moistened.
6. Fill greased mini-muffin tins with batter.
7. Bake for 15–20 minutes, until toothpick inserted into the center comes out clean.
8. Cool 10 minutes, remove muffins from pans, and drizzle with glaze made from icing sugar and lemon juice.

*—Betty*

# BREAD FOR THE JOURNEY
# EACH CHILD *a* WORLD *of* POSSIBILITIES

*"For I know the plans I have for you," declares the* LORD, *"plans to prosper you and not to harm you, plans to give you hope and a future."*

—JEREMIAH 29:11 (NIV)

{ The gift of a newborn can bring such joy into our lives. Oh, how my spirit rejoiced each time I heard the wonderful news that we were going to be parents! I remember those early days of parenthood as if they happened yesterday: staring down at the innocent and perfect face of our sleeping newborn child, being filled with awe at God's marvelous creation, and praying for God's blessing upon that new life. Within each child lives a world of possibilities from God.

Sadly, not all new life happens under ideal circumstances. For twenty years I volunteered with our local crisis pregnancy center as a crisis line counselor, and I heard the stories of women and men who found themselves in desperate situations, needing support in dealing with their pregnancies. We can't understand why some children grow up feeling unloved and neglected. We ask why a child is born with serious health concerns or why a baby or child who was wanted and prayed for suddenly dies. These

*Every birth reminds us that life itself is a miracle.*

questions leave us feeling deep sadness and helplessness. But God is the creator of all life, regardless of circumstances. Every birth reminds us that life itself is a miracle.

As a mother, I know that the love a parent has for a child is incredibly powerful, and that the desire to protect, guard, and nurture that child is immense. But God's love is far more powerful than even a parent's love. The Lord has placed intrinsic value and hope in each person, in the newborn life and in your life as well. Jeremiah 29:11 says, "'For I know the plans I have for you,' declares the LORD, 'plans to prosper you and not to harm you, plans to give you hope and a future.'"

Life is vulnerable, fragile, and precious. Ask yourself: *what difference can I make in someone's life?* I encourage each of you to walk alongside another in both good and difficult times and to whisper gently, lovingly, "God loves you. God has a wonderful plan for you, with hope for your future. Trust in the God of hope; he alone is sovereign." ৵

*—Charlotte*

38

Beatriz Photography / www.beatrizphotography.com

# CELEBRATING *Childhood*

Pizza and chicken nuggets, ice cream sandwiches and caramel apples: such treats call out to the child in each of us. Many of our favorite childhood memories involve the foods that we enjoyed and the people we enjoyed them with. You will find new and creative ways of serving these age-old favorites right here.

## CELEBRATE WITH

*Let the little children come to me and do not hinder them, for to such belongs the kingdom of heaven.*
—MATTHEW 19:14 (ESV)

# BETTY REFLECTS *on* CHILDHOOD

I recently visited the farm where I grew up, and although it is now abandoned, the wonderful memories linger.

As a little girl, I loved playing with my doll. I also enjoyed pretending that an old car that was sitting in our yard was my house. My mom gave me chipped dishes and a few tattered and torn crocheted doilies. These castoffs were precious to me as I decorated the car, and it became a special place where I loved to spend time.

*My childhood wasn't all play. We had chores to do, and everyone pitched in.*

Another memory is playing by the creek that flowed through our property. My girlfriends and I would walk along the edges, into the dense green foliage, chatting and listening to the birds sing. We were sure that we were the only ones who knew about this enchanted, secret place!

My childhood wasn't all play. We had chores to do, and everyone pitched in. In summer we picked beetles off the potato plants and put them in a jar. Dad gave us a penny for every three beetles. I don't recall that he counted them, but I sure did! Then there were the never-ending jobs of pulling weeds in the garden, picking berries, and doing housework. Off the farm, my family would hoe beets for a beet-grower to earn extra money. I remember those long rows of beets and how I would receive twenty-five cents a row. That was my share to keep. Money was scarce, and I couldn't keep all my earnings.

My dad's uncle and aunt lived in a little house on our property for a few years. I would often go to their house midafternoon, knowing that *Faspa* (coffee break) was going to be served soon, and I would offer to help set the table. My dad's aunt made the best cream cookies. Looking back, I am sure she knew that those cookies were the reason I was there!

I did not go to Sunday school and seldom attended church. Then a church from a nearby town started Sunday school classes in our country school. There was little to do in a rural farming area on a Sunday afternoon, so I decided to go. This is where I first heard that Jesus loved me and died for my sins so that I could be forgiven and have eternal life. Although I did not accept him into my heart at the time, the seed had been planted. I knew that I wanted this for my life. It wasn't until I was in my late twenties that the seed took solid root and I accepted Jesus as my Savior.

I have so many precious memories of my childhood, but the most important one was learning that Jesus loves me. ❧

—*Betty*

# APPLE CIDER

## SERVES 20

- 10 pounds / 4.5 kg apples of assorted varieties (about 20 apples)
- 3 lemon slices, with peel

- 4 cinnamon sticks
- 1 tablespoon / 15 ml whole allspice
- ½ cup / 125 ml maple syrup, or more to taste

1. Wash, peel, core, and roughly slice apples into a large pot, filling up to ¾ full. Add lemon slices, cinnamon, and allspice. Add water to nearly cover.
2. Bring to a boil and then turn heat to low. Cover and simmer for 3 hours, stirring occasionally.
3. Stir in maple syrup and taste. If necessary, add additional syrup.
4. Put a colander over another large pot to catch the juice. Using a measuring cup, transfer pulp and juice to the colander.
5. Stir pulp with a wooden spoon to extract excess juice. Put the pulp on a large square of cheesecloth, hold over the pot, and squeeze out remaining juice.
6. Serve the cider either hot or chilled.

## TIPS

- To make pure apple juice that children will love, use only the lemon peel and maple syrup and omit the spices. Adjust the sweetness to taste, chill, and serve.
- The pulp can be transferred to freezer bags to use later in baking apple bread.
- To freeze cider, ladle the juice into wide-mouth jars, leaving 1 inch / 2.5 cm at the top for expansion, screw lids onto jars, and place in freezer. Thaw at room temperature.

I have fond memories of my mom using up all the apples on the farm, one tree at a time: from the early Transparent apples, to the Gravenstein, and finally to the Northern Spy. The freezer was full of applesauce, apple pies, and apple juice to enjoy all winter long. Our winters are relatively mild on the south coast of British Columbia, so we take advantage of the few snow days we get by bundling up, playing outside, and later sipping hot apple cider by the fire. This is a simple, lightly spiced cider that can be made without a juicer and that has just a touch of sweetness.

*—Lovella*

47

# ORANGE PEACH SMOOTHIE

**SERVES 4–6**

This is lovely with fresh ripe peaches when they are in season. For the rest of the year, having canned peaches in the pantry and orange juice in the freezer makes it easy to prepare this smoothie.

- ➤ 10 ice cubes
- ➤ 1 15-ounce / 425-g can sliced peaches, or 3 fresh peaches, peeled, pitted, and cut into quarters
- ➤ 1 cup / 250 ml frozen orange juice concentrate
- ➤ 2 tablespoons / 30 ml blue agave sweetener or honey

1. Put all ingredients into a blender and blend until smooth.
2. If needed, add extra orange juice for desired consistency.
3. Serve immediately.

*—Ellen*

# CHICKEN NUGGETS

## YIELDS 30 NUGGETS

- 3 chicken breasts
- ¾ cup / 175 ml dry bread crumbs
- ⅓ cup / 75 ml Parmesan cheese, grated
- ¼ teaspoon / 1 ml salt
- ½ teaspoon / 2 ml Italian seasoning
- ¼ teaspoon / 1 ml pepper
- ⅓ cup / 75 ml butter, melted

1. Preheat oven to 400° F / 205° C.
2. Cut chicken into pieces the size of small nuggets.
3. Combine dry ingredients in a bowl to make crumbs.
4. Dip nuggets into butter and then into crumb mixture.
5. Place in a single layer on a parchment-lined baking sheet.
6. Bake for 20 minutes until golden brown.

Your children will love this simple, healthy, baked version of chicken nuggets. Dip nuggets in your favorite sauce; our favorites are honey dill or plum sauce. Serve with carrot and celery sticks.

*—Betty*

The crust I use for these mini-pizzas is my favorite quick dough. This is appropriate because these have become tea party fare. When my youngest daughter was little, I started hosting tea parties for her with her cousins, who were close in age. At first it was something to do when all the girls came over after school, but now it has become a birthday tradition. About twice a year, we combine the birthdays that are close together. The girls get to pick out their favorite teacup, and we change our names to some kind of flower, speak with a British accent, and make sure our pinkies are up in the air as we sip. We share silliness and laughter around the table.

# MINI-PIZZAS

## YIELDS 18 MINI-PIZZAS

### CRUSTS

- 2 cups / 500 ml flour
- 1 tablespoon / 15 ml sugar
- 1 tablespoon / 15 ml baking powder
- ½ teaspoon / 2 ml salt
- ½ cup / 125 ml butter, cold
- ¾ cup / 175 ml milk

1. Preheat oven to 425° F / 220° C.
2. Sift together dry ingredients.
3. With a pastry blender or 2 knives, cut in butter to make coarse crumbs.
4. Add milk and stir only until blended.
5. Knead the dough no more than 8–10 strokes.
6. Roll the dough to about ¼-inch / 0.5-cm thick.
7. Cut into circles. These can be any size you wish; to make about 18 mini-pizzas, cut into 3-inch / 7-cm circles.
8. Place crusts onto greased baking pans.

### SAUCE AND TOPPINGS

- 1 5.5-ounce / 156-ml can tomato paste
- 5.5 ounces / 156-ml water
- 1 tablespoon / 15 ml olive oil
- ½ teaspoon / 2 ml dried basil
- ½ teaspoon / 2 ml dried oregano
- ½ teaspoon / 2 ml dried thyme
- ½ teaspoon / 2 ml onion powder
- ¼ teaspoon / 1 ml garlic powder
- 1 teaspoon / 5 ml hot pepper sauce
- 1 teaspoon / 5 ml sugar
- Salt and pepper to taste
- Mozzarella cheese
- Pepperoni and other favorite toppings

1. Mix all but the last two ingredients together and spoon onto pizza crusts.
2. Top with desired amount of mozzarella cheese and favorite toppings.
3. Bake for 10–12 minutes or until cheese bubbles.

### TIP

- You can cut pepperoni slices into children's initials to personalize their pizzas.

*—Charlotte*

# HOMEMADE POTATO CHIPS

## SERVES 4

- ➤ 4 medium potatoes, unpeeled
- ➤ 4 tablespoons / 60 ml olive oil
- ➤ Salt to taste

1. Slice the potatoes paper thin, using a sharp knife or mandoline.
2. Use 1 tablespoon oil per potato. Place 1 sliced potato and oil into plastic bag and shake.
3. Cover a microwavable plate with parchment paper.
4. Arrange oiled potato slices in a single layer on parchment paper.
5. Salt lightly.
6. Cook in the microwave oven up to 7 minutes or until lightly browned. The cooking time will vary by microwave. If the chips have not browned, they will not be crisp.
7. Repeat step 6 until all potato slices are used.

### TIPS

- A mandoline slicer is a perfect tool to give potatoes a consistent, even slice.
- To use the correct amount of parchment paper, trace the microwave plate onto the parchment and then cut out the circle.

—*Marg*

Potato chips have always been my weakness, and my kids love them too. This year my grandsons and their cousins from Calgary dug up the potatoes and washed and brushed them while I sliced them. They eagerly waited and watched through the microwave's window as the chips turned golden brown. Homemade potato chips are gluten free and contain no artificial flavors, artificial colors, or trans fats. Can it get any better than that?

# CHILI MEAT POCKETS

## YIELDS APPROXIMATELY 4 DOZEN

### CHILI MEAT FILLING

- 1 pound / 500 g ground beef
- ¾ cup / 175 ml onion, finely chopped
- 1½ tablespoon / 22 ml chili powder, or to taste
- 2 envelopes or 2 cubes beef bouillon, crumbled
- 1 pound / 500 g cheddar cheese, sliced ¼-inch / 0.5-cm thick

1. Brown ground beef and onion until meat is cooked through. Drain fat.
2. Add chili powder and beef bouillon powder to the meat mixture. Cook a little longer, stirring well, until seasonings are incorporated. Do not add water.
3. Let cool while you make the pastry. This makes enough filling for 2 batches of pastry; freeze half the filling to use the next time you make chili meat pockets.
4. Cut cheese into rectangles about 1 x 1½ inches / 2.5 x 3.5 cm and set aside.

### PASTRY

- 1 cup / 250 ml cottage cheese
- 1 cup / 250 ml stick margarine
- 2¾ cups / 675 ml flour
- 2 tablespoons / 30 ml wheat germ

1. Preheat oven to 375° F / 190° C.
2. Place all pastry ingredients in a food processor and pulse until dough begins to stick together. If mixing by hand, cut margarine and cottage cheese into dry ingredients and then mix by hand until mixture holds together and becomes somewhat sticky.
3. Divide dough into 4 pieces. On a floured surface, roll out each piece to about ⅛-inch / 0.25-cm thick.
4. Cut circles using a cutter about 3½ inches / 9 cm in diameter.
5. Place 1 piece cheddar cheese on one side of each circle. Top with about 1 tablespoon / 15 ml meat filling.
6. Fold in half and crimp edges together using a fork. Prick tops with the fork to let out the steam while baking.
7. Place on lightly greased or parchment-lined baking sheets. Bake for about 15–20 minutes or until pockets are lightly browned.
8. Serve with ketchup or red pepper jelly for dipping.

### TIPS

- Vary the spices to make different flavored lunch pockets. For a Mexican lunch pocket, substitute taco seasoning for the chili powder and Monterey Jack cheese for the cheddar. For a pizza pocket, use basil and oregano, a smear of tomato paste, and mozzarella cheese.
- One way to cut out even circles of dough is to use a cutter made from an empty yogurt container.

*—Bev*

These meat pockets were popular lunch items with our children. Let the pockets cool to room temperature and then freeze them in airtight bags. When it is time to make lunches, grab a couple from the freezer, pop them into a sandwich bag, add some fruit and a cookie, and lunch making is done. Alternatively, serve these as an appetizer when friends come over to watch a game or a movie.

# CHOCOLATE CAKE POPS

**YIELDS 2 DOZEN**

## CAKE

- ¾ cup / 170 g butter
- ½ cup / 60 g cocoa powder
- 4 eggs
- 1¼ cup / 250 g sugar
- 1 teaspoon / 5 ml vanilla extract

- ½ cup / 125 ml milk
- 1¼ cup / 180 g quinoa flour
- 1 teaspoon / 5 g baking powder
- ½ teaspoon / 2 g baking soda
- ½ teaspoon / 2 g salt

1. Preheat oven to 350° F / 175° C.
2. Melt butter in the microwave. (Bring butter just to melting point; do not overheat.) Stir in the cocoa powder, mixing until perfectly smooth.
3. In a separate bowl, beat together eggs and sugar until fluffy.
4. Blend butter and cocoa mixture into eggs.
5. Add vanilla and milk.
6. Mix quinoa flour, baking powder, baking soda, and salt, blending well.
7. Add dry ingredients to liquids and beat until smooth.
8. Pour into a greased 9 x 13-inch / 22 x 33-cm cake pan and bake for 40 minutes, until a toothpick inserted in the center comes out clean.
9. Cool completely.

## ICING

- ¼ cup / 55 g butter, softened
- ¼ cup / 30 g cocoa powder
- ¼ cup / 60 ml milk

- 1 teaspoon / 5 ml vanilla extract
- 2 cups / 250 g icing sugar

1. Place softened butter in a bowl and mix in cocoa powder.
2. Add milk and vanilla and beat, by hand or with a mixer, until smooth.
3. Add 3 cups / 375 g icing sugar, or enough to make a stiff icing.
4. Set aside.

## OTHER INGREDIENTS

- 1 cup / 250 g white chocolate wafers or candy, melted
- 1 cup / 250 g dark chocolate wafers or candy, melted

- 1 package skewers or lollipop sticks
- Candy sprinkles (optional)

Cake pops are popular, but as a rule, they are rather sugar-laden and contain little nutritional value. Not only are these cake pops gluten free; they also offer the health benefits of quinoa flour. So go ahead: enjoy more than one!

1. Crumble half of the cold cake into a bowl to make even, fine crumbs. You could freeze the remainder of the cake for individual servings.
2. Add enough icing to cake crumbs to make a mixture that holds together.
3. Chill for about an hour.
4. Press the crumbly dough into rounds with your hands or into individual shapes by using a cookie press or a standard cake pop pan.
5. Let cake pops firm up in refrigerator.
6. Slip a skewer or lollipop stick into each cake pop.
7. For icing, melt chocolate wafers in the microwave, being careful not to overheat.
8. Dip each cake pop into the melted chocolate, letting excess chocolate drip off. When coating is partially set, decorate as desired.
9. Serve in a vase or on top of pieces of cake.

**TIPS**

- I find that one skewer is not quite strong enough to hold the cake pop. Two skewers wound together with curling ribbon not only works great but also looks pretty.
- To make the melted chocolate the right consistency for smooth dipping, add oil, a little at a time.
- You can serve these cake pops unwrapped or wrapped in cellophane and tied with ribbon. Be creative!

*—Julie*

55

# CHOCOLATE CRISPY RICE ROLL

## YIELDS 30–36 SLICES

### ROLL

- 1 cup / 250 ml corn syrup
- ¾ cup / 175 ml sugar
- 1 cup / 250 ml smooth peanut butter
- 3 tablespoons / 45 ml butter
- 6 cups / 1.5 L crispy rice cereal

### FILLING

- ½ cup / 125 ml butter
- 3 tablespoons / 45 ml milk
- 2 cups / 500 ml icing sugar
- ⅔ cups / 150 ml cocoa powder
- 1 teaspoon / 5 ml vanilla extract

1. Line an 11 x 17-inch / 28 x 43-cm baking sheet with wax paper.
2. In a large pot over medium heat, bring corn syrup and sugar to a boil. Add peanut butter and butter, stirring until smooth.
3. Remove from heat and mix in crispy rice cereal. Press into prepared cookie sheet with wet hands.
4. In a medium saucepan, melt butter. Remove from heat and add milk, icing sugar, cocoa, and vanilla, stirring until smooth. This mixture should be thick but spreadable—not runny. If too thick, add 1 tablespoon / 15 ml milk.
5. Spread over flattened cereal mixture and roll up jelly-roll style, starting at long end and shaping gently to form a uniform roll. Wrap wax paper around the roll and refrigerate several hours until set but not too hard.
6. Using a large, sharp knife, slice into ½-inch / 1.5-cm slices. Press down with both hands on knife rather than using a sawing motion.
7. Keeps well in fridge or freezer.

*TIP*

- To make this recipe gluten free, choose a brand of crispy rice cereal that does not have malt flavoring as an ingredient. ⓖ

*—Anneliese*

There is something about this peanut- and chocolate-flavored crispy rice cereal roll that still surprises my taste buds in a pleasant way every time I take a bite. These slices can be nicely packaged in a cellophane bag and tied with a ribbon. Because the slices keep so well, they were one of my favorite items to send to my kids while they were at college.

# ICE CREAM SANDWICHES

## YIELDS 12 SANDWICHES

- ½ cup / 125 ml butter, room temperature
- 1 cup / 250 ml sugar
- 1 egg
- 1 teaspoon / 5 ml vanilla extract
- 2 cups / 500 ml flour

- ½ teaspoon / 2 ml baking powder
- 1 teaspoon / 5 ml baking soda
- ½ cup / 125 ml cocoa powder, plus more for dusting pans
- 1 cup / 250 ml milk
- 1 2-quart / 2-L container ice cream of any flavor

1. Preheat oven to 400° F / 205° C.
2. Line 2 10 x 15-inch / 25 x 38-cm baking pans with parchment paper and lightly grease with butter. Dust buttered parchment with cocoa powder, making sure that the pans are completely coated.
3. Cream together butter, sugar, egg, and vanilla until smooth.
4. In a separate bowl, stir together all dry ingredients.
5. Alternately add milk and dry ingredients into butter mixture until batter is smooth. Divide batter between pans. Bake for 7 minutes. Cake is thin and does not take long to bake. Do not overbake, as the edges will become dry.
6. When cakes are baked, place a cooling rack the size of your baking pans on top of each hot cake and flip. Remove pans and immediately pull off parchment paper. Allow cakes to completely cool.
7. Remove the carton from a brick of ice cream. Using an electric or serrated knife, cut the brick of ice cream into ¾-inch / 2-cm slices.
8. Working quickly, lay ice cream slices over 1 sheet cake, still on the cooling rack. Using cooling rack for support, flip second cake over on top of the ice cream, making a large sandwich. Remove top cooling rack. Lay a piece of plastic wrap over top cake and flip the entire sandwich. Remove cooling rack (which is now on top) and wrap the whole ice cream sandwich with plastic wrap.
9. Place in freezer until completely frozen.
10. When ready to cut into individual sandwiches, remove from freezer. Remove plastic wrap and place large sandwich on cutting board. Working quickly, measure and then cut into 12 equal rectangular sandwiches.
11. Wrap individual sandwiches in parchment paper. Tie with a ribbon or place a sticker on the fold of the parchment. Place wrapped ice cream sandwiches in an airtight container and freeze until ready to serve.

Sweet little packages tied up in bows will become a favorite treat for young and old. Strawberry or mint chocolate chip may be the kids' favorite choice of ice cream, while choosing mocha chocolate ripple or raspberry cheesecake will turn these ice cream sandwiches into gourmet delights that adults will love.

*—Kathy*

# TIE-DYED RAINBOW CAKE

**SERVES 16**

## CAKE

- 2 16.25-ounce / 461-g white cake mixes
- 4 eggs
- ½ cup / 125 ml vegetable oil
- Water
- Gel food coloring

1. Preheat oven to 350° F / 175° C.
2. Prepare 2 9-inch / 22-cm round pans by lining bottoms with parchment paper and spraying with cooking spray.
3. Empty both cake mixes into a large mixing bowl.
4. In a 4-cup / 1-L measuring cup, combine eggs and oil; add enough water to make 3 cups / 750 ml liquid.
5. Add liquids to the cake mix and stir until combined; then beat on medium speed for 1 minute.
6. Divide batter equally into 6 individual bowls.
7. Add gel coloring to each to create a rainbow of colors: if possible, use purple, blue, green, yellow, orange, and red. In the first pan, drop half the purple batter into the center. Carefully add half the blue batter right on top of the purple, followed by green, yellow, orange, and red. Do not stir at all!
8. In the second pan, use remaining batter in the reverse order, beginning with the red.
9. Bake for about 40 minutes or until toothpick inserted in center comes out clean.
10. Cool completely before removing from pans.
11. Frost when cool.

*TIP*

- Gel coloring is available anywhere cake decorating supplies are sold. Liquid food coloring will not produce the same vibrant colors.

## FROSTING

- 2 packages vanilla instant pudding (4-serving size)
- 2 cups / 500 ml milk
- 1 16-ounce/ 1-L tub frozen whipped topping, thawed
- Sprinkles (optional)

1. Combine pudding mix with milk and beat for 1 minute.
2. Fold in whipped topping.
3. Cut a thin slice off the top of 1 cake layer to create a level top. Place layer on cake plate.
4. Spread a generous amount of frosting over first layer.
5. Top with second layer.
6. Frost top and sides of cake.
7. Decorate with sprinkles, if desired.
8. Refrigerate until ready to serve.

*—Judy*

Our oldest grandchildren are twin girls, and over the years they have enjoyed many fun cakes. For their tenth birthday, I baked them a tie-dyed rainbow cake. It was a hit! Since that time, they have helped bake tie-dyed cakes for a cakewalk at their school, and more recently they enjoyed a tie-dyed rainbow cake at a sleepover with their friends. If you are looking for a cake to brighten someone's day, look no further.

61

The first time I ever ate a caramel apple was at a fair in the city. Although they can now be found in stores year-round, nothing can replace a homemade caramel apple made with an apple straight from the orchard. Biting through the sweet, creamy coating into the juicy crunch of a fresh apple will give you one more reason to look forward to apple-picking season!

After the apples are dipped and the caramel on the apples is no longer hot to touch, children can have fun decorating their own caramel apples. My favorite is a fine dusting of Himalayan pink salt that is then dipped in freshly roasted chopped walnuts.

# CARAMEL APPLES

## YIELDS 12–15 APPLES

- 12–15 apples of various sizes
- Popsicle or craft sticks
- 2 cups / 500 ml brown sugar
- 1 cup / 250 ml golden corn syrup
- ¼ cup / 60 ml maple syrup
- ½ cup / 125 ml butter
- 1⅓ cup (14-ounce / 300-ml can) sweetened condensed milk
- 1 teaspoon / 5 ml maple or vanilla extract
- Crushed nuts, small candies, freshly cracked Himalayan pink salt (optional)

1. Wash and dry apples.
2. Using fine sandpaper, scuff the sides of the apples very gently to help the caramel adhere.
3. Push sticks into the stem end of each apple and set aside.
4. Prepare several baking sheets by either lining them with parchment paper or greasing heavily.
5. Combine brown sugar, corn syrup, maple syrup, butter, and sweetened condensed milk in a medium saucepan. Stir over medium heat until butter is melted.
6. Raise heat to medium high and stir constantly until the caramel comes to a boil.
7. Lower heat to medium and stir constantly to avoid scorching until a candy thermometer reaches soft-ball stage, 235° F / 113° C. This will take 15–20 minutes. Using a heat-safe silicone spatula to scrape the bottom of the pan will help prevent scorching. Remove from heat and cool about 5 minutes until thermometer reads 200° F / 93° C. Stir in extract.
8. Dip the apples into the caramel and then into crushed nuts or candies, if desired. Set onto prepared cookie sheets.
9. Store in the refrigerator. Very fresh apples will keep in the refrigerator for 1 week.

*TIP*

- This recipe is not safe for children to make themselves. Keep children away from the stove while preparing the caramel, as the intense heat of the caramel could cause severe burns.

*—Lovella*

## THE BUD

Back door slamming, he bounced in,
Front teeth missing, what a grin!
Mysteriously hiding something behind him;
Should I ask where he had been?
The yard is exciting, there's much to see.
Then, oh so proudly, he handed it to me—
A beautiful rosebud in perfect splendor
With words shyly spoken in awe and wonder.
"It smells like strawberries!" he said,
"And I wish it could stay like this forever!"
The look in his eyes, the sound of his voice,
Oh, sweet little boy among boys!

In the evening as I tuck him into bed
And watch him drifting off to sleep,
I remember the moment and the words he said.
I ponder the things I'd like to keep,
The things I wish could stay forever—
His purity and innocence, his unspoiled joy.
But the world is waiting, with all its wonder
And like the bud, he can't always stay a boy.
At the end of the day I won't know where he's been
And as I reach to smooth that wisp of hair,
A prayer rises up from deep within,
"Dear Lord, please always keep him in your care."

—*Anneliese*

(BASED ON AN EXPERIENCE
RECORDED ON JUNE 8, 1989.)

## BREAD FOR THE JOURNEY
# WRITING *on the* HEARTS *of* CHILDREN

*Your word is a lamp to my feet and a light to my path.*

—PSALM 119:105 (ESV)

As my thoughts turn back to my childhood, I can say that I have reason to celebrate. "Tell me the stories of Jesus, write on my heart every word": these words from a Sunday school song became my heart's desire from a young age.

My mom treasured and protected the hearts of her children like they were precious jewels. She made wise and healthy deposits into our lives each day through setting an example, talking about Jesus, reading the Bible, and praying with us. I can still hear her soft voice singing hymns and choruses throughout the day. Once tucked into bed, I could hear her singing songs about Jesus and his love. The words became familiar and have stayed with me, nourishing my soul.

*When we share God's Word with children around us, we are passing on the greatest story ever told.*

My dad was never one for taking us shopping, but I remember one morning he told us that on Saturday he planned to take us to the Christian bookstore. When Saturday came, he explained that he wanted us to walk around the store and read the plaques that had Scripture verses printed on them. He told each of us to pick one that had a verse on it that we liked and that he would buy it for us to take home and hang in our rooms. I remember as if it were yesterday reading the verses on many plaques and then stopping at one with a verse that I knew by memory. It read, "Thy word is a lamp unto my feet, and a light unto my path. Psalm 119:105." I had made my choice. Later that day I hung the plaque on my bedroom wall. This plaque came with me when I left home. God's Word has shed the needed light on my lifelong pathway.

God's Word is a precious gift. When we make a practice of opening it up, its message will come alive in our hearts and we will feel the nearness of God. His love and faithfulness, even in the most difficult times, will be a comfort and will bring hope and light to our pathway when we feel hopeless and lost. God's Word is a source of encouragement, joy, and inspiration, renewing us day by day. It's a message for all generations, one we have shared with our own children and now share with our grandchildren. When we share God's Word with children around us, we are passing on the greatest story ever told. ✎

*—Kathy*

# CELEBRATING *Marriage*

It is so fitting to celebrate the union of marriage, where Jesus performed his first miracle and kept the celebration going. Join us around a beautiful tea table spread with delicacies that will be enjoyed by all who gather to honor the new bride and groom.

## CELEBRATE WITH

*Let love and faithfulness never leave you . . . write them on the tablet of your heart.*
—PROVERBS 3:3 (NIV)

# LOVELLA REFLECTS *on* MARRIAGE

*A*s a three-year-old, I walked down the aisle as Auntie Betty's flower girl in my pink organza dress. Seeing a bride for the first time, radiantly beautiful beside her handsome groom, left a big impression on me. A few years later, two of my older brothers married, and I again practiced walking down the aisle while lighting candles. My dreams of being a bride began.

I relished the idea of marriage, and as a teenager, I spent precious time with my best friends, Nancy and Shirley, laying out the important qualifications of a husband. While I envisioned my wedding gown with a long train and a veil edged in lace, I dreamed of a good-looking, romantic, musically talented, and (naturally) wealthy husband. Before my search could even begin, I was drawn to a boy in English class who was shy, tidy, and kind. By the time that course was finished, we considered ourselves to be in love and he signed my grade-nine yearbook with, "To my dear Lovella." Terry and I spent the remaining years of high school lunch hours sitting at the end of school corridors, sharing ketchup chips and ice cream sandwiches and thinking toward our life together.

*As we show mercy to each other in our shortcomings, we believe that our relationship is a gift from God.*

It never once occurred to me then that I should look beyond attraction and friendship. While I sensed that his musical talent and romantic sensitivities still needed some work, I no longer worried about wealth, since he had a part-time job as a grocery clerk and full-time work at the store lined up after graduation. If any of the qualifications I had previously deemed important were lacking, I was certain that they would develop, at least in part, after marriage.

My beloved came to the marriage with a quiet spirit, a faithful heart, a natural ability to keep everything around him clean, and most of all, a desire to love me. Rather than expecting the supercharged romance promised by films and television shows, I learned over the years to see the gentle, daily tokens of his love all around me. I had never even wondered if he would love children, but as I see him now with our grands, I realize in a new way that he was a wonderful daddy who taught his sons by example how to grow up to be men worthy of their wives' respect.

Occasionally, we tuck our grands into bed and tell them stories of long ago. Our oldest grandgirlie has asked to hear the story of when Grammie was a bride, and she is not content to have the story end with the wedding trip. Perhaps it is a ploy to keep the story going, but it reminds me that the story of a marriage should have many chapters. When she says to Grandpa, "I want to hear about how Grammie is a bride up to today," she is trusting that the love story continues.

I often marvel at God's grace in how I was led to my life partner, but then I look at the example of my parents and remember how they loved each other well. They gave each of their children a priceless advantage by praying for us as we entered into marriage. (The photographs in the field show me wearing my mother's wedding dress from 1942 and my granddaughter in the flower-girl dress that I wore at my aunt's wedding in 1962. My mother sewed both of these dresses as well as my wedding gown, shown here in our wedding photograph from 1978.)

We've shared life together as husband and wife for thirty-five years now, and we are still finding joy and contentment in the commitment. As we show mercy to each other in our shortcomings, we believe that our relationship is a gift from God. Because we are so thankful, we invest our homegrown skills by mentoring other couples as they prepare for marriage. We hope to be an encouragement and inspiration for wherever their road may lead. May we be faithful in passing on the beauty of marriage. ❧

—*Lovella*

# WHITE GRAPE AND LIME SPARKLING PUNCH

## SERVES 24

In my home this punch is known as the "Christmas punch" because it is pale green and looks quite festive in the punch bowl with frozen cranberries floating on top. Ice cubes containing wee slices of lime or edible flowers are a nice touch as well. Light and refreshing, it is a great party punch any time of the year! An added bonus is that spills won't leave stains like red beverages do.

➤ 1 11.5-ounce / 340-ml can frozen white grape juice concentrate

➤ 1 12-ounce / 355-ml can frozen limeade concentrate

➤ 8 cups / 2 L water

➤ 1–2 quarts / 1–2 liters citrus-flavored carbonated beverage

1. Mix frozen juice concentrates with water.
2. Add citrus-flavored beverage to taste.
3. Serve in punch bowl, adding ice and garnishes.

*—Judy*

# PUFF PASTRY SPIRALS

## YIELDS APPROXIMATELY 30 SPIRALS

- ➤ 1 package frozen puff pastry (2 sheets)
- ➤ Honey Dijon mustard
- ➤ About 4 slices honey ham, thinly sliced
- ➤ ¾ cup / 175 ml fresh Parmesan cheese, finely grated, divided
- ➤ 2 tablespoons / 30 ml spreadable cream cheese
- ➤ Red or green pesto

## HAM AND PARMESAN SPIRALS

1. Roll one sheet of puff pastry to about ¼-inch / 0.5-cm thick.
2. Spread with a thin amount of honey Dijon mustard.
3. Add a layer of thinly sliced honey ham.
4. Top with ½ cup / 125 ml finely grated Parmesan cheese.
5. Gently and tightly roll each short end of the pastry toward the center. Slice into ½–¾ -inch / 1–2-cm slices.

## CREAM CHEESE AND PESTO SPIRALS

1. On the second sheet of rolled-out puff pastry, spread a thin layer of cream cheese. Top with a thin layer of pesto.
2. Sprinkle with remaining ¼ cup / 60 ml Parmesan cheese.
3. Starting at the shorter end of the pastry, roll it up in a pinwheel fashion.
4. Cut into ½–¾-inch / 1–2-cm slices.

## BAKING INSTRUCTIONS

1. Place spirals on parchment-lined baking sheets. Bake at 400° F / 205° C for 10–15 minutes or until puffed and golden brown.

*TIP*

- These can be made ahead of time and kept in the refrigerator until ready to bake if you want to serve them warm. They also taste good at room temperature.

*—Charlotte*

Since these puff pastries are so quick and easy to make, I bake them up the day of the party. They add nice variety to a table of appetizers with delicate, savory flavors. They also make a nice complement to a pear salad for a special luncheon.

# TEA SANDWICHES

## WEST COAST CHICKEN SALAD SANDWICHES
### YIELDS 24–32 SANDWICHES

### CHIMICHURRI

- 4 garlic cloves, minced
- ½ jalapeño pepper, minced
- ½ lime, juiced
- 3 tablespoons / 45 ml red wine vinegar
- 2 tablespoons / 30 ml extra light olive oil
- ½ cup / 125 ml fresh parsley, finely chopped
- ½ cup / 125 ml fresh cilantro, finely chopped
- 1 teaspoon / 5 ml kosher salt

### OTHER INGREDIENTS

- 2 dozen mini-croissants
- 2 cups / 500 ml roasted chicken breast, cubed
- 2 cups / 500 ml jicama, peeled and cubed
- 2 tomatillos, husked, rinsed, and diced
- ½ red onion, chopped
- ½ cup / 125 ml mayonnaise

These are not your mother's chicken salad sandwiches. The freshness of the chimichurri gives these tea sandwiches an unexpected level of flavor. You'll be pleasantly surprised with the nice crunch the jicama gives the filling. Jicama, a root vegetable, and tomatillos, a relative of tomatoes with a papery outer husk, are used in Mexican cuisine and can be found in grocery stores or specialty stores.

### CHIMICHURRI INSTRUCTIONS

1. Combine garlic, jalapeño, and lime juice in a small mixing bowl.
2. Whisk in vinegar and olive oil.
3. Stir in parsley, cilantro, and salt.
4. Cover and let stand for at least 2 hours.

### SALAD INSTRUCTIONS

1. In a large bowl, mix the chicken, jicama, tomatillos, and red onion.
2. Stir in the chimichurri sauce and fold in the mayonnaise. For a creamier filling, add more mayonnaise to taste.
3. Slice open mini-croissants and fill generously with chicken salad filling.
4. Arrange on a 3-tiered plate stand or single platter and serve immediately.
5. Refrigerate any leftover filling.

*—Ellen*

77

Scoring the cucumbers instead of peeling them completely gives the little sandwich rounds an effect that will add to the visual beauty of your tea table.

# CUCUMBER TEA SANDWICH BITES
## YIELD 24–36 SANDWICH ROUNDS

- 1 8-ounce / 250-g tub whipped cream cheese
- 1 tablespoon / 15 ml seasoned rice vinegar
- 3 tablespoons / 45 ml fresh chives, chopped
- 2 large or 6 small cucumbers
- 1 loaf bread of choice, thinly sliced

1. Set aside ¼ cup / 60 ml of the whipped cream cheese to use for piping.
2. Mix together remaining cream cheese, rice vinegar, and 2 tablespoons / 30 ml chives. (Reserve remaining 1 tablespoon / 15 ml chives for garnish.)
3. Wash and score cucumbers with a fork or lemon zester instead of peeling.
4. Slice the cucumbers uniformly.
5. Using a 1½-inch / 4-cm diameter round cookie cutter, cut out 24–36 rounds of bread.
6. Spread each round of bread with the cream cheese mixture.
7. Top each prepared round with 1 large or 3 small cucumber slices.
8. Pipe a little mound of cream cheese on the center of the cucumber slices and sprinkle with reserved chives.
9. Arrange on a 3-tiered plate stand or single platter to serve.

*—Ellen*

# EGG-FILLED SPIRALS

## YIELDS 24 SPIRAL SANDWICHES

- 8 hard-boiled eggs, chopped
- ¼ cup / 60 ml dill pickles, minced
- 2 tablespoons / 30 ml
  fresh dill weed, minced
- 2 tablespoons / 30 ml
  fresh chives, minced
- ½ cup / 125 ml mayonnaise
  or salad dressing
- ½ teaspoon / 2 ml salt, or to taste
- 1 loaf soft whole wheat
  or white bread

1. Mix together all the filling ingredients and chill.
2. Using a serrated or electric knife, cut crusts from bread. Slice bread lengthwise into ⅓-inch / 1-cm slices. You will need 4 slices for 1 recipe of filling.
3. Spread egg filling ⅓-inch / 0.75-cm thick on bread.
4. Roll up spirals from the short end and wrap in plastic wrap. Refrigerate overnight.
5. Using a serrated or electric knife, cut each roll into 6 slices and place on tray.

*—Lovella*

Egg-salad sandwiches are timeless favorites that grace nearly every tea sandwich tray. My mom often made open-faced bun sandwiches with this egg filling. Egg filling can be dressed up for special occasions by rolling tea sandwiches into spirals. Most bakeries will be happy to slice bread to your specifications. The dill pickles and herbs are optional in this filling.

## GLUTEN-FREE SANDWICHES ⓖⒻ

Any of the tea sandwiches can be made gluten free by using a gluten-free mayonnaise and serving them on gluten-free bread.

# CROISSANTS

## YIELDS 24

- 5 teaspoons / 25 ml active dry yeast
- ½ cup / 125 ml lukewarm water
- ½ cup / 125 ml milk
- ¼ cup / 60 ml sugar

- 2 teaspoons / 10 ml salt
- 3 tablespoons / 45 ml butter, melted and cooled
- 2½ cups / 625 ml unbleached flour
- 1 cup / 250 ml unsalted butter, chilled

1. Add yeast to lukewarm water in a mixing bowl. Let rest 5 minutes.
2. Add milk, sugar, salt, melted butter, and flour to the yeast mixture and stir until most of the flour is absorbed. Knead with the dough hook attachment on a mixer for 5 minutes or by hand until smooth and elastic.
3. Shape dough into a rectangle, place into a freezer bag, and refrigerate for 12 hours or overnight.
4. On the next day, dust counter lightly with flour and roll the dough into a rectangle that measures 9 x 25 inches / 23 x 64 cm.
5. Lightly score the dough into 3 parts.
6. Slice chilled butter into thin pieces as shown and divide evenly to cover ⅔ of the dough. Fold the unbuttered section over ⅓ of buttered side, and then fold over once more as you would a letter. Pinch the edges gently to seal in butter. Cover loosely with plastic wrap and allow to rest for 15 minutes.
7. Dust counter very lightly with flour. Roll dough back into the original size, and fold again into thirds as one folds a letter.
8. Wrap the dough in wax or parchment paper and place in a lidded container. Refrigerate for approximately 1 hour.
9. Repeat seventh and eighth steps 4 times.
10. Remove from refrigerator, roll back to the original size, and slice in the middle down the length of the dough.
11. Cut each long slice into 6 even pieces to make 12 squares. Cut each of these squares on the diagonal, as shown, to make 24 triangles.
12. Each triangle will have 2 long edges and 1 short edge. The long edges may not be quite the same length. Beginning at the short end, roll up to the tip of the triangle, ending with the tip underneath the croissant. Turn the 2 ends toward one another to shape into a crescent.
13. Place croissants on a cookie sheet, allowing room for them to rise. Cover with a tea towel and then with a plastic bag, and allow them to rise for 1 hour before baking. Or place immediately side by side in a lidded container and freeze. To bake frozen croissants, place on cookie sheets and allow to thaw and rise until doubled, up to 7 hours, in a cool place before baking.
14. Bake in a preheated 400° F / 205° C oven for 12–15 minutes or until golden brown.

I first learned to make croissants in foods class in high school, and I am grateful that my teacher saw the method as valid in understanding how flakes form in pastry. This recipe requires more patience than expertise, and I expect that most cooks will find it satisfying to create such beautiful delicacies for special events.

## TIPS

- Croissant pastry should never become warm during preparation. If the butter begins to melt, the layers will collapse.
- The pastry is chilled between rollings to allow the gluten to relax and make the pastry easier to work with. When chilling the dough, it is important that the dough not dry out. I use parchment paper and a rectangular cake pan with a lid. This makes it easy to do the repeat steps of chilling and rolling.
- Use a light hand with dusting flour onto counter. If the pastry is sticking, use a bit more flour. It is important that the pastry does not tear, as that will allow the butter to escape.
- At first you will be able to see where the butter slabs are, but eventually they will become unnoticeable as they become rolled thin to form flakes.
- Bake until golden brown. The layers inside must be baked or they will not be light and flaky.

*—Lovella*

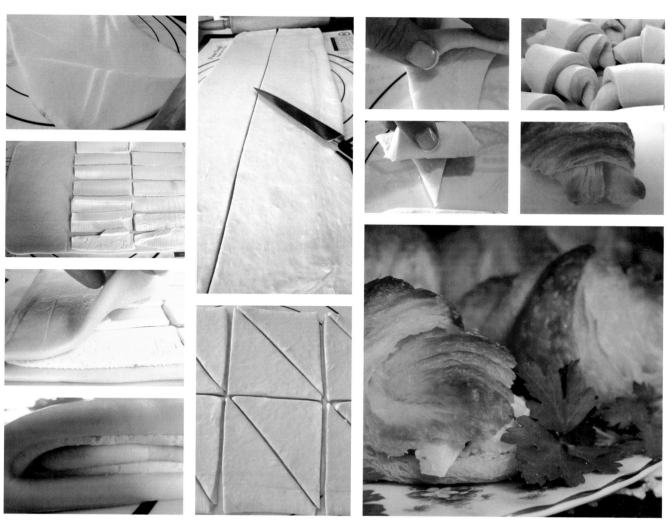

# SMOKED SALMON *and* MUSHROOM TURNOVERS

**YIELDS 4 DOZEN**

As this recipe combines several of our favorite appetizers and flavors, this has become a family favorite. Though these turnovers initially take a bit of time to prepare, they can be made weeks in advance and pulled out of the freezer and baked as guests are walking in the door.

## PASTRY

- 8 ounces / 250 g cream cheese
- ⅓ cup / 75 ml butter
- 1 cup / 250 ml flour

1. Cube cream cheese and butter. Combine with flour in a food processor until fine crumbs form. Alternatively, in a medium mixing bowl, cream together cream cheese and butter and then stir in the flour.
2. Turn mixture out onto a long piece of plastic wrap. Pressing together using the plastic wrap, form a flattened rectangle. Wrap in plastic wrap and chill for 30 minutes.

## FILLING

- 2 tablespoons / 30 ml butter
- ¾ cup / 175 ml onion, finely diced
- 1½ cup / 375 ml white button mushrooms, finely diced
- 2 tablespoons / 30 ml fresh lemon juice
- ¼ cup / 60 ml cream cheese
- 1 cup / 250 ml smoked salmon, finely chopped
- ¼ cup / 60 ml fresh dill weed, minced
- 1 egg, beaten, for egg wash

1. While the pastry is chilling, melt butter in a large frying pan and add the onion, mushrooms, and lemon juice. Sauté over medium heat until tender and the liquid has evaporated.
2. Stir in cream cheese, mixing until the cream cheese has melted.
3. Add the salmon and dill, stir to combine, and remove from heat. Cool mixture for 15 minutes in refrigerator.

## ASSEMBLING TURNOVERS

1. Sprinkle flour on a pastry mat and roll pastry into a large rectangle 24 x 14 inches / 60 x 35 cm.
2. Using a 2½-inch / 6-cm round cutter, cut out rounds of dough and put 1 teaspoon / 5 ml filling in the center. Fold dough together and pinch the edges shut to make a crescent shape. Collect the leftover dough, re-roll it, and make more turnovers until all the dough and filling have been used up.

3. Arrange the turnovers on parchment-lined baking sheets, brush with a beaten egg, prick with a fork, and put in the freezer until firm. Store the pastries in a sealed container in the freezer.

4. To bake, remove as many pastries as you want to serve and put them on a parchment-lined baking sheet about an inch apart. Bake frozen at 375° F / 190° C for about 15–20 minutes or until golden brown. Serve immediately.

*TIP*

- If there is some leftover filling as you make the turnovers, enjoy it on a cracker.

*—Lovella*

These wonton cups would make a pretty base for a variety of prepared fillings, warm or cold, sweet or savory.

# CRAB *and* MANGO CUPS

## YIELDS 4 DOZEN

- 1 package wonton wrappers
- 2 tablespoons / 30 ml canola oil
- 1 16-ounce / 454-g package imitation crabmeat
- 2 small mangoes, peeled and diced
- 2 ribs celery, finely chopped
- 1–2 tablespoons / 15–30 ml fresh dill weed, minced
- 2 tablespoons / 30 ml fresh chives, finely chopped
- 1 tablespoon / 15 ml red bell pepper, finely chopped (optional)
- ⅓ cup / 75 ml mayonnaise (approximately)
- Juice from ½ lime
- Salt and pepper

## CUPS

1. Preheat oven to 375° F / 190° C.
2. Working with 12 wonton wrappers at a time, lay the wrappers on your counter or pastry sheet.
3. Lightly brush both sides with oil.
4. Sprinkle one side sparingly with salt.
5. Fit each wrapper into a mini-tart tin cup, folding and pressing the wrapper into the sides to form a cup, making sure the 4 corners are pointing up.
6. Bake until cups are brown and crisp, about 8–9 minutes.
7. When cups are cool, remove from tins and store until needed in an airtight container. They should be used within 2 or 3 days.

## FILLING

1. Finely chop imitation crab and place in a medium mixing bowl.
2. Add remaining ingredients, using only half the mayonnaise to start and adding more if necessary. Do not make the filling too moist, as the mango will add moisture as it sits.
3. Season to taste with salt and pepper.
4. Just before serving, fill each wonton cup with crab-mango filling and garnish with a bit of dill. Serve immediately.

*TIPS*

- Wonton wrappers come in a block package and can be found in the produce section of major grocery stores.
- You will need 4 dozen wrappers. Store any unused wrappers in the refrigerator to use within a week. You can halve the recipe if you like.

*—Bev*

# ALMOND CREAM STRAWBERRIES

## YIELDS 30

- ¾ cup / 175 ml cream cheese
- ½ cup / 125 ml sour cream
- ½ cup / 125 ml icing sugar
- ¼ teaspoon / 1 ml almond extract
- 1 teaspoon / 5 ml vanilla extract
- 30 fresh strawberries
- Toasted almonds

1. In a small bowl, beat cream cheese, sour cream, icing sugar, and extracts until fluffy.
2. Cut a deep X in the tip of each strawberry.
3. Gently spread apart the center of the strawberry, keeping the berry whole. Pipe cream cheese mixture into each berry.
4. Chill until set.
5. Garnish berries with toasted almonds before serving.

—*Betty*

These festive cream-filled strawberries are beautiful, easy to make, and the perfect treat for any special occasion. If serving them as a dessert, allow at least three strawberries per person.

# BEST-KEPT SECRET SCONES *with* CRÈME FRAÎCHE

## YIELDS 9 SCONES

### SCONES

- ¼ cup / 60 ml applesauce
- ½ cup / 125 ml vanilla yogurt
- 2 eggs
- ¼ cup / 55 g butter, softened
- ½ cup / 125 ml milk
- Zest of ½ lemon (approximately ½ teaspoon / 2.5 ml) (optional)
- 1 teaspoon / 5 ml almond extract
- ½ cup / 65 g millet flour

- ¼ cup / 50 g white rice flour
- ½ cup / 95 g white corn flour
- ½ cup / 75 g tapioca starch/flour
- ¼ cup / 30 g cornstarch
- 4 teaspoons / 30 g baking powder
- ¼ teaspoon / 2 g baking soda
- ¼ teaspoon / 2 g salt
- 2 tablespoons / 25 g sugar
- 1 teaspoon / 3 g xanthan gum

Biscuits were something I missed on a gluten-free diet until I came up with this recipe. These scones are flavorful and light and . . . shhhhhh . . . gluten free!

1. In the bowl of a mixer, combine applesauce, yogurt, eggs, butter, milk, lemon zest, and almond extract. Mix until well blended.
2. Sift together dry ingredients.
3. Add dry ingredients all at once to liquids and beat on high speed until smooth and elastic, about 1 minute.
4. Drop by spoonfuls onto a greased baking sheet. Alternatively, make rings of folded parchment paper, as shown, to shape scones.
5. Bake at 375° F / 190° C for 20 minutes or until nicely browned.
6. Serve warm or cool.

*TIPS*

- To make rings, fold 12 x 5-inch / 30 x 12-cm strips of parchment paper twice lengthwise. Staple into 3-inch / 8-cm diameter rings that are 1½ inches / 4 cm high. Using parchment-paper rings controls the shape of the scones and encourages them to rise instead of flattening.
- You can vary these scones by adding ½ cup / 125 ml blueberries, dried cranberries, or raisins. These keep well and are still great the next day.

Crème fraîche is wonderful whipped, sweetened, and used as a dessert topping or as a filling. It can be used in place of whipped cream or as a substitute for a layer of cream cheese in desserts. Crème fraîche holds its shape without weeping; no stabilizers are required.

## CRÈME FRAÎCHE

➤ 2 cups / 500 ml whipping cream          ➤ 2 tablespoons / 30 ml buttermilk

1. Pour whipping cream into glass jar; microwave until just barely lukewarm.
2. Add buttermilk and stir well.
3. Cover with plastic wrap and set on kitchen counter for 24 hours. If it is not set, let it sit a while longer.
4. Refrigerate for several hours.
5. Use plain or whip it with sugar as a substitute for whipped cream.

*TIP*

• Serve scones with strawberries and crème fraîche that has been whipped, sweetened with sugar, and flavored with vanilla extract.

*—Julie*

# LEMON SHORTBREAD TARTS

## YIELDS 40–48 MINI-TARTS

### TARTS

- 1 cup / 250 ml butter, room temperature
- ½ cup / 125 ml icing sugar
- 1¼ cups / 300 ml flour
- ½ cup / 125 ml cornstarch
- 1 teaspoon / 5 ml lemon zest

1. Using a pastry blender or 2 knives, cut butter into combined dry ingredients and lemon zest, blending until well incorporated.
2. Dust with flour and use a spatula to gather into a ball. Cover with plastic wrap and chill for 1 hour.
3. Using about ⅓ of the pastry at a time, roll out on a flour-dusted surface, to about ⅛-inch / 0.25-cm thick, dusting with more flour as needed.
4. Cut out circles, using a 2½-inch / 6-cm round cookie cutter or glass.
5. Using a spatula, gently lift each circle and place over top of a mini-muffin tin cavity. Do not push down in the center; rather, gently push sides of pastry so that it drops in.
6. Gather remaining scraps of pastry and re-roll. If too soft, chill for a while. Repeat until all the pastry is used, making sure to roll it out quite thin. Prick bottoms with a fork.
7. Cover tarts with plastic wrap and freeze to set. Bake frozen tarts the day before or the day of serving.
8. Bake at 325° F/ 160° C for about 15 minutes, until light golden in color. About 5 minutes into baking time, you can push the centers down gently, using your finger, if they swell too much. Baking time can vary according to the type of pans used. Do not overbake.
9. Cool before removing from pans. Gently twirl tarts with finger and remove, or turn pans upside down onto a clean tea towel and tap bottoms to help tarts drop out.
10. Fill with lemony cheese filling a few hours before serving.

# LEMONY CHEESE FILLING

- 8 ounces / 250 g cream cheese, room temperature
- 10 ounces / 300 ml sweetened condensed milk
- 4 tablespoons / 60 ml lemon juice
- 1 teaspoon / 5 ml vanilla extract

1. Beat cream cheese with mixer until very creamy.
2. Gradually beat in sweetened condensed milk and then lemon juice and vanilla.
3. For easiest, smoothest filling, fill tarts right away. Top with any kind of berry and a tiny slice of kiwi.
4. Just before serving, dust with icing sugar. Leftovers will keep for a few days in fridge.

*TIP*

- Do not store tarts in a sealed container. Tarts can sit at room temperature for several hours but should be refrigerated for longer periods.

*—Anneliese*

The recipe for these delightful little cheesecakes was a family secret until my cousin by marriage, Alvina, shared it with me and I begged her to allow me to let the world know. Many people have enjoyed these tarts at wedding showers and longed for the recipe, so here it is!

# RASPBERRY CAKE ROLL

**SERVES 12**

## CAKE

- 6 eggs, separated
- ¼ teaspoon / 1 g cream of tartar
- 1 cup / 200 g sugar, divided
- 1 tsp / 5 ml vanilla extract
- ¼ cup / 30 g arrowroot powder/ starch/flour
- ¼ cup / 50 g brown rice flour
- ½ cup / 95 g white corn flour
- ½ teaspoon / 2 g salt
- ½ teaspoon / 2 g baking powder
- ½ teaspoon / 2 g xanthan gum
- Icing sugar (for dusting tea towel)

It is the filling that makes this cake roll stand out as special and is well worth the extra effort.

1. Preheat oven to 350° F / 175° C.
2. Beat egg whites until foamy. Add cream of tartar and ¼ cup / 50 g sugar. Beat until stiff (but not dry) peaks form. Set aside.
3. In mixer bowl, beat 6 egg yolks with ¾ cup / 150 g sugar and vanilla until light-colored and fluffy.
4. Combine and sift dry ingredients, then add them to the yolk mixture and beat until smooth.
5. Fold in beaten egg whites until well incorporated.
6. Spoon batter into an 11 x 17-inch / 28 x 43-cm baking sheet lined with parchment paper.
7. Bake for 25–30 minutes until toothpick inserted into the center comes out clean.
8. Turn upside down on a tea towel that has been liberally dusted with icing sugar. Remove parchment paper and cut away any crisp edges.
9. Starting at the shorter edge, roll up with the tea towel.
10. Let sit until cool. While cake is cooling, make filling.

# RASPBERRY FILLING

- 2 cups / 500 ml whipping cream
- 1 teaspoon / 5 ml
  vanilla pudding mix
- 8 ounces / 250 g cream cheese,
  softened
- ¾ cup / 90 g icing sugar
- ⅔ cup / 175 ml raspberry jelly
  (recipe follows)

1. Beat whipping cream with vanilla pudding mix until stiff. Set aside.
2. Whip softened cream cheese with icing sugar.
3. Beat raspberry jelly into cream cheese mixture.
4. Add whipped cream and beat just until blended.

# RASPBERRY JELLY

- 1½ cup / 375 ml raspberries,
  frozen or fresh
- 1 cup / 200 g sugar
- 2 teaspoons / 10 g pectin

1. Crush raspberries with a potato masher in a small saucepan, and bring berries to a boil to maximize juice.
2. Press through a sieve to remove all seeds. About 1 cup / 250 ml juice will remain.
3. Add sugar and fruit pectin to the juice. Bring this mixture to a rolling boil that can't be stirred down.
4. Cook for 1 minute. Pour into jar and cool. This makes 1 cup / 250 ml raspberry jelly.

# ASSEMBLING CAKE ROLL

1. Carefully unroll cake from the tea towel.
2. Spread filling over the cake, saving enough for the top of the roll.
3. Re-roll cake, taking care to not squeeze out the filling.
4. Use leftover filling to decorate the top of cake roll, and decorate as desired.
5. Refrigerate until needed.

*—Julie*

# NANAIMO BARS

## YIELDS 50 BARS

### BOTTOM LAYER / CRUMB BASE

- ½ cup / 125 ml unsalted butter
- ⅓ cup / 75 ml cocoa powder
- ¼ cup / 60 ml sugar
- 1 egg, lightly beaten
- ⅔ cup / 150 ml walnuts, finely chopped
- 1 cup / 250 ml fine unsweetened coconut
- 1⅓ cup / 325 ml graham cracker crumbs (approximately)

1. Line a 9 x 13-inch / 22 x 33-cm baking dish with aluminum foil.
2. In a medium saucepan, partially melt butter and remove from heat. Alternatively, put the butter in a microwave-safe bowl and melt until it is nearly but not entirely melted. If the butter is too hot, it will instantly cook the egg when you add it.
3. Add the cocoa and sugar and whisk until smooth.
4. Add a small amount of the warm mixture to the slightly beaten egg and whisk to temper the eggs (see tips). Return to the saucepan or bowl and whisk until smooth.
5. Return to heat and stir until mixture has thickened. Alternatively, put mixture back in the microwave for about 1 minute, whisking after 30 seconds. Your mixture should be like custard. This process will cook the egg and thicken the mixture.
6. Add walnuts and coconut, stirring until well combined.
7. Add the graham crackers last. Don't add all the crumbs at once; some brands of graham cracker crumbs are more powdery and can dry out the mixture. If the mixture is too dry, it will crumble later when slicing. Spread the mixture into the prepared pan, press firmly, and chill for 1 hour.

### SECOND LAYER / CREAM FILLING

- ½ cup / 125 ml unsalted butter, softened
- 2 tablespoons / 30 ml unsweetened custard powder (see tips)
- 2 cups / 500 ml icing sugar
- 3 tablespoons / 45 ml heavy cream

1. Cream the butter with a mixer. Add the custard powder and combine well.
2. Beat in the icing sugar and then drizzle in the cream a bit at a time to make a smooth, thick icing. Spread over the chilled crumb base using an offset spatula, smoothing as much as possible. Refrigerate until firm.

## THIRD LAYER / CHOCOLATE GLAZE

> 6 squares semi-sweet chocolate

> 3 tablespoons / 45 ml unsalted butter

1. Combine chocolate and butter in a microwave-safe bowl and heat for 30 seconds, then stir well. Continue heating in the microwave, stirring at 30-second intervals until it is perfectly smooth. Alternatively, stir mixture on the stove over very low heat until smooth. Take chilled bar out of the refrigerator and spread on the melted chocolate using an offset spatula. Resting the pan on the counter, shake it back and forth a few times to level the chocolate.
2. Refrigerate for a few minutes until it begins to set. Remove from refrigerator and score the bars with a sharp, thin-bladed knife, just through the chocolate layer.
3. Return to the refrigerator and chill until firm. Use foil to lift from pan and finish slicing the bar. Keep refrigerated.

*TIPS*

- To "temper" eggs means to avoid scrambling them when adding hot liquid. A small amount of hot liquid is added to the eggs to slowly raise the temperature of the eggs.
- Custard powder is basically cornstarch (or corn flour) with vanilla flavoring and yellow food coloring. If custard powder is unavailable, substitute the same amount of cornstarch and add a teaspoon of vanilla powder (which can usually be purchased at stores selling cake decorating supplies, online, or sometimes at Asian markets) or pure vanilla extract.
- As you heat the chocolate layer, make sure that no droplets of water or steam get into the chocolate or it will become grainy and lose its smooth, glossy texture.
- Scoring the top layer before it is completely firm will help to prevent the chocolate from cracking when you slice it.

*—Lovella*

I've been making Nanaimo bars since my early teens. They are a British Columbian treat named after the city that first made them popular. They have always been my favorite bar, and I have many memories attached to them. When my mom and I invited my bridesmaids, Shirley and Elsie, and my future mother-in-law over to wrap the traditional fruit cake for our wedding favors, I made these bars to serve with tea. The result on that particular day was memorable for all the wrong reasons. The crumb base crumbled, the cream filling was runny, and the chocolate cracked. Much to my dismay, my mom served them and, in her effort to encourage my baking efforts, raved about how tasty they were. Since then I have perfected the recipe and now I share it with you. I am thankful for the memory of long ago that still makes me smile.

93

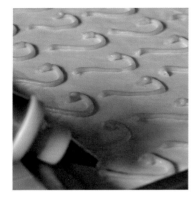

# CREAM PUFF SWANS

## YIELDS 24–30

### SWAN BODIES

- ½ cup / 125 ml butter
- ½ teaspoon / 2 ml salt
- 1 cup / 250 ml water
- 1 cup / 250 ml flour
- 4 eggs

1. Line baking sheets with parchment paper or grease and dust with flour. Preheat oven to 450° F / 230° C.
2. In a small saucepan, bring butter, salt, and water to a boil.
3. Remove from heat and quickly add flour, stirring vigorously, until it completely loosens from the sides of the pot.
4. Add eggs one at a time, beating well after each, until smooth.
5. For necks, fill a decorating tube or bag with about ½–¾ cup / 125–175 ml batter. Using a large (⅛-inch / 0.30-cm) writing tip #58, pipe out 30–40 question marks, each 2½-inches / 6-cm tall.
6. Bake the necks for about 5 minutes. Check frequently to make sure they do not darken beyond a light golden color. To keep them from getting too dark underneath, insert oven rack a little higher than the center of the oven.
7. For bodies, drop the remaining pastry by rounded teaspoon onto prepared cookie sheets. Bake at 450° F / 230° C for the first 10 minutes, then lower temperature to 350° F / 160° C and bake for 25–30 more minutes. Allow bodies and necks to cool before filling.

# VANILLA CUSTARD FILLING

- ➤ 2 cups / 500 ml milk, divided
- ➤ ¼ cup / 60 ml cornstarch
- ➤ 2 tablespoons / 30 ml sugar
- ➤ ⅛ teaspoon / 0.5 ml pure vanilla powder (or 1 teaspoon / 5 ml vanilla extract)
- ➤ 2 egg yolks
- ➤ 1 cup / 250 ml whipping cream

1. In a saucepan over medium heat, bring 1½ cup / 375 ml milk to a boil.
2. In the meantime, in a small bowl, mix cornstarch, sugar, vanilla, and just a small amount of the remaining ½ cup / 125 ml milk to make a paste. Beat in egg yolks, stirring until smooth, and then add the rest of the milk.
3. When milk in the pot begins to boil or skin forms on top, pour in the egg mixture, stirring constantly with a whisk, until smooth and bubbly. Cover with plastic wrap and cool in ice water or fridge.
4. When pudding has cooled completely, beat whipping cream in mixing bowl until stiff peaks form. Then beat in pudding just until well blended, adding 1 teaspoon / 5 ml sugar, if desired.

# ASSEMBLING THE SWANS

1. To make bodies, slice off the top ⅓ of each puff and set aside. Fill with vanilla custard.
2. Insert the necks, leaning them slightly backward on the front end of each swan. If bodies are slightly elongated, be sure it sits correctly.
3. To make wings, cut previously set-aside tops in half and insert, cut side into filling, so that the wings stand up at an angle.
4. Place on shiny silver tray or mirror for lake effect. Using a small sieve, dust with icing sugar.

*TIP*

- These can be prepared the day ahead and refrigerated. To keep them from getting soft, do not cover. You can put them in a large refrigerator drawer if you are concerned about them catching odors from other refrigerated items.

*—Anneliese*

Cream puffs have always been a favorite of mine. When I saw them shaped into swans at a party many years ago, I decided to try them, using my mother's basic recipe. The first time I made them was for my daughter's first birthday. Since then they have become a favorite for special occasions, especially for events related to weddings or baby showers.

Because some cultures use ducks as symbols of mating for life, wedding swans have added special meaning to this picture for me. Just for fun, when preparing for a baby shower, try making one or two large swans with a number of small ones trailing behind.

Needless to say, these pastries never fail to bring smiles, and they really are not as fussy as they first appear. The bodies can be baked ahead of time and frozen to fill on the day of serving.

Refrigerate for at least a few hours to set, before serving.

95

This recipe brings back memories of my mom baking hundreds of icicles for my wedding. These crispy dainties are great for adding to trays at showers, family gatherings, or Christmas celebrations. Generally I mix the dough in the evening, put it in the refrigerator, and roll it out first thing in the morning on the day I want to serve them. It takes less than an hour to twirl and bake them. There's no fuss after that, and the kitchen smells wonderful.

# ICICLES / *ZUCKERHÖRNCHEN*

## YIELDS 48–60 TWISTS

### PASTRY

- ½ cup / 125 ml butter
- 2 eggs
- ½ cup / 125 ml whipping cream
- ½ cup / 125 ml warm water
- ½ teaspoon / 2 ml salt
- 2½ cups / 625 ml flour
- 1½ tablespoon / 20 ml instant yeast

### VANILLA SUGAR COATING

- 1 cup / 375 ml sugar
- ¼ teaspoon / 1 ml pure vanilla powder

### CINNAMON SUGAR COATING

- 1 cup / 375 ml sugar
- 1 teaspoon / 5 ml cinnamon

1. Melt and cool butter until just warm.
2. In a large mixing bowl, beat eggs. Then add cream, water, salt, and butter, stirring well.
3. In a separate bowl, mix yeast into flour and add to wet ingredients, stirring until smooth. Shape mixture into a ball, dusting with more flour if needed. Cover and refrigerate for 6 hours or overnight.
4. Preheat oven to 350° F / 180° C.
5. Line two large baking sheets with parchment paper. Alternatively, grease and flour baking sheets well.
6. Divide dough into 2 parts. Taking 1 part at a time, shape into a log. Spread vanilla sugar coating or cinnamon sugar coating on rolling surface, and then roll each log into a 6 x 15-inch / 15 x 38-cm rectangle. As you roll, keep spreading sugar coating under and over top, using up to ½ cup / 125 ml for each half.
7. Cut into ½-inch / 1.25-cm strips. To form "ringlet" icicles, twirl each strip around the upper part of your right index finger, slip off, and push into a tight ringlet as you place it on the baking sheet.
8. Bake for 20 minutes or until light golden in color. If parchment paper wasn't used, remove icicles before they cool. These freeze well. Thaw uncovered.

*—Anneliese*

# VANILLA BABYCAKES

## YIELDS 36–40

- 1 cup / 250 ml sugar
- 1¾ cup / 425 ml cake flour
- 1½ teaspoon / 7 ml baking powder
- ½ teaspoon / 2 ml baking soda
- ½ teaspoon / 2 ml salt
- ¼ cup / 60 ml butter, room temperature

- 2 large eggs
- ⅓ cup / 75 ml sour cream
- ¼ cup / 60 ml grapeseed oil
- 2 teaspoons / 20 ml pure vanilla extract
- ⅔ cup / 150 ml liquid French vanilla coffee creamer

1. Preheat oven to 350° F / 175° C.
2. Measure dry ingredients into a large bowl. Stir well to blend and then sift. Set aside.
3. Beat together butter and eggs until creamy yellow in color.
4. Add sour cream, oil, vanilla, and coffee creamer. Beat well.
5. Add sifted dry mixture to wet mixture and beat just until everything is incorporated.
6. Fill paper baking mini-cups to ¾ full.
7. Bake for about 10 minutes. To test for doneness, poke with a toothpick. If it comes out with a bit of wet batter, bake another minute or 2 and then test again. These babycakes will be creamy white in color when done.
8. Remove babycakes from pans onto a cooling rack. When completely cooled, frost with butter-cream frosting.

## BUTTERCREAM FROSTING

- ½ cup / 125 ml unsalted butter, room temperature
- ½ cup / 125 ml high-ratio shortening, room temperature (see tips)
- 4 cups / 1000 ml icing sugar, sifted

- ½ teaspoon / 2 ml salt
- 4 tablespoons / 60 ml milk
- 2 teaspoons / 10 ml clear vanilla extract

1. Beat together butter and shortening until fluffy.
2. Add sugar and salt and beat well. Add milk and vanilla. Beat until frosting is smooth.
3. To frost babycakes, spoon buttercream into a pastry bag fit with piping tip.
4. Pipe frosting onto babycakes and decorate as you wish.

## DECORATING SUGGESTIONS

- Edible flowers
- Edible disco dust to add a shimmer
- Purchased candy flowers

When love is in the air, take the time to bake something extra special. These vanilla babycakes have a delicate crumb, and the buttercream frosting is creamy smooth. Topped with pretty edible flowers and a dusting of disco dust, which adds a shimmer, these babycakes will be enjoyed by all those gathering for the celebration.

# PRESERVING EDIBLE FLOWERS

1. Small pansies are edible and perfect for decorating babycakes. Make sure your flowers have not been sprayed or fed any fertilizer.
2. Pick pansies the same day that you will be serving the babycakes.
3. Gently wash flowers and lay on paper towels to dry. Once dry, place flowers on a flat glass plate.
4. Pour a small amount of lemon juice into a bowl. Dip a small paint brush into lemon juice and gently dab onto flower petals.
5. Using the same paint brush, gently paint the flower petals with egg wash. (To make an egg wash, mix 1 tablespoon / 15 ml meringue powder with 2 teaspoons / 10 ml water. Stir until you have a thin white liquid.)
6. Place flowers, uncovered, in the refrigerator for several hours. The petals will become slightly firm, but this process helps to preserve the flowers' shape and color.
7. Using a small tweezers, carefully pick up flowers and place on top of frosted babycakes. The flowers will stay fresh-looking for approximately 8 hours.

## TIPS

- High-ratio shortening holds more liquid and sugar than regular store-bought shortenings. It is very white in color and contains emulsifiers that help stabilize and whip better. Your frosting will have a smoother texture with a less greasy taste. High-ratio shortening can be purchased at some bakeries and specialty cake shops or online.
- For best results, keep decorated babycakes in a sealed container in refrigerator until ready to put onto serving tray.
- These babycakes freeze well with or without frosting for up to a month. Do not freeze edible flowers.

*—Kathy*

## BREAD FOR THE JOURNEY
# BRIDAL SHOWER BLESSING

*An excellent wife who can find?*
*She is far more precious than jewels.*
*The heart of her husband trusts in her,*
*and he will have no lack of gain.*
*She does him good, and not harm,*
*all the days of her life.*

—PROVERBS 31:10-12 (ESV)

{ *L*ord of heaven and earth,
you are the architect of marriage.
We pray for your hand of blessing on this new couple.
Guard each of their hearts with your Word.
May they grow closer to you as they follow you and may
they grow closer to each other as husband and wife.
May love grow generously in their lives.
Fill their relationship and home with your peace and joy,
and may they remain faithful to you and to each other as
they grow old together.
We bring these requests to you as we celebrate these lives
you have brought together.
In your name we pray,
Amen. ❧

*—Ellen*

# CELEBRATING *Family*

Family dinners are a beloved tradition in each of our homes. Featured in this section are some of the home-style menus that have been favorites at our tables over the years.

## CELEBRATE WITH

*May the Lord bless you . . . May you live to see your children's children.*
—PSALM 128:5-6 (NIV)

# JUDY REFLECTS ON FAMILY

*T*he year was 1926, and the family had gathered at the home of the grandparents in southern Russia. Grandmother wanted a photo of the grandchildren, dressed in all their finery and having a tea party. It was the year that my mother was born, so she is missing from the photograph of all the cousins. I doubt they knew it would be the last time they would all sit around the table together. Due to political upheaval, the family was soon scattered. Some left for Canada. My mother's family followed several years later, and her grandparents were exiled to Siberia. All they had left of their time together were the memories, the traditions, and the photograph.

*There is something special about everyone gathering around the table at Grandma's house.*

There is something special about everyone gathering around the table at Grandma's house. It's where cousins become good friends, where favorite family foods are shared, and where stories from the old days are told time and time again. Several decades later, cousins again gathered around the table. I have fond memories of time spent at my grandmother's table. In those days, the adults ate first. What a novel concept! Once they were finished with their meal, the table was re-set for all of us children, the cousins. The food was every bit as good as the meal at the first seating. Sunday supper always included *Zwieback* (double-decker buns), *Kotletten* (cold meatballs), potato salad, Jell-O salad, and an assortment of Grandma's trademark cookies. In the summer, Grandma would organize a cousin picnic, and she would serve watermelon and *Rollkuchen* (fried bread). When my own children arrived, time spent at Grandma's table was always special for them. She knew exactly what each of the grandchildren enjoyed eating and prepared it for them. And she always had treats.

I have no idea how this happened so quickly, but now I am the grandmother and the cousins are gathering around my table. I love to have the family come home for all those special occasions. We celebrate birthdays, holidays, and other milestones in life. Who better to share those moments with than family? We bought a larger dining room table so that we can all fit around it. There is no second seating! It is crowded, but we always seem to find room to add one more spot. Usually the cousins run off to play after we eat, while the adults take their time dining and chatting. They all return for dessert!

Just like my great-grandmother in Russia did so long ago, I enjoy having my grands around the table. I began hosting tea parties with the oldest granddaughters many years ago on Valentine's Day. When their brother arrived, he did not want to be left out. Now they all come and we have a grand tea party, whatever the occasion may be.

We never know what tomorrow may bring, but as long as it is today, we will celebrate our family.

Gathering around the table with family is about cementing family ties, carrying on traditions, and caring for each other. ✎

*Gathering around the table with family is about cementing family ties.*

—*Judy*

# MANGO CHICKEN SALAD

## SERVES 6 AS MAIN DISH

This is our family's favorite version of a mango chicken salad. One of my favorite suggestions is to keep some grilled teriyaki chicken in the freezer. Take it out and in a moment's notice, you are ready to serve a bowl of healthy and delicious goodness. I have often used this dish as a main course with a side of corn on the cob or freshly roasted potatoes. Add a slab of fresh apple *Perishky* for dessert and everyone's happy!

## SALAD

- 3 cups / 750 ml chicken breast, cooked and chopped
- 2 cups / 500 ml cabbage or Chinese cabbage, chopped
- 2 cups / 500 ml romaine hearts, chopped
- 1 cup / 250 ml carrots, shredded
- 2 cups / 500 ml red bell pepper, chopped
- 2 cups / 500 ml ripe mangoes, chopped
- 2 cups / 500 ml fresh bean sprouts
- ½ cup / 125 ml green onions, chopped
- ½ cup / 125 ml fresh cilantro, chopped
- ½ cup / 125 ml toasted sunflower or sesame seeds

1. Toss together all salad ingredients in a large serving bowl.
2. Add half the dressing to the salad. Toss again, adding more dressing until you are satisfied with the flavor.
3. Serve immediately.

## DRESSING

- ⅓ cup / 75 ml bottled peanut sauce
- ¼ cup / 60 ml hoisin sauce
- 1 tablespoon / 15 ml red wine vinegar
- 1 tablespoon / 15 ml toasted sesame oil
- 1 teaspoon / 5 ml ginger root, grated

1. Whisk together all dressing ingredients in a small bowl.
2. Cover and refrigerate until ready to use.

*—Marg*

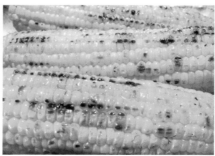

# SIRLOIN STROGANOFF
## *with* BUTTERED NOODLES

**SERVES 8–10**

## MEAT

- 2 tablespoons / 30 ml butter
- 1 cup / 250 ml yellow onion, finely chopped
- 1 large leek, rinsed well and finely chopped (about 2 cups / 500 ml)
- 1 large carrot, grated
- 2 pounds / 1 kg boneless top sirloin steak, cut into ½-inch / 1.5-cm strips or chunks
- ½ teaspoon / 2 ml garlic powder
- ½ teaspoon / 2 ml onion powder
- ⅛–¼ teaspoon / 0.5–1 ml cayenne pepper
- ½ teaspoon / 2 ml dried oregano
- 1 teaspoon / 5 ml kosher salt
- ½ teaspoon / 2 ml pepper, freshly ground
- 2 tablespoons / 30 ml flour
- 3 tablespoons / 45 ml beef stock or water
- 3 cups / 750 ml beef stock
- 1 bay leaf
- 1 teaspoon / 5 ml dried thyme

1. In a large pot, melt butter over medium-high heat.
2. Add chopped onion and sauté for 2 minutes.
3. Add leek and carrot, stirring until soft, about 4 minutes.
4. Add the steak, garlic powder, onion powder, cayenne, oregano, salt, and pepper. Cook until beef is browned, about 4 minutes.
5. In a small bowl, combine flour and 3 tablespoons / 45 ml beef stock or water to make a slurry.
6. Add to the pot and blend well. Let cook for 2 minutes.
7. Add the 3 cups / 750 ml beef stock, bay leaf, and thyme, stir well, and bring to a boil.
8. Lower heat to medium-low and simmer, partially covered, until meat is tender, about 1–1½ hours.
9. While the meat is simmering, prepare the mushrooms. Close to the end of the cooking process, start the noodles.

...................................................................................

Stroganoff is a family favorite at our house. Because of its Russian roots, I want to keep the tradition of this great dish alive in our family. We enjoy it with whole green beans and a crusty loaf of bread.

# MUSHROOMS

- 2 tablespoons / 30 ml butter
- 2 tablespoons / 30 ml olive oil
- 1 pound / 500 g fresh mushrooms, cleaned and sliced
- 3 garlic cloves, minced
- 3 sprigs fresh thyme
- 2 tablespoons / 30 ml Cognac or brandy
- ¼ teaspoon / 1 ml salt
- ⅛ teaspoon / 0.5 ml pepper
- 2 tablespoons / 30 ml sour cream
- 1 tablespoon / 15 ml Dijon mustard

1. In a large skillet, melt butter with olive oil. Add mushrooms and blend well.
2. Add garlic, thyme, and Cognac or brandy.
3. Sprinkle mushrooms with salt and pepper.
4. Sauté until mushrooms are browned and cooked through. Set aside to add to the pot of meat.
5. When meat is tender, remove pot from the heat, fold in the mushroom mixture, sour cream, and mustard, discarding the thyme sprig and bay leaf.
6. Taste and adjust seasoning, if needed.

# BUTTERED NOODLES

- 12–16 ounces / 350–500 g wide egg noodles
- 2 tablespoons / 30 ml butter
- 2 tablespoons / 30 ml chopped fresh parsley for garnish

1. Cook the noodles in a large pot of boiling, well-salted water until tender.
2. Drain the noodles and toss with butter.
3. Serve the stroganoff mixture over the noodles. Garnish with chopped parsley and more sour cream, if desired.

*—Ellen*

111

This is a simple version of chicken cordon bleu. I serve this with brown rice and a salad. Assemble this dish early in the day, refrigerate, and then put it in the oven just before the family walks in for dinner. It's a no-fuss meal, so you will have time to set a pretty table with special touches to welcome your loved ones.

# CHICKEN CORDON BAKE

## SERVES 9

- 4 cups / 1000 ml chicken, cooked and cubed
- 2 cups / 500 ml ham, cooked and cubed
- 1 cup / 250 ml Swiss cheese, grated
- ¼ cup / 60 ml butter

- ⅓ cup / 75 ml flour
- 2¼ cups / 550 ml milk
- ½ teaspoon / 2 ml dry mustard
- ⅛ teaspoon / 0.5 ml nutmeg
- ¼ teaspoon / 1 ml salt
- ½ teaspoon / 2 ml pepper

1. Preheat oven to 350° F / 175° C.
2. Layer chicken, ham, and cheese in a greased 9 x 13-inch / 22 x 33-cm baking dish.
3. In a medium pot, melt butter and stir in flour. Add milk and whisk until smooth.
4. Add dry mustard, nutmeg, salt, and pepper.
5. Cook over medium heat, stirring until thickened.
6. Pour sauce over meat and cheese and sprinkle with crunchy topping (below).
7. Bake for 30 minutes.

## CRUNCHY TOPPING

- 2½ cups / 625 ml coarse bread crumbs
- ¼ cup / 60 ml butter, melted

- ½ cup / 125 ml cheddar cheese, grated

1. Mix together bread crumbs, cheese, and melted butter.

*—Betty*

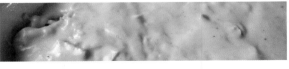

# ORANGE-SAUCED RIBS

## SERVES 4–6

- 2 pounds / 1 kg pork back ribs
- ½ cup / 125 ml bottled chili sauce
- ¼ cup / 60 ml ketchup
- 2 or 3 garlic cloves, minced
- ½ cup / 125 ml orange juice
- ¼ cup / 60 ml soy sauce
- ¼ cup / 60 ml honey
- 1 tablespoon / 15 ml Worcestershire sauce
- 1 tablespoon / 15 ml dry mustard
- Hot pepper sauce to taste (optional)

1. Heat grill until very hot (400° F / 205° C).
2. Cut each rib rack into 2 pieces.
3. Sear ribs on grill until browned and juices are sealed in. If your grill is very hot, this will take about 15 minutes.
4. Cut each half rack into 2 pieces again and place in roaster. Ribs can be refrigerated overnight at this point if desired.
5. Preheat oven to 375° F / 190° C.
6. To make the sauce, combine remaining ingredients and mix well. Pour sauce over ribs and cover tightly, first with foil and then the roaster lid.
7. Bake for 50 minutes.
8. Reduce heat to 325° F / 160° C and baste ribs. Cover with the foil again and bake for an additional 1–2 hours, basting several times. Ribs are done when meat pulls away from the bone.
9. Arrange ribs on platter and cover with foil until serving.
10. Whisk remaining sauce in roaster, thickening if desired with 1–2 teaspoons / 5–10 ml cornstarch dissolved in 1 tablespoon / 15 ml water.
11. Serve the ribs and pass the sauce.

"Pig ribs," as my grandson calls them, never fail to please when our out-of-town children and grandchildren come for a visit. Garlic mashed potatoes pairs well with these ribs.

### TIPS

- Give yourself plenty of time to bake the ribs. How long the ribs bake depends on their thickness. It's much better to have the meat falling off the bone than underdone and tough.
- If the sauce seems to be getting too thick, add up to ½ cup / 125 ml water.

*—Bev*

113

# MAPLE-GLAZED SALMON *with* LEMON-BUTTERED SHRIMP

**SERVES 6**

- 6 4-ounce / 114-g sockeye salmon fillets (fresh, or frozen and thawed)
- ½ cup / 125 ml maple syrup
- ½ cup / 125 ml soy sauce
- 2 teaspoons / 10 ml butter
- ½ pound / 226 g small shrimp
- 2 tablespoons / 30 ml olive oil
- 2 tablespoons / 30 ml butter
- Juice of 1 lemon
- 2 garlic cloves, minced
- 2 tablespoons / 30 ml parsley, minced

1. Place salmon fillets, maple syrup, and soy sauce in a zip-close plastic bag. Seal and marinate in refrigerator for 1 hour.
2. Heat a grill pan or large nonstick pan over medium heat. Add 2 teaspoons / 10 ml butter, remove salmon from marinade, and place on pan with skin facing up. Fry until evenly glazed and cooked on the bottom, and then flip over and continue on medium heat until the salmon flakes in the thickest part.
3. As soon as the salmon goes in the pan, place shrimp and remaining ingredients in a small saucepan and bring to a simmer. Serve the shrimp over the salmon or with crusty baguette slices. Drizzle shrimp sauce over the salmon.

*TIPS*

- I purchase my shrimp in the frozen section. Look for cooked, peeled, and deveined shrimp.
- To make this recipe gluten free, use gluten-free soy sauce. ⓖ

This family favorite is quick to prepare and cook, and it has been a staple in our home for many years. I rarely measure the marinade ingredients but rather adjust for the number of fillets I plan to serve. The maple syrup gives the salmon a beautiful glaze that is as appealing to the eye as it is to the palate. Living on the West Coast, we have fresh salmon available year-round. Even so, I always keep frozen wild sockeye salmon pieces and frozen shrimp in the freezer to quickly thaw on days when I don't plan dinner ahead of time. Serve the salmon with a bright green vegetable and coleslaw, and you have a healthy meal in no time.

*—Lovella*

# SPAGHETTI SAUCE *and* MEATBALLS

**SERVES 6**

## SPAGHETTI SAUCE

- 3 tablespoons / 45 ml olive oil
- 1 medium onion, finely chopped
- 3 garlic cloves, minced
- 1 pound / 500 g lean ground beef
- ½ pound / 250 g ground hot Italian sausage
- 1 22-ounce / 680-ml can tomato sauce
- 1 14-ounce / 398-ml can diced tomatoes
- 1 5.5-ounce / 156-ml can tomato paste
- 1¼ cup / 300 ml boiling water
- 2 beef bouillon cubes
- 1 teaspoon / 5 ml salt
- ½ teaspoon / 2 ml pepper, freshly ground
- 2 bay leaves
- ½ teaspoon / 2 ml red pepper flakes
- 1 teaspoon / 5 ml Italian seasoning
- 1 teaspoon / 5 ml dried oregano
- 1 tablespoon / 15 ml sugar
- ¼ cup / 60 ml Parmesan cheese, grated
- ¼ cup / 60 ml fresh parsley, finely chopped
- ½ red bell pepper, finely chopped

1. In a large heavy pot, heat oil over medium heat.
2. Add onion and garlic. Sauté until they begin to lightly brown.
3. Add ground beef and Italian sausage, stirring to crumble meat until it is just cooked through.
4. Add tomato sauce, diced tomatoes, and tomato paste. Stir well to combine. Once sauce begins to bubble, turn down to simmer.
5. Pour boiling water over bouillon cubes and stir to dissolve. Add to meat sauce.
6. Add spices, cheese, parsley, and red pepper. Stir well. Cover and let simmer. Make meatballs (below) and add to sauce. Simmer sauce and meatballs for 3 hours. If sauce becomes too thick, add a small amount of water.

## MEATBALLS

- ½ pound / 250 g lean ground beef
- ½ pound / 250 g ground hot Italian sausage
- ½ onion
- 1 tablespoon / 15 ml milk
- 1 egg
- ¼ cup / 50 ml fine bread crumbs
- ½ teaspoon / 2 ml salt
- ¼ teaspoon / 1 ml pepper
- ¼ teaspoon / 1 ml garlic powder
- ¼ teaspoon / 1 ml ground dried oregano
- 1 tablespoon / 15 ml dried parsley

1. Preheat oven to 400° F / 205° C.
2. Place ground beef and Italian sausage in a mixing bowl.
3. Using a blender or food processor, purée onion and add to meat.

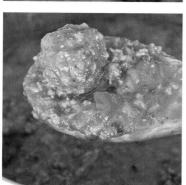

4. Whisk together milk and egg. Stir in bread crumbs. Add this mixture, along with the remaining ingredients, to the meat. Mix well by hand.
5. Form meatballs (about the size of a golf ball) and place on parchment-lined baking sheet.
6. Bake meatballs for 13 minutes. Add baked meatballs to meat sauce.
7. When ready to serve, cook pasta according to package directions. Serve immediately with spaghetti sauce and meatballs.

**TIP**

- Use mild Italian sausage in the sauce and meatballs if your family prefers a less spicy dish.

Sitting down for supper together as a family can be one of the most important and fun times during the day. Midweek activities often leave little time for preparing suppers. A pot of spaghetti sauce is an easy and satisfying meal. This recipe can be doubled and the extra frozen for a second meal. Serve with breadsticks or crusty bread and a side salad.

*—Kathy*

117

# BBQ BEEF ON A BUN

## SERVES 6–8

> 1 boneless chuck roast (about 3 pounds / 1.5 kg)

> 1 28-ounce / 796-ml can tomatoes

1. Cut roast into 3–4 pieces.
2. Place roast and tomatoes in a slow cooker.
3. Cook on low overnight or about 10 hours, until meat is tender.
4. Drain juices and shred the cooked beef with 2 forks.

## SAUCE

> 1 tablespoon / 15 ml vegetable oil
> 1 medium onion, chopped
> 1 cup / 250 ml celery, chopped
> 1 garlic clove, minced
> 1 cup / 250 ml water
> 1 cup / 250 ml ketchup
> ¼ cup / 60 ml vinegar
> 3 tablespoons / 45 ml brown sugar, packed

> 1 tablespoon / 15 ml Worcestershire sauce
> 2 teaspoons / 10 ml dried parsley flakes
> 1 teaspoon / 5 ml chili powder
> 1 teaspoon / 5 ml prepared mustard
> ½ teaspoon / 2 ml dried oregano
> ½ teaspoon / 2 ml salt
> ¼ teaspoon / 1 ml cayenne pepper

If the meat lovers in your life are wondering, "Where's the beef?"—well, here it is! This recipe became a family favorite decades ago and has gone to potlucks, on camping trips, and even on a family picnic at the beach. Add corn on the cob or potato salad and coleslaw and call it a meal.

1. Sauté onion and celery in oil until tender.
2. Add remaining sauce ingredients and heat through.
3. Add to shredded beef and simmer in slow cooker for about 1 hour before serving.
4. Serve on submarine rolls or round buns.

### TIPS
- You can use a variety of meat cuts instead of the roast. Try flank steak, round steak, or beef brisket.
- To make this recipe gluten free, use gluten-free Worcestershire sauce and serve on gluten-free rolls. GF

*—Judy*

# APPLE TENDERLOIN STEW

## SERVES 8

- 1 tablespoon / 15 ml olive oil
- 2 pounds / 1 kg pork tenderloin, cut into 2-inch / 5-cm cubes
- Dash salt and pepper
- 4 tablespoons / 60 ml cornstarch, divided
- 1 onion, sliced
- 2 garlic cloves, minced
- 1 1-quart / 900-ml carton low- or no-sodium chicken broth
- 8 medium potatoes, peeled and cubed
- 4 carrots, sliced
- ½–1 teaspoon / 2–5 ml dried rosemary
- ½ teaspoon / 2 ml ground dried sage
- ½ teaspoon / 2 ml dried thyme
- 2 red-skinned apples, cored and cubed
- 1 large yam, peeled and cubed
- ¼ cup / 60 ml fresh parsley, chopped

1. Heat oil in a large skillet or pot on medium heat.
2. Combine pork cubes with salt, pepper, and 2 tablespoons / 30 ml cornstarch.
3. Brown the pork in batches. After all the meat is browned, return to pot.
4. Add onion slices and garlic and cook until the onions are softened.
5. Add 1 cup / 250 ml chicken broth to deglaze the pan and loosen all the brown bits at the bottom.
6. Add remaining chicken broth, potatoes, carrots, rosemary, sage, and thyme, and cook 15 minutes.
7. Add the apples and yam and cook 15 minutes longer.
8. Mix the remaining 2 tablespoons / 30 ml cornstarch with a little cold water, stirring well to dissolve the cornstarch. Add the cornstarch mixture to the stew and cook for about 5 more minutes or until the liquid is thickened.
9. Stir in chopped parsley at the end of the cooking time.

### TIP

- To make this recipe gluten free, use gluten-free chicken broth. 🅖🅕

—*Charlotte*

There is something comforting about stew simmering in the pot: the aroma fills the air and the kitchen gives off an inviting warmth on cool days. Freshly baked buns coming out of the oven add the message "Welcome home!" as the family comes in out of the cold. I have fond memories of coming home to my mother and the scents of dinner cooking. These memories I will always cherish.

This stew is made with pork tenderloin, a tender meat that is low in fat and doesn't require a long cooking process—it can be ready in less than an hour. When pork tenderloin is on sale, this dish is an economical entree to feed the family. Serve with a crisp side salad and fresh buns.

# GERMAN COUNTRY-FRIED STEAK DINNER

### SERVES 6–8

## STEAK

- 2 pounds / 1 kg round or sirloin steak, thinly sliced
- Seasoning salt
- Salt and pepper
- Garlic powder
- 3 eggs, beaten
- ¾ cup / 175 ml flour, white or whole wheat
- Oil for browning

1. Tenderize thinly sliced beef using a meat mallet. To cut your own, cut regular steaks into palm-sized pieces and then slice through horizontally, once or twice, before tenderizing them.
2. Sprinkle tenderized steak with seasoning salt on 1 side and salt, pepper, and garlic powder on the other side.
3. Prepare 2 shallow bowls: 1 with beaten eggs and 1 with flour.
4. Pour about 2–3 tablespoons / 30–45 ml oil into a large nonstick or stainless steel frying pan, set on medium heat.
5. Dip each slice of steak into egg, coat with flour, and then place in heated frying pan.
6. Brown steaks on both sides, repeating with added oil for extra batches. Place on an ovenproof plate, cover, and keep warm on low oven heat, or serve immediately.

# GRAVY (OPTIONAL)

- 1 shallot, small onion, or mushrooms, sliced
- 1½–2 tablespoons / 22–30 ml white flour
- Water, milk, or cream
- White wine (optional)
- Salt and pepper to taste

1. To make gravy, add sliced shallot, onion, or mushrooms to pan drippings from steak. Stir until caramelized.
2. Place flour in small jar with about ½ cup / 125 ml water, milk, or cream and shake up well. Add to caramelized shallots, onions, or mushrooms. Cook, stirring and adding more liquid (about 2 cups / 500 ml) until mixture reaches desired consistency. Add salt and pepper to taste.
3. Alternatively, deglaze pan with ½ cup / 125 ml wine, adding liquids mixed with flour after wine is reduced by half. Add salt and pepper to taste. Serve gravy as desired, on side dish or meat.

# SUGGESTED SIDE DISHES

1. *Spaetzle*. Caramelize a diced onion in 2 tablespoons / 30 ml butter. Then stir in 1 pound / 500 g cooked *Spaetzle*. Add butter to taste. (*Spaetzle* are German pasta that can be homemade or purchased ready to cook.)

2. Cooked red cabbage and apples. Cook the following for 45–60 minutes, stirring when needed.

- 2 tablespoons / 30 ml oil
- ½ medium onion, diced
- 1 small head red cabbage, sliced
- 2 apples, chopped
- ¼ cup / 60 ml vinegar
- ½ cup / 125 ml sugar
- 1 teaspoon / 5 ml salt

3. Cucumber and tomato salad with favorite dressing.

## TIP

- You can also purchase tenderized steaks that are ready to eat, but they will not be as thin as if you tenderize them yourself. In some areas you can buy meat sliced for *Rouladen*.

*—Anneliese*

This recipe is not only a method for making a steak stretch farther; it was a family favorite in my home as I grew up. My husband fondly remembers the sandwiches my mother packed from these leftover steaks for one of our picnics when we were dating. They have been his favorite ever since.

# BREADED VEAL *SCHNITZEL*

## SERVES 6

- 6 veal cutlets
- 1 cup / 160 g arrowroot powder/ starch/flour
- Salt to taste
- 2 eggs (beaten)
- 2 cups / 150 g gluten-free bread crumbs (see below)
- Oil for frying

My family prefers simple meals, and because three out of six of us have celiac disease, our meals are also gluten free. We still enjoy breaded meat like chicken fingers or veal *Schnitzel*, which I made for a recent Thanksgiving dinner. My kids never tire of my bacon-and-onion green beans as the vegetable side dish served with our favorite meat and mashed potato dinners.

1. Pound each veal cutlet to less than ¼-inch / 0.6-cm thick. Placing the meat in an open plastic storage bag makes for easier pounding.
2. Salt both sides of cutlet.
3. Prepare 3 bowls: 1 with the arrowroot powder, 1 with the beaten eggs, and 1 with the bread crumbs.
4. Dip each cutlet first into the arrowroot powder. Shake off excess powder and then dip it into the egg and then into the bread crumbs. Do not press the crumbs into the meat.
5. Fry the cutlets in oil over medium heat for about 8 minutes each side, depending on thickness, until crumbs are nicely browned and crisp.
6. Serve immediately.

## GLUTEN-FREE BREAD CRUMBS

- 1 teaspoon / 5 g sugar
- 1 teaspoon / 5 g unflavored gelatin
- ½ cup / 125 ml warm water
- 1½ tablespoon / 12 g active dry yeast
- 1 egg
- ½ cup / 125 ml milk
- 2 tablespoons / 30 ml oil
- ¼ cup / 30 g white bean flour (or sorghum flour)
- ⅓ cup / 35 g oat flour (gluten-free)
- ¾ cup / 105 g millet flour
- ⅓ cup / 40 g tapioca starch/flour
- ¼ cup / 40 g arrowroot powder/ starch/flour
- ½ teaspoon / 3 g salt
- ½ teaspoon / 2 g xanthan gum

1. Mix sugar and gelatin in a cup and add the warm water. Stir well and then add the yeast, stirring again. Allow yeast to proof for several minutes.
2. In a mixing bowl, beat egg, milk, and oil. Add yeast mixture.
3. Blend together the dry ingredients and add all at once to the liquids.
4. Stir and then beat on high speed for 2 minutes.
5. Scrape dough into a loaf pan.

6. Let rise uncovered in a warm place until loaf rises above the top of the pan. This will take about 30 minutes.
7. Bake bread in a preheated 350° F / 175° C oven for 55 minutes. Let cool slightly in pan, then turn out on a wire rack to cool completely.
8. When bread has cooled, use a food processor to make it into crumbs.
9. Let the crumbs dry in a bowl for a day, stirring occasionally.

### TIPS

- Not all gluten-free breads make good crumbs, but this one does. And if the bread falls slightly during baking, don't worry!
- Store dry crumbs in freezer for later use in breaded meats or as a casserole topping.
- Using less xanthan gum is better than using too much. A general rule is to use not more than ½ teaspoon / 2 g xanthan gum per 1 cup / 120 g flour.

*—Julie*

# BREAD FOR THE JOURNEY
# FAMILY FAITH PASSED ON

*"Love the* LORD *your God with all your heart and with all your soul and with all your strength. These commandments that I give you today are to be on your hearts. Impress them on your children. Talk about them when you sit at home and when you walk along the road, when you lie down and when you get up. . . . be careful that you do not forget the* LORD, *who brought you out of Egypt, out of the land of slavery."*

—DEUTERONOMY 6:5-7, 12 (NIV)

{ I marvel at how God created the family to provide a safe and loving environment in which children can grow. It is in this setting that he instructs us, as parents and grandparents, to teach our children about him in the way that we go about everyday life. Teaching and modeling our love for God does not happen only by attending church. Some of my earliest and most vivid memories of learning about God are of my paternal grandmother telling me about her hardships in Russia and the heavenly home she was waiting for. While she strummed her guitar, teaching me the lyrics to *"Gott ist die Liebe,"* or as I sat on her bed, combing her long, graying hair which she would then twist into a tiny bun, she described heaven as if she had been there.

*No matter our background, we all have a story to tell.*

The stories my grandparents and parents shared with me over the years ingrained in me an awareness of God's protection and leading, beginning with our Anabaptist forebears fleeing Europe to live in Russia and eventually bringing us to a country where we can enjoy peace and prosperity. In spite of hunger, imprisonment, war, family separation, and the loss of loved ones, our grandparents continued to trust in God even when communism banned all manner of religious practice. Their faith, and God's provision through it all, is a story to share, sometimes even through a simple thing such as preparing our "strange" ethnic foods. If *Borscht* and *Zwieback* give me an excuse to tell my grandchildren of our past, then they are good things. As grandparents, especially, we have a legacy of time and experience to draw on for wisdom and patience as we remember God's patience with us.

No matter our background, we all have a story to tell. Not all of us have ancestors who worshiped God, but all of us have the chance to begin a new story of hope by accepting God's invitation to become part of his family. By learning to love and forgive, lending a listening ear, and letting our family know that we are praying for them, we can pass on the greatest gift we have: a personal relationship with a loving God, expressed in daily life. ✏

*—Anneliese*

Beatriz Photography  www.beatrizphotography.com

125

# CELEBRATING *Outdoors*

Whether you are at the ocean or beside a stream, on the mountain or in the valley, in the forest or on the plain, or simply on your own back patio: food always seems to taste better in the great outdoors. Here is a collection of a few of our favorite outdoor recipes.

## CELEBRATE WITH

*When I consider your heavens, the work of your fingers, the moon and the stars, which you have set in place, what is mankind that you are mindful of them, human beings that you care for them?*
—PSALM 8:3-4 (NIV)

# KATHY REFLECTS *on the* OUTDOORS

As a family, we have camped often over the years. I love to wake early to watch the fog lift over the lake, or sit in the evening to watch the moon rise from behind the mountain while we wait for that first star to appear. As I sit here at a picnic table overlooking Harmen Lake in beautiful British Columbia, I look up and marvel at God's creation of the heavens, moon, and stars. I also reflect back to a time fifteen years ago when we saw the stars in the night sky over the jungle of Peru.

*We prayed, shared a meal, and visited around their family table.*

In 1997, we had the privilege to take our teenage daughters to Trujillo, Peru, where our cousin Pam was working as a missionary with the young people in a local church. On the morning of our tour into the jungle of Tarapoto, there was a knock on the door. We were greeted by our hostess, Zaida, a tiny woman in a red dress who was beaming from ear to ear. I was instantly intrigued by this dear woman. She hugged each of us and then began to sing us a welcome song. We didn't understand a word she sang, but her joy was evident and we felt very welcomed. She motioned for us to climb into the back of an old pickup truck. As we bumped along the rough road, we came to a roadside coconut stand along the bank of a river. We couldn't pass up the opportunity, so we placed our orders with the man and watched as he effortlessly shimmied up the tree with his machete, and coconuts began falling to the ground. Then he cut them open, added a straw, and we drank our fresh coconut milk.

Nearby, we observed the daily activities of the busy riverbank. Women with babies tied to their backs were washing dishes and doing laundry, while some children swam and others collected water. As we stood, taking it all in, Zaida once again began to sing. We recognized the song and began to sing along in English. "This is the day that the Lord has made. We will rejoice and be glad in it. These are the friends that the Lord has given." Tears filled our eyes as we shared our common love for Jesus there along the bank of the river.

Back in the truck, we crested a hill where we could see Zaida's family waiting for us. After exchanging smiles and waves, we introduced ourselves and they invited us into their home. After the long, dusty ride, someone suggested that we might enjoy a swim; how could we say no? We smiled as Zaida dove into the river, dress and all, joining the children who obviously loved her. Not wanting to miss out, I reluctantly walked into the river, which was used for many necessities.

Later we gathered in the outdoor kitchen where the meal was being prepared. There in the jungle we prayed, shared a meal, and visited around their family table. As the sun began to set, we said goodbye and returned to the city. My memory of our day with Zaida will always be punctuated by the image of her diving into the river in her red dress, enjoying God's creation with joyful abandon. ✍

*—Kathy*

# WRANGLERS

## FOR EACH WRANGLER YOU WILL NEED:

- ➤ 1 piece of bread
- ➤ 1 slice of bacon
- ➤ 1 egg
- ➤ Salt and pepper to taste

1. Using a cookie cutter or glass, cut a 2-inch / 5-cm hole out of the center of the slice of bread. Set aside.
2. Cut bacon slice in half.
3. Place bacon halves side by side 2 inches / 5 cm apart on a griddle or in a skillet over a campfire. Wranglers can also be made on the stove over medium-high heat.
4. Brown bacon on 1 side, and then flip each piece onto the other side.
5. Immediately place bread over bacon.
6. Crack egg into the hole and turn heat to medium.
7. Season lightly with salt and pepper. Cook just until egg white begins to set.
8. Flip the wrangler over and continue cooking until egg yolk is of desired doneness.
9. Serve immediately.

*—Bev*

I spent a summer as a camp counselor over forty years ago, and one of the skills we taught our campers was how to cook this "all-in-one" breakfast on the surface of a gallon-sized juice can set over a small fire. Since that time, wranglers have become a breakfast favorite in our family all year round but especially on camping trips. They are not only delicious; there's only one pan to wash!

# CAMPFIRE BANANA BOATS

- ➤ 1 banana per person
- ➤ Peanut butter or hazelnut spread (optional)
- ➤ Chocolate chips
- ➤ Caramel chips

- ➤ Mini-marshmallows (white or colored)
- ➤ 12-inch / 30-cm square aluminum foil for each banana boat
- ➤ Ice cream, chopped nuts, coconut, or sprinkles (optional)

1. Leaving the skin on, slice down the inner curve of each banana, through the skin and most of the banana. Be careful not to slice through the skin on the opposite side.
2. Gently open the slice wide enough to stuff with the toppings of your choice.
3. Spread with peanut butter or hazelnut spread first, if desired.
4. Layer the chocolate chips, caramel chips, and mini-marshmallows.
5. Carefully wrap each banana in foil.
6. Place in the coals of a campfire or on the grill rack above the fire for about 4 minutes per side. Turn with tongs at the halfway point.
7. Remove from fire, unwrap, and enjoy.

**TIPS**

- Banana boats can be cooked on an outdoor grill for 5–10 minutes or until bananas are soft and marshmallows are melted.
- A scoop of ice cream and a sprinkling of chopped nuts, coconut, or sprinkles make it a banana boat deluxe!

*—Judy*

This gooey, simple treat is a camping trip favorite in our family. Everyone creates their own dessert with the toppings of their choice. Although we don't always have access to ice cream when we are camping, a scoop of vanilla ice cream on the piping hot banana boat is a nice touch.

133

# RIVER WALK GUACAMOLE
## *with* WALKING TACOS

**SERVES 4**

## GUACAMOLE

- Juice of 1 small orange
- Juice of 1 lime
- 2 large avocados
- 1 small Roma tomato, diced

- ½ jalapeño pepper, minced
- 2 tablespoons / 30 ml red onion, chopped
- 1 tablespoon / 15 ml fresh cilantro, chopped
- 1 teaspoon / 5 ml coarsely ground sea salt

1. Squeeze juice of orange and lime into bowl.
2. Peel and pit avocado. Add to the bowl and chop coarsely, using 2 knives.
3. Fold tomato, pepper, onion, and cilantro into avocado mixture. Add salt.
4. Refrigerate until ready to serve.

*TIP*

- The key to good guacamole is using an avocado at its peak. It should be dark-skinned and somewhat soft when squeezed. The guacamole should be somewhat chunky, not mashed.

## WALKING TACOS

- Ground beef
- Taco seasoning mix
- Tomatoes, chopped
- Lettuce, shredded
- Salsa

- Cheese, grated
- Sour cream
- Guacamole, chopped onions, and other toppings of your choice
- Individual lunch-sized bags of nacho chips or corn chips (1.5 ounce / 45 g each)

1. Brown and drain ground beef; add taco seasoning and prepare according to directions on package.
2. Prepare and arrange all toppings on a tray, along with the hot meat.
3. To serve, gently crush an individual bag of nacho chips. Then open the bag by slicing along the side. Start adding your chosen toppings, beginning with the meat. Stir up the walking taco with a disposable fork, and then eat it right out of the bag!

*TIP*

- Small canning jars work great as bowls for the toppings.

*—Judy*

One of the most popular attractions in Texas is the San Antonio River Walk. It is a great place to stroll or take a riverboat cruise, and there are restaurants galore from which to choose. On our most recent visit, we walked by a bistro where they were making fresh guacamole as the patrons watched. Before long we found ourselves sitting at one of their tables. We ordered a "guacamole-for-two" salad, which was prepared right at our table as we watched. It was good to the last lick, and we could have ordered another . . . and another! Instead, I asked the server to share the recipe and I took notes. We have been enjoying a copy-cat version of their famous guacamole ever since.

This is not so much a recipe as it is an idea. It is a fun way to feed kids of all ages while camping, on a picnic, or in your own backyard. I first heard about walking tacos from my brother, who lives in the Midwest and says they are a favorite at ballgames, fundraisers, and picnics in their area. Maybe I was the last one on the block to hear about them, but we have been enjoying them on picnics and camping trips over the past few years. No dishes required!

135

# FRESH-CUT SUMMER SALSA

## YIELDS 6 CUPS

Our friends Richard and Dorothy Friesen are naturally gifted in hospitality, opening their home in friendship as well as business at their beautiful inn. At times I have helped Dorothy chop this salsa as she prepared to serve luncheons.

We eat this salsa as a condiment in our home year-round, but we especially enjoy it in the summer when the produce grows fresh in the garden. At first glance, this recipe might not seem to make a camping menu easier, but one of the last things I do before we pull our travel trailer onto the highway is to pick the bell peppers, jalapeños, onions, and tomatoes. We keep a little jar of the seasonings packed in the trailer. Once we are settled in our camping spot, I chop up the fresh vegetables so that we can enjoy this salsa during our time away from home. The vinegar base keeps the salsa fresh for several days, and it is a great accompaniment to tacos, nachos, quesadillas, taco salads, and burgers.

- ¾ cup / 175 ml white vinegar
- ¼ cup / 60 ml fresh lime juice
- 1 5.5-ounce / 156-ml can tomato paste
- 4 teaspoons / 20 ml sugar
- 1 teaspoon / 5 ml salt, or to taste
- 1 teaspoon / 5 ml paprika
- ½ teaspoon / 2 ml dried oregano
- ½ teaspoon / 2 ml cumin
- 1 green bell pepper, diced
- 1 yellow bell pepper, diced
- 1 red bell pepper, diced
- 1 cup / 250 ml white onion, finely chopped
- 2–4 jalapeño peppers, minced
- 4½ cups / 1 L fresh tomatoes, seeded and diced
- 2 garlic cloves, minced
- Small handful of fresh cilantro, chopped, to taste

1. Combine vinegar, lime juice, tomato paste, sugar, salt, paprika, oregano, and cumin in a small container with a lid. Refrigerate or place in cooler.
2. In a large bowl, combine bell peppers, onion, jalapeño peppers, tomatoes, and garlic.
3. Add the vinegar-tomato mixture and cilantro. Stir to combine.
4. Keep chilled.

*TIP*
- Use rubber gloves to mince the jalapeño peppers.

—*Lovella*

# COBB SALAD

## SERVES 4 AS A MAIN DISH

### SALAD

- ½ head iceberg lettuce, finely chopped
- ½ head romaine lettuce, finely chopped
- 1 medium tomato, chopped
- 2 cups / 500 ml cucumber, diced
- 2 grilled chicken breasts, chopped
- 2 hard-boiled eggs, sliced
- 1 cup / 250 ml grilled corn kernels
- 1 cup / 250 ml crumbled feta cheese

1. Mix greens together and place in a large serving bowl.
2. Arrange remaining ingredients in rows across the lettuce bed as shown. By the time you have finished assembling the salad, multiple strips of ingredients will cover the lettuce bed.
3. Just before serving, pour the dressing over the salad and toss thoroughly.

This colorful main-course salad is the perfect meal to share with friends on the patio in the summertime. What is more special than creating a salad displaying fruits and vegetables from your own garden? Instead of adding the bacon to the salad, it has been whipped up into the dressing, giving the salad its rich flavors. You can really use any vegetables you want and make your own special Cobb salad. Use your imagination and have fun.

### DRESSING

## YIELDS 1 CUP / 250 ML

- 3 strips bacon
- 2 tablespoons / 30 ml bacon drippings
- 2 tablespoons / 30 ml water
- ⅛ teaspoon / 0.5 ml sugar
- ¾ teaspoon / 3 ml salt
- 1 tablespoon / 15 ml lemon juice
- ½ teaspoon / 2 ml Worcestershire sauce
- 2 tablespoons / 30 ml balsamic vinegar
- ¼ teaspoon / 1 ml Dijon mustard
- 2 garlic cloves, minced
- 5 tablespoons / 75 ml olive oil

1. Cook bacon in a frying pan until crisp, reserving 2 tablespoons / 30 ml of the drippings.
2. Using a blender or hand (immersion) blender on high speed, purée all the ingredients, including bacon and reserved bacon drippings, except for olive oil.
3. Continue blending, adding the olive oil slowly. Blend well.
4. Keep refrigerated until ready to serve.

*TIP*

- To make this recipe gluten free, use gluten-free Worcestershire sauce and gluten-free Dijon mustard. ⓖ

*—Marg*

137

# CHICKEN SLIDERS *with* PINEAPPLE SALSA

**YIELDS 16–18 SLIDERS**

Watch these tender little burgers disappear at your next backyard barbecue!

## CHICKEN SLIDERS

- 1 pound / 500 g ground chicken breast
- 3 tablespoons / 45 ml saltine crackers, finely crushed
- 1 tablespoon / 15 ml pineapple juice (reserved from salsa, next page)
- 3 tablespoons / 45 ml thick teriyaki sauce
- 1 teaspoon / 5 ml dried parsley
- 2 tablespoons / 30 ml onion, grated
- ¼ teaspoon / 1 ml salt
- ½ teaspoon / 2 ml pepper
- ½ cup / 125 ml thick teriyaki sauce (to use for glazing after sliders come off grill), plus more for basting
- 16–18 small slider buns

1. Place all ingredients (except last 2) in a mixing bowl. Using your hands, gently mix together until all ingredients are well incorporated.
2. Form small meatballs and flatten in the palm of your hand to make patties that are no larger than 3 inches / 7 cm in diameter.
3. Place on parchment-lined baking sheet until ready to grill.
4. Grill chicken sliders, basting with teriyaki sauce on both sides. These are very delicate and small, so be careful when flipping and watch that they don't burn. Cook sliders until a meat thermometer registers 165° F / 74° C.
5. Heat ½ cup / 125 ml teriyaki sauce and pour into a glass baking dish. When sliders come off the grill, place into warmed sauce to glaze.
6. Toast split buns if desired, and place meat on buns. Top with pineapple salsa. Serve immediately.

*TIP*

- If you make these burgers ahead of time, stack the uncooked patties with parchment paper between the layers and cover. Patties will keep in the refrigerator for up to 12 hours.

# PINEAPPLE SALSA

- 1 12-ounce / 375-ml can pineapple tidbits
- 2 tablespoons / 30 ml fresh lime juice
- 2 tablespoons / 30 ml olive oil
- 1 garlic clove, crushed
- ¼ teaspoon / 1 ml red pepper flakes
- 1 teaspoon / 5 ml sugar
- 1 jalapeño pepper, finely diced
- ¼ cup / 60 ml red bell pepper, finely diced
- ¼ cup / 60 ml red onion, finely diced
- 1 tablespoon / 15 ml fresh cilantro, finely chopped
- 1 tablespoon / 15 ml fresh parsley, finely chopped
- ½ teaspoon / 2 ml salt
- ¼ teaspoon / 1 ml pepper

1. Drain pineapple tidbits, reserving 1 tablespoon / 15 ml of the liquid for the sliders.
2. Squeeze lime juice into a glass bowl and add drained pineapple and olive oil.
3. Stir in garlic, pepper flakes, and sugar.
4. Stir vegetables and herbs into pineapple mixture. Add salt and pepper.
5. Refrigerate for at least 2 hours.

*—Kathy*

# NAAN BITES *and* SPINACH DIP

## SERVES 10

- 1 teaspoon / 4 g sugar
- 1 teaspoon / 4 g unflavored gelatin
- ½ cup / 125 ml warm water
- 1½ tablespoon / 12 g yeast
- ¼ cup / 60 ml oil
- ¼ cup / 80 ml sour cream or yogurt
- 1 egg
- 1 cup / 120 g millet flour
- ¼ cup / 35 g white bean flour or brown rice flour

- ¼ cup / 35 g brown rice flour
- ½ cup / 65 g tapioca starch/flour
- ¼ cup / 35 g sweet rice flour
- ½ teaspoon / 5 g xanthan gum
- 1 teaspoon / 10 g baking powder
- 1 teaspoon / 10 g salt
- Sweet rice flour (extra)
- Oil for frying

*Naan* bites are good with soup, salad, or served with a favorite dip, such as the spinach dip recipe included here. My granddaughter likes them with melted cheddar cheese on top.

1. Mix sugar and unflavored gelatin in a small bowl. Add warm water and yeast. Allow yeast to proof for several minutes.
2. In the bowl of a mixer, blend oil, sour cream or yogurt, and egg.
3. Add yeast mixture and mix.
4. Mix together dry ingredients.
5. Add dry ingredients all at once to liquids, mix, and then beat on high for 1 minute.
6. Turn dough out onto parchment paper, liberally dusted with sweet rice flour, and knead in extra sweet rice flour (up to ¼ cup until dough is easy to handle).
7. Roll out into a 12 x 22-inch / 30 x 56-cm rectangle, turning and dusting to avoid sticking.
8. Using a pizza cutter, cut rectangle of dough into 1 x 2-inch / 2.50 x 5-cm pieces.
9. Heat oil in skillet until hot. Fry dough rectangles until nicely browned on both sides.

*TIPS*

- With gluten-free yeast baking, think smaller quantities. It is better to make a recipe twice than doubling.
- Humidity makes a big difference; recipes that turn out great in summer can flop in winter! So if in doubt, hold back a little of the liquid and carefully watch the consistency of the dough. Adding more liquid is much preferable to trying to add more flour.
- Using enough oil to let the dough pieces float ensures that little oil is absorbed into the dough.

# SPINACH DIP

- 10-ounce / 300-g package of chopped frozen spinach, thawed
- 1 cup / 250 ml sour cream
- ½ cup / 125 ml gluten-free mayonnaise
- ½ teaspoon / 2 ml gluten-free Worcestershire sauce
- 1 garlic clove, crushed
- 1 teaspoon / 3 g gluten-free seasoning mix
- Salt and pepper to taste
- 1 cup / 80 g cheese, shredded

1. Press water out of thawed spinach using a sieve and paper towels. Set aside.
2. Mix together sour cream, mayonnaise, Worcestershire sauce, garlic, and seasonings.
3. Add shredded cheese. Then add spinach to the mixture, stirring well.
4. Refrigerate until ready to serve.

—*Julie*

A variety of seasoning mixes can be used in this dip. My favorite is a bacon-chive seasoning mix. A pizza mix of cheese works well in this recipe.

# STUFFED SWEET MINI-PEPPERS

## YIELDS 6 STUFFED PEPPERS

➤ 6 sweet mini-peppers

➤ ¾ cup / 175 ml soft cream cheese

## CHOOSE ONE OF THE FOLLOWING

➤ ¼ cup / 60 ml smoked salmon, flaked

➤ ¼ cup / 60 ml dried apricots, finely chopped

➤ ¼ cup / 60 ml dates, finely chopped

1. Wash peppers. Slice off tops to make little caps. Scoop out seeds and membranes from inside of peppers, making sure not to break through the outer skins.
2. Stir together cream cheese and salmon, dates, or apricots.
3. Using a small spoon, carefully fill peppers to the top and place pepper caps on top.
4. Heat grill or oven to 375° F / 190° C.
5. Place filled peppers onto a pepper rack. Roast for 15–20 minutes. Cream cheese filling will puff up slightly as it bakes. The skins will become tender, wrinkled, and slightly charred.
6. Serve immediately.

*TIP*

- If you don't have a pepper rack, place peppers in a baking pan that has sides high enough for peppers to stand against while roasting. The peppers need to be standing upright while roasting so that the filling does not run out.

*—Kathy*

This little medley of peppers will add color to your next backyard barbecue side dishes. Tri-colored peppers work well for this recipe. Depending on your main course, choose either a savory or a sweeter fruit addition for the cream cheese filling.

143

# CAMPERS' STEW / *GUISO*

## SERVES 8

- 2 tablespoons / 30 ml cooking oil
- 1 double-link smoked farmer sausage, sliced
- 1 large onion, chopped
- 1 green pepper, chopped
- 2 garlic cloves, chopped
- 1 teaspoon / 5 ml chili powder (optional)
- 1 teaspoon / 5 ml dried oregano (optional)
- 1 28-ounce / 796-ml can of tomatoes
- 1 cup / 250 ml salsa (optional)
- Salt and pepper to taste
- 6½ cups / 1.5 L water (or more)
- 5 cups / 1250 ml rotini noodles

This rustic, no-fuss dish has become a beloved family favorite. My husband, Tony, was born in Paraguay and introduced this dish to me when we were first married. It is such a simple yet delicious meal, cooked in a cast iron pot and usually over an open fire. You can use any kind of meat, sausage, or chicken, which can be cooked with either noodles or rice and some kind of tomato base; I can't decide whether this version or one with chicken and rice is my favorite. Traditionally the only spices added are salt and pepper, but I like to add a little something extra. Serving *guiso* is my favorite way to show hospitality: you eat the meal outside, use no fancy table settings, serve it right out of the pot, and have very little to prepare or to clean up. This is the meal I request for my birthday every year; it sure beats going out to a crowded restaurant!

1. Start the fire in the fire pit. Let the flames come down a bit.
2. Place a cast iron pot over the flame to heat up. Add oil and heat.
3. Brown sausage and then add onion, pepper, garlic, and, if desired, chili powder and oregano. Cook until softened.
4. Add the tomatoes and salsa and bring to a boil.
5. Add the uncooked noodles and pour the water into the stew.
6. Watch the stew closely to make sure that there is enough water; add more water if it begins to get too dry.
7. Cook the noodles until they are *al dente*. They should not be too soft. At this point the dish should look a bit soupy.
8. Take the pot off the heat and let it sit for 10–15 minutes before serving. The stew thickens as it stands.

*TIPS*

- *Guiso* can also be cooked inside on the stove. The stovetop version tastes good, but it doesn't have the smoky flavor of outdoor cooking.
- The noodles will continue to cook while the stew sits, which is why the noodles should only be cooked *al dente* before being taken off the heat; otherwise, they will become too soft and mushy.
- Serve *guiso* with a crusty bread. For our family, pickles on the side are a must.

*—Charlotte*

145

# GRILLED LATTICE-TOPPED APPLES

## SERVES 4

- 4 Granny Smith apples
- 4 tablespoons / 60 ml butter
- 4 tablespoons / 60 ml honey
- 1 teaspoon / 5 ml cornstarch
- 1 teaspoon / 5 ml cinnamon
- 1 unbaked pastry shell, rolled out flat
- ¼ cup / 60 ml apple juice

1. Heat grill to 375° F / 190° C.
2. Cut tops off apples and discard.
3. Scoop out the flesh from the apples, making a hollow in each one as shown. Discard cores and seeds.
4. Finely chop the apple flesh into a small bowl.
5. In a small saucepan, melt together butter and honey.
6. Remove from heat and stir in cornstarch and cinnamon. Pour over chopped apples and stir to combine.
7. Spoon filling into hollowed-out apples.
8. Using a pastry wheel or a sharp knife, cut thin strips of pastry.
9. Weave strips of pastry over each apple to form a lattice top.
10. Place apples in a cast iron or heavy pan that can go on a grill.
11. Pour apple juice into pan around the base of the apples.
12. Place apples on grill. Close grill lid and bake for 45 minutes or until apple filling is soft when poked with a sharp knife.
13. Remove from heat and arrange on serving dishes.
14. Serve as is or with a scoop of ice cream and caramel sauce.

Whether we are grilling out on the deck or at a campsite, grilled lattice-topped apples have become one of our favorite desserts. Once the main course comes off the grill, the apples go on. The apples and filling soften while the woven pastry browns to apple-pie perfection.

*—Kathy*

147

# SWEET AND SALTY GRANOLA

**SERVES 12**

- 3 cups / 750 ml rolled oats
- ⅔ cup / 150 ml almonds, coarsely chopped
- ⅔ cup / 150 ml cashews, coarsely chopped
- ⅔ cup / 150 ml pumpkin seeds

- ¾ cup / 175 ml coconut, unsweetened and shredded
- ½ cup / 125 ml brown sugar
- ¼ cup / 60 ml grapeseed oil
- ¼ cup / 60 ml maple syrup
- ¾ teaspoon / 3 ml sea salt

My niece, who is a doctor of naturopathic medicine, has given me suggestions on healthy eating; this is her granola recipe. Instead of almonds, cashews, and pumpkin seeds, I have sometimes substituted hazelnuts, walnuts, and macadamia nuts. You can add ⅔ cup dried fruit to the granola after it has cooled. This recipe makes a great snack for a family camping trip. It doesn't take long to make, and you may find yourself doubling the ingredients.

1. Preheat oven to 250° F / 125° C.
2. Mix first 6 ingredients in a large bowl.
3. Mix grapeseed oil, maple syrup, and sea salt together.
4. Carefully pour the liquid over the oats mixture, stirring gently with a wooden spoon.
5. Spread granola in a 10 x 15-inch / 25 x 38-cm greased baking pan.
6. Bake for 75 minutes. Do not stir.
7. Allow the granola to cool and store in an airtight container.

*TIP*

- This recipe can be adapted for people with celiac disease if you use gluten-free rolled oats.

*—Marg*

# PEANUT BUTTER CARAMEL POPCORN

## SERVES 20

- 20 cups / 4.5 L popped popcorn (¾ cup / 175 ml unpopped kernels)
- 3 tablespoons / 45 ml butter
- ¾ cup / 175 ml brown sugar, lightly packed
- ¾ cup / 175 ml corn syrup
- ¾ teaspoon / 3 ml salt
- ½ cup / 125 ml peanut butter
- 2 teaspoons / 10 ml vanilla extract
- ¼ teaspoon / 1 ml cayenne pepper
- 1 cup / 250 ml peanuts
- 2 cups / 500 ml peanut butter chips
- 2 teaspoons / 10 ml shortening, divided
- ¾ cup / 175 ml chocolate chips

1. Preheat oven to 250° F / 120° C.
2. Melt butter in a medium saucepan over medium heat.
3. Stir in brown sugar, corn syrup, and salt.
4. Bring to a boil, stirring constantly. Continue to boil for 3 minutes without stirring.
5. Remove from heat and whisk in peanut butter, vanilla, and cayenne pepper.
6. Pour over popped popcorn, stirring until popcorn is well coated.
7. Transfer coated popcorn onto a large greased baking sheet.
8. Bake for 1 hour, stirring every 15 minutes.
9. Remove from oven, cool completely, and break into pieces. Stir in peanuts.
10. In a small bowl, combine peanut butter chips and 1 teaspoon / 5 ml shortening. Melt in microwave until smooth, stirring every 30 seconds. Drizzle over popcorn and toss to combine.
11. In another small bowl, combine chocolate chips and 1 teaspoon / 5 ml shortening. Melt in microwave until smooth, stirring every 30 seconds. Drizzle over popcorn. Don't stir. Set aside until chocolate hardens before serving.
12. Store in a cool place in covered containers.

*—Betty*

This is a delicious snack to take along when you go camping or to eat while sitting around a bonfire in the backyard. Adults will love the extra zing that cayenne pepper provides; if serving this to children, you might want to omit it.

BREAD FOR THE JOURNEY

# GLIMPSES *of* GOD'S HANDIWORK

*The heavens declare the glory of God, and the sky above proclaims his handiwork.*

—PSALM 19:1 (ESV)

It has been a privilege to raise our family in beautiful British Columbia. We are blessed with diverse and amazing places to enjoy, and we experience God's creation right in our own backyard. Since my children were young, we have celebrated outdoor adventures together as a family. I remember taking them for walks around the glistening emerald lakes. I remember their silhouettes in the evening sun. I remember them jumping off bridges into icy cold water. I remember buckling up their boots and untangling their skis. I remember sitting around evening campfires and strumming a guitar while their tired heads nodded off to sleep. These times have brought us together to stand in awe of God's beauty around us.

*These times have brought us together to stand in awe of God's beauty around us.*

In winter, when the clouds part, we can see endless snow-capped mountains towering above us. There is nothing more exhilarating than making fresh powdery tracks down the mountainside with our skis, inhaling and exhaling breaths of crisp air, feeling the fresh chilly breezes on our faces, and listening to nature speak its own language. During the summer months, these mountains are transformed into moss-carpeted rain forests, which allow for endless hours of hiking, cycling, fishing, and camping. We can watch a vibrant sun setting over a rich, rugged landscape dotted with pristine lakes and rivers. A day's hike up the Joffre Trail at Whistler, capped by the Matier Glacier, allows us to lose ourselves in the backcountry, away from the crowded cities.

The song "Creation Calls" by Brian Doerksen invites us to discover the stunning glimpses of God's masterpiece which allow us to glorify, worship, and draw our minds to new places of intimacy with him. The last words of the song—"I believe just like a child"—invite us to come back to a childlike state of wonder. Returning to the lakesides and mountains year after year, generation after generation—these things help us enjoy the simple pleasures of this earth with our children and grandchildren, build lifelong memories, and share God's truth.

There is nothing like the feeling of standing in the great outdoors and listening to the voice of God. Such moments of intimacy reinforce my relationship with God the Creator. ✑

*—Marg*

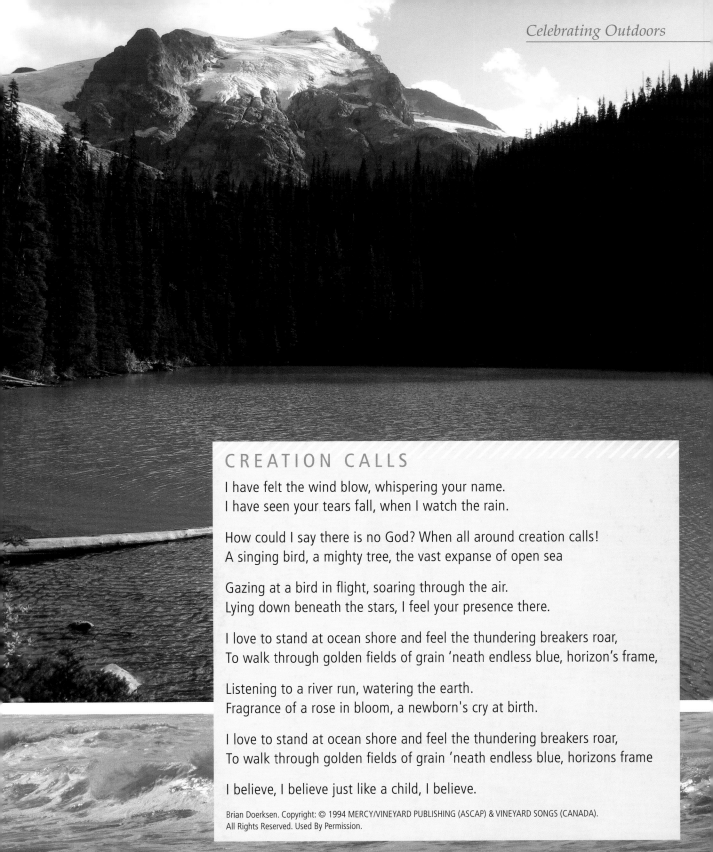

## CREATION CALLS

I have felt the wind blow, whispering your name.
I have seen your tears fall, when I watch the rain.

How could I say there is no God? When all around creation calls!
A singing bird, a mighty tree, the vast expanse of open sea

Gazing at a bird in flight, soaring through the air.
Lying down beneath the stars, I feel your presence there.

I love to stand at ocean shore and feel the thundering breakers roar,
To walk through golden fields of grain 'neath endless blue, horizon's frame,

Listening to a river run, watering the earth.
Fragrance of a rose in bloom, a newborn's cry at birth.

I love to stand at ocean shore and feel the thundering breakers roar,
To walk through golden fields of grain 'neath endless blue, horizons frame

I believe, I believe just like a child, I believe.

Brian Doerksen. Copyright: © 1994 MERCY/VINEYARD PUBLISHING (ASCAP) & VINEYARD SONGS (CANADA).
All Rights Reserved. Used By Permission.

# CELEBRATING
## *Community*

A neighborhood block party, barbecue, or potluck can bring your community together and open doors for relationships. This chapter comprises some of our favorite recipes to serve larger groups; these have been tested by time, yet are fresh for you to share.

## CELEBRATE WITH

*Each of us should please our neighbors for their good, to build them up.*
—ROMANS 15:2 (NIV)

# JULIE REFLECTS *on* COMMUNITY

*I* love that the meaning of the word from which *community* was derived is "with/together." Community resonates with the sound of our deepest need: to belong. Over recent years, I have become aware that changes in society profoundly affect how people find and experience community. I grew up at a time when Sunday dinners were a weekly special; company was welcomed and expected. "Set the table," "clear the table," "wash the dishes," and "dry the dishes" were assigned chores and were a daily norm. Today, family gathered around the table is no longer a given. Observing people's lives around me today, I look back on my life and realize how much I have taken for granted. I have been blessed with a sense of belonging throughout my life.

## FAMILY

The first and most basic community is our family. I was the firstborn in a family of four siblings and grew up in a rural setting. Our farm bordered that of my grandparents, and I remember the countless times I trod the path between our farms just to say "hi" to Grandma in the kitchen or to see what Grandpa was doing outside, to listen to my uncle play guitar or to talk to my aunts. Then there were the extended family gatherings, to which all the family members would come. I knew where I belonged. Even today, I live close to my daughter, son-in-law, and granddaughters, and our lives intertwine on an almost daily basis. (The far right photograph shows me with my daughter, Romay, and granddaughters Elise and Elora.)

## CHURCH

Born into a Mennonite family, I experienced church as a very big part of my life. My parents first took me to church when I was two weeks old, and I was married in the same church eighteen years later (the photograph from the 1960s shows my church, West Abbotsford Mennonite Church). Though the church was large, it was like extended family.

Everyone knew who was related to whom and where the family connections were. We worshiped together, visited together, grew up together, and celebrated together. I belonged.

## NEIGHBORHOOD

My neighborhood also fed my sense of belonging. Everyone knew everyone who lived on our country road, and there was no need to lock doors or worry about children being safe. There was always time to visit, either over the fence or in each other's homes.

## SCHOOL

During my elementary years I attended a small, two-room schoolhouse, where a new student was a rare excitement. (In the school picture, I am seated at the left end of the second row.) Teachers did not come and go. Miss Cooper, my teacher for grades four through six, was the principal of the school for three generations of students. I belonged.

## CITY

I was three months old when my parents moved to Abbotsford, buying the twenty acres where I grew up. I lived in Abbotsford for the next fifty-eight years. I was part of its changes, its growing, yet always I knew I belonged; it was home.

## COMMUNITY

Seven years ago we moved to Chilliwack to be near our children, and we bought into a community complex where most of us are retired. Our clubhouse is a meeting place for weekly coffee mornings and monthly potluck meals. We watch each other's homes, share life memories, and enjoy the fellowship of being "with/ together" in so many ways. Again, I belong!

I celebrate the people in my life who have created communities that have provided for me a sense of belonging, love, and security. They are a blessing from God, and I am so grateful! ❧

*—Julie*

157

# CHILI CHEESE DIP

## SERVES 10 AS AN APPETIZER

### CHILI
**SERVES 4 AS A MAIN DISH**

- 1 pound / 500 g lean ground beef
- 1 medium onion, chopped
- ½ each red and green bell pepper, chopped
- 1 stalk celery, chopped
- 1 7.2-ounce / 213-ml can tomato sauce
- 1 5.5-ounce / 156-ml can tomato paste
- 1 cup / 250 ml water
- ½ cup / 125 ml ketchup
- 1 tablespoon / 15 ml chili powder
- Salt and pepper to taste
- 1 tablespoon / 15 ml Worcestershire sauce
- 1 cup / 250 ml kidney beans, rinsed and drained
- 1 cup / 250 ml black beans, rinsed and drained

1. Brown ground beef in a skillet over medium-high heat.
2. Drain and place in a saucepan.
3. Add remaining ingredients and simmer for 30 minutes or until thick.
4. Serve hot, or cool the chili, package in 1- or 2-cup / 250- or 500-ml portions, and freeze to use for chili cheese dip.

### ASSEMBLING THE DIP

- 1 8-ounce / 250-g package cream cheese, room temperature
- 2 cups / 500 ml chili
- 2 cups / 500 ml cheese, grated (half mozzarella and half sharp cheddar)

1. Preheat oven to 350° F / 175° C.
2. Spread cream cheese over the bottom of a shallow 10 inch / 25 cm ovenproof casserole or 9 x 13 inch / 22 x 33 cm ovenproof glass pan.
3. Spoon chili over the cream cheese, spreading almost to the edges.
4. Sprinkle the grated cheese generously over the top.
5. Bake for about 20 minutes or until the cheese topping has melted and begins to bubble around the edges.
6. Serve with baguette slices or whole-grain tortilla chips.

The next time you serve chili to your family, freeze the leftover chili and use it for this dip. Nothing could be simpler, and your guests will finish this hot and cheesy dip in short order. Watch it disappear!

*TIPS*

- For this dish, you can use the homemade chili recipe above or use canned chili with meat and beans.
- Use a brick of cream cheese rather than the kind packaged in a plastic tub.
- You can easily halve or double the amounts to suit the size of your group.
- To make this recipe gluten-free, use kidney beans and black beans that come in a can without any sauce. Also use gluten-free Worcestershire sauce. ⓖⓕ

*—Bev*

# BLACK BEAN MANGO SALSA

## SERVES 12 AS A SIDE DISH

Say the word "salsa," and I'm in. This recipe has now become a favorite in our home. It easily adapts to substituting and adding a variety of vegetables that have crunch.

- 2 ripe mangoes, peeled and coarsely chopped
- 1 cup / 250 ml red onion, diced
- 2 jalapeño peppers, stemmed, seeded, and finely diced
- 2 cups / 500 ml celery, chopped
- 1 cup / 250 ml jicama, peeled and coarsely chopped (see tips)
- 2 cups / 500 ml fresh-cut cooked corn
- 1 cup / 250 ml fresh cilantro, chopped
- 1 15.5-ounce / 439-g can black beans, rinsed and drained
- 1 cup / 250 ml fresh lime juice
- 4 tablespoons / 60 ml honey
- ½ cup / 125 ml olive oil
- Sea salt and freshly ground pepper to taste

1. Combine all ingredients in a large bowl.
2. Season with salt and pepper.
3. Serve as an appetizer with your favorite tortilla chips or use as a topper for grilled chicken.

*TIPS*

- Consider adding honey to this recipe if the mangoes are not sweet enough.
- This salsa may be prepared and refrigerated up to one day ahead.
- Jicama is a Mexican turnip with a sweet, nutty taste. If you do not have access to jicama, simply use 1 cup / 250 ml water chestnuts instead.

*—Marg*

# GREEN BEAN *and* FETA SALAD

## SERVES 10–12

- 1 pound / 500 g fresh green beans
- 1 head Romaine lettuce
- 1 cup / 250 ml cherry tomatoes
- 1 cup / 250 ml crumbled feta cheese
- ½ cup / 125 ml Kalamata olives
- 4 green onions, chopped, *or*
- ½ red onion, slivered

1. Steam the green beans until tender crisp.
2. Place beans in ice-cold water to stop the cooking, drain and dry in a paper towel.
3. Layer torn lettuce leaves in a platter or a bowl.
4. Layer the tomatoes and green beans. Top with feta cheese and olives.
5. Drizzle vinaigrette over the salad and top with green or red onions.

## SUN-DRIED TOMATO VINAIGRETTE

- ½ cup / 125 ml olive oil
- ⅓ cup / 75 ml red wine vinegar
- 1 teaspoon / 5 ml Dijon mustard
- 4 sun-dried tomatoes packed in oil
- 1 large garlic clove
- 1½ teaspoon / 7 ml dried oregano
- 1 tablespoon / 15 ml fresh parsley
- 1½ teaspoon / 7 ml sugar
- Salt and cracked pepper to taste

1. Put all the ingredients except olive oil into the blender.
2. Pulse together to finely chop the sun-dried tomatoes and garlic.
3. Drizzle olive oil in a slow and steady stream, with the blender running, to emulsify.

*TIPS*

- Frozen whole green beans can easily be substituted for the fresh beans.
- If you'd like to serve a hot side dish instead of a cold salad, serve the steamed green beans hot, drizzled with a bit of dressing and a sprinkle of feta cheese.
- To make this recipe gluten free, choose a brand of Dijon mustard that is gluten free. ⓖ

*—Charlotte*

Our family likes to eat a variety of salads. When it comes to potlucks, salads are great to bring. This is not a common salad, and it adds a nice variety to any potluck meal. If you enjoy Mediterranean flavors, give this one a try. The size of the recipe is easy to adjust, depending on how many you need to serve. At a potluck where there are many dishes, this salad can easily serve sixteen.

# STRAWBERRY SPINACH SALAD

## SERVES 16 AS A SIDE DISH

- 1 10-ounce / 283-g bag of spinach
- 1 medium head iceberg lettuce, chopped coarsely
- 1 long English cucumber, sliced
- 1 cup / 250 ml red onion, thinly sliced

- 3 cups / 750 ml strawberries
- Zest of 1 lemon
- Sugared almonds (recipe below)

1. Layer half of the spinach and lettuce in a large bowl. Store the mixture of the other half for refill.
2. Layer half of the onion and cucumbers on top of the lettuce bed. Store the other half for refill.
3. Quarter and slice strawberries vertically. Spread half over top of salad. Reserve half for refill.
4. Garnish salad generously with lemon zest. Top with a handful of sugared almonds.

## LEMON POPPY VINAIGRETTE

- 3 large lemons or ⅔ cup / 150 ml lemon juice
- 2 teaspoons / 10 ml onion, grated
- ½ cup / 125 ml rice vinegar
- ½ cup / 125 ml olive oil
- 1½ teaspoon / 7 ml salt

- ½ teaspoon / 2 ml pepper, freshly ground
- ½ cup / 125 ml sugar
- 4 teaspoons / 20 ml poppy seeds
- 2 garlic cloves, pressed

1. Prior to extracting lemon juice, use a zester or fine grater to make the lemon zest used in the salad. Store lemon zest in refrigerator to be used as garnish prior to serving.
2. Place all remaining ingredients in a container and shake vigorously.
3. Refrigerate 1 hour before serving. Shake again before using.

## SUGARED ALMONDS

- 1 cup / 250 ml whole almonds

- ⅓ cup / 75 ml sugar

1. Cook almonds and sugar over low heat, stirring constantly until sugar is melted and almonds are coated.
2. Cool and break apart.
3. Store at room temperature.

*—Marg*

Have you ever been to a salad bar that looks demolished? Let's avoid that. I generally chop and prepare all the ingredients in advance, using half of them to make a full-size platter and storing the rest in a sealed container. Then, when the dish needs replenishing, I top it with the remaining ingredients. Adding strawberries and almonds to the top of this salad give it a colorful and fresh look, and the vibrant colors, along with the lemon zest, are the features that make this salad stand out among the rest. We prepared this for the one hundredth birthday party in honor of my husband's father.

# BAKED POTATO BAR

## SERVES 20

- 20–25 large russet potatoes
- Chili made with 3 pounds / 1.5 kg lean ground beef (see recipe on page 158)
- 12 cups / 3 L broccoli and cauliflower
- 2 cups / 500 ml cheese sauce (next page)

- 4 cups / 1 L cheddar cheese, grated
- 6 cups / 1.5 L Greek salad (see tip)
- 3 cups / 750 ml fresh salsa (see recipe on page 136)
- 3 cups / 750 ml corn, cooked
- 3 large onions, thinly sliced

- 16 slices bacon
- ¾ cup / 175 ml butter, cubed into single servings
- 2 cups / 500 ml sour cream or plain yogurt
- 1 cup / 250 ml fresh chives, chopped
- Salt and pepper

## A FEW HOURS BEFORE DINNER

1. Set out all the serving dishes on a kitchen island or serving table, thinking through what will go into each dish and the most practical order.
2. Scrub potatoes, let dry, and set out on an extra-large, parchment-lined baking sheet.
3. Prepare your favorite chili recipe and keep warm in a slow cooker.
4. Cut broccoli and cauliflower into bite-sized pieces and place in a pot, ready to steam.
5. Prepare vegetables for Greek salad and fresh salsa. Chop chives and grate cheese. Refrigerate all.
6. Place corn in a pot or dish, ready to heat.
7. Crisp bacon, crumble, and set aside
8. Caramelize onions by cooking in a heavy pan with a bit of olive oil, stirring often, until golden. Set aside.

## ONE AND A HALF HOURS BEFORE DINNER

1. Brush potatoes with olive oil, poke with a fork, and place in a 400° F / 205° C oven.

## HALF AN HOUR BEFORE DINNER

1. Lightly steam broccoli and cauliflower and prepare cheese sauce.
2. Mix Greek salad, heat corn, and reheat onions.
3. Set out all ingredients, as well as butter, sour cream, salt, and pepper.
4. Just before serving, remove potatoes from the oven and cut a long slit in the top of each potato. To open potatoes, squeeze both ends toward the center.

Although this meal is more of an idea than a recipe, it is an enjoyable way to prepare for and host a group. You could also ask guests to bring designated toppings and make it a potluck. Amounts can easily be adjusted according to the number you are serving, and possibilities for variety are endless. Pulled pork with coleslaw and baked beans or salmon with steamed asparagus and hollandaise could accompany a potato bar. It is an easy way to please both vegetarians and meat lovers. Sweet potatoes are also a great option.

# CHEESE SAUCE

- 2 tablespoons / 30 ml butter
- 2 tablespoons / 30 ml flour

- 1½–2 cups / 375–500 ml milk
- 1 cup / 250 ml cheddar cheese, grated

1. Melt butter in saucepan. Using whisk, stir in flour.
2. Gradually add milk, stirring until bubbly. Add cheese and stir until melted.
3. Pour cheese sauce over broccoli and cauliflower and transfer into a small slow cooker, if desired, to keep warm.

*TIP*

- Greek salad is easy to make; simply chop and mix cucumbers, peppers, tomatoes, olives, and feta cheese. Add your favorite dressing.

*—Anneliese*

# BARBECUE MEATBALLS

**SERVES 14**

- 3 pounds / 1.5 kg ground beef
- ¾ cup / 175 ml evaporated milk
- 2 eggs
- ¾ cup / 175 ml dry bread crumbs
- 2 teaspoons / 10 ml chili powder
- 2 teaspoons / 10 ml salt
- ½ teaspoon / 2 ml pepper

These zesty meatballs are an excellent dish to take to a potluck lunch. This recipe can be doubled quite easily if you need to serve a larger crowd.

1. Preheat oven to 400° F / 205° C.
2. Combine ingredients, shape into small meatballs, and place in single layer on a greased baking pan.
3. Brown meatballs in oven for 15 minutes, then remove baking pan and lower oven temperature to 350° F / 175° C.
4. Transfer meatballs to a roaster pan. Pour barbecue sauce over meatballs.
5. Cover pan and bake for 1 hour.

## BARBECUE SAUCE

- 1¾ cups / 425 ml bottled barbecue sauce
- ¼ cup / 60 ml sweet chili sauce
- ½ cup / 125 ml rhubarb jam (or your choice of jam)

1. Whisk sauce ingredients together until smooth.

*—Betty*

# CALICO BEAN BAKE

**SERVES 15**

- 3 14-ounce / 398-ml cans baked beans in tomato sauce
- 2 19-ounce / 540-ml cans red kidney beans, drained and rinsed
- 1 19-ounce / 540-ml can lima beans or mixed beans, drained and rinsed
- ½ pound / 250 g bacon, cut into 1-inch / 2.5-cm pieces

- 2 cups / 500 ml onion, chopped
- 2 garlic cloves, minced
- 1 cup / 250 ml ketchup
- ¼ cup / 60 ml brown sugar
- 2 teaspoons / 10 ml prepared mustard
- 2 teaspoons / 10 ml salt
- ¼ cup / 60 ml vinegar

1. Preheat oven to 350° F / 175° C.
2. Combine beans in a large bowl and set aside.
3. Fry bacon until crisp.
4. Sauté onions and garlic until tender.
5. Mix ketchup, brown sugar, mustard, salt, and vinegar.
6. Combine all ingredients.
7. Place in covered roaster and bake for 1½–2 hours.

This is a great dish for a crowd and is easy to double or triple. It is always a favorite side dish at barbecues and has been a staple at many barn parties we have hosted over the years. Leftovers, frozen in foil pans, are perfect for your next camping trip.

*TIP*

- Cans of beans come in many different sizes, with a standard-sized can holding about 2 cups / 500 ml. A few ounces/mls more or less won't make any difference. Mix and match the beans of your choice to equal about 12 cups / 3 L beans.

*—Judy*

# PUNCH BOWL TRIFLE

## SERVES 32

### ORANGE CHIFFON CAKE

- 2 cups / 500 ml flour
- 1½ cup / 375 ml sugar
- 3 teaspoons / 15 ml baking powder
- 1 teaspoon / 5 ml salt
- 6 large eggs, separated
- ½ teaspoon / 2 ml cream of tartar
- ½ cup / 125 ml vegetable oil
- ¾ cup / 175 ml orange juice
- 2 tablespoons / 30 ml orange zest

1. Preheat oven to 325° F / 160° C.
2. In a large mixing bowl, sift together the first 4 dry ingredients.
3. Separate egg whites from yolks, being careful not to break any yolks. Pour egg whites into a clean glass bowl. Set yolks aside in a smaller bowl.
4. Add cream of tartar to egg whites and beat at high speed until stiff peaks form when you pull the beaters up. Do not overbeat the egg whites, as that will cause the whites to become dry and the cake will not rise properly.
5. To egg yolks, add oil, orange juice, and orange zest, and beat together.
6. Pour egg yolk mixture into sifted dry ingredients and beat well.
7. Gently fold egg whites into the batter until just incorporated.
8. Pour batter into an ungreased tube pan.
9. Bake for 1 hour and 10 minutes.
10. Immediately after baking, invert cake onto a jar to cool.

*TIP*

- This orange chiffon cake is not only good in the trifle but also as a cake for any special occasion. Slice whole cake into 3 layers and fill with orange cream filling, then frost with whipped cream.

### ORANGE FILLING

- 2 4-ounce / 135-g boxes (6-serving size) cooked vanilla pudding mix
- 3 cups / 750 ml orange juice
- Juice from one large orange
- 2 tablespoons / 30 ml orange zest

1. Combine all filling ingredients in a medium saucepan.
2. Place over medium heat. Stir constantly until pudding thickens. This will be a very thick mixture. Remove from heat and cool.
3. Add 2 cups / 500 ml whipped cream (below) into cooled orange filling. Whip until well combined.

## WHIPPED CREAM

- 6 cups / 1.5 L whipping cream
- 4 tablespoons / 60 ml white sugar
- 1 tablespoon / 15 ml pure vanilla extract

1. Pour cream into mixing bowl. Beat on high speed for 2 minutes.
2. Add sugar and vanilla and whip until cream is set.
3. Save the whipped cream that is not blended into the orange filling to layer in the trifle.

## FRUIT

Vary the choice of fruit to your liking. Save some of the fruit to decorate the top of the trifle.

- 1½ cup / 375 ml blueberries
- 3 nectarines, thinly sliced
- 1½ cup / 375 ml raspberries
- 1½ cup / 375 ml blackberries
- 1½ cup / 375 strawberries, thinly sliced
- 2 kiwis, thinly sliced

## ASSEMBLING THE TRIFLE

1. Remove cooled cake from pan. Pull cake apart into small, golf ball–sized pieces and place into a large bowl.
2. In a large glass punch bowl or serving bowl, spread ¾ cup / 175 ml orange filling over the bottom. Top with a layer of cake pieces; a layer of whipped cream; then a layer of each fruit.
3. Continue to layer filling, cake, whipped cream, and fruit. As you add layers, place pieces of fruit around the edges of the bowl for a nice visual effect.
4. The top layer should be whipped cream. Decorate with additional fruit.
5. Cover and refrigerate trifle for at least 8 hours or overnight.

*—Kathy*

This trifle would be a spectacular finale for your next gathering. The orange chiffon cake and orange filling add a burst of citrus flavor. A trifle loaded with fresh fruit and cream— well, who can resist?

# GLUTEN-FREE VERSION OF TRIFLE

## YIELDS 4 SERVINGS

If you would like to have a gluten-free choice for your guests, simply replace the cake with small meringue cookies, available in many super-markets.

Using a 4½-cup / 1-L glass bowl in which to assemble the trifle, substitute 10–12 meringue cookies for cake. Assembling a small gluten-free trifle at the same time that you make the large one will only take away approximately 3 cups / 750 ml of the filling and fruit from the larger trifle. You will have a slice or two of chiffon cake left over if you make the gluten-free option.

*—Kathy*

# CHOCOLATE SHEET CAKE

**SERVES 24**

## CAKE

- 1 cup / 250 ml butter or margarine
- 1 cup / 250 ml water
- ¼ cup / 60 ml cocoa powder
- 2 cups / 500 ml sugar
- 2 cups / 500 ml flour
- ½ teaspoon / 2 ml salt
- 1 teaspoon / 5 ml baking soda
- 2 eggs
- 1 cup / 250 ml sour cream
- 1 teaspoon / 5 ml vanilla extract

1. Preheat oven to 350° F / 175° C.
2. Combine butter, water, and cocoa in a large saucepan over medium heat, stirring until mixture comes to a boil.
3. Remove from heat and add sugar. Cool slightly.
4. Add flour, salt, and baking soda. Stir until smooth.
5. Add eggs, beating with whisk.
6. Add sour cream and vanilla. Mix well.
7. Pour into a greased 10 x 15-inch / 25 x 38-cm jelly roll pan.
8. Bake for 20–25 minutes or until a toothpick inserted in the center comes out clean.
9. Spread frosting (recipe below) over warm cake.

## FROSTING

- ½ cup / 125 ml butter
- 4 tablespoons / 60 ml cocoa powder
- 4 tablespoons / 60 ml milk
- 2½ cups / 625 ml icing sugar
- 1 teaspoon / 5 ml vanilla extract
- ½ cup / 125 ml chopped pecans

1. Combine butter, cocoa, and milk in a saucepan and bring to a boil. Remove from heat.
2. Add icing sugar and stir until smooth.
3. Add vanilla and pecans.

Everyone seems to have a favorite chocolate cake recipe; this has been our family favorite for more than three decades. It has gone to picnics and potlucks through the years, and it can always be cut into smaller pieces to feed the multitudes! It is simple to make, convenient to transport, and easily served straight from the pan.

*—Judy*

# CHOCOLATE PEANUT BUTTER CHEESECAKE

## SERVES 12

## CRUST

- ½ cup / 60 g millet flour
- ¼ cup / 35 g tapioca starch/flour
- ¾ cup / 80 g almond flour
- 2 tablespoons / 16 g cocoa powder
- ¼ cup / 50 g sugar
- ⅓ cup / 80 ml butter, melted

1. Preheat oven to 350° F / 175° C.
2. Mix together flours, cocoa powder, and sugar. Stir in melted butter.
3. Press crumb mixture into an 11-inch / 28-cm springform pan. Bake for 15 minutes. Cool.

## FILLING

- 1 cup / 250 ml whipping cream
- 1 teaspoon / 5 g instant vanilla pudding mix
- 2 8-ounce / 250-g packages cream cheese, room temperature
- 1 cup / 200 g sugar
- 2 tablespoons / 30 ml butter, melted
- 2 tablespoons / 16 g cocoa powder
- ¾ cup / 175 g smooth peanut butter
- 1¼ cups / 225 g chocolate melting wafers
- 3 tablespoons / 45 ml milk
- 1 cup / 250 ml whipped cream
- Peanuts for garnish

1. Whip whipping cream with instant vanilla pudding mix. Set aside.
2. In a large bowl, beat cream cheese with sugar.
3. Mix cocoa into melted butter in a small bowl, stirring until smooth, and then add to cream cheese, beating until smooth and an even color.
4. Beat in the peanut butter.
5. Stir in the whipped-cream mixture until evenly mixed.
6. Pour over the cooled crust, smoothing the top.
7. Melt chocolate wafers with milk in the microwave, 30 seconds at a time to avoid overheating. Stir after each 30-second interval, and continue until all wafers are melted.
8. Spread chocolate mixture over the cheesecake filling.
9. When chocolate is set, pipe whipped cream around the edge. Add peanuts for garnish and to alert any guest with a peanut allergy of the ingredients.
10. Refrigerate until serving.

## TIPS

- This cheesecake can be made a day ahead.
- Crème fraîche (see recipe on page 87) can be substituted for the whipped cream.

*—Julie*

I made this dessert for a potluck that was hosted by a family whose home was a nut-free zone. Instead of the peanut butter, I used a no-peanut spread from my grocery store. In my opinion, spreads that list toasted soy as the first ingredient are superior in taste, texture, and color to those that are made from peas. For the almond flour in the base, I substituted quinoa flour.

173

These moist, tender sweet rolls have been taken to choir socials, school meetings, workplace lunchrooms, and care group, and the baking sheets have always come home empty. After they are baked and iced, they can be placed on cookie sheets, frozen, and then transferred to freezer containers where they can be kept until needed. Simply remove one or several from the container and thaw at room temperature.

# LEMON ROLLS

## YIELDS 2 DOZEN

### DOUGH

- 1½ cup / 375 ml milk
- ¾ cup / 175 ml lard or shortening
- 1 cup / 250 ml cold water
- 3 eggs
- ¾ cup / 175 ml sugar
- 2 teaspoons / 10 ml salt
- 2 tablespoons / 30 ml instant yeast
- 8–9 cups / 1.8–2 L flour

### FILLING

- ¼ cup / 60 ml butter, melted
- ½ cup / 125 ml sugar

1. Heat milk and lard or shortening together over medium heat until the fat melts. Add cold water.
2. In a large mixing bowl, beat eggs until light. Add sugar and salt and beat until frothy.
3. Add the warm liquids to the egg and sugar mixture.
4. Combine the yeast with 2 cups / 500 ml flour and add to the liquid.
5. Add remaining flour, a cup at a time, until the dough is able to be kneaded on a floured surface. Knead until smooth.
6. Place dough in a large bowl and cover with plastic wrap and a tea towel; allow to rise until doubled, about an hour.
7. While the dough is rising, make the lemon curd (next page).
8. Gently roll the dough into a 36 x 10-inch / 90 x 25-cm rectangle. Spread with melted butter and sprinkle with sugar.
9. Starting with the long side, roll up the dough. Slice into 1¼-inch / 3-cm slices. Place rolls on a greased baking pan. Space the rolls close together but not touching so they have room to rise.
10. Cover with a tea towel and let rise until doubled.
11. Put 1 teaspoon of lemon curd in the center of each roll.
12. Bake in a preheated 350° F / 175° C oven for 15–20 minutes or until lightly browned.
13. Allow to cool and then spread with icing.

# LEMON CURD

- ½ cup / 125 ml sugar
- 1 tablespoon / 15 ml cornstarch
- 3 egg yolks, beaten
- Juice of 1 large lemon
- Enough water to make 6 tablespoons / 90 ml liquid when combined with lemon juice
- ¼ cup / 60 ml butter, cubed

1. In a small saucepan, mix sugar and cornstarch.
2. Stir in egg yolks, lemon juice, and water.
3. Stir over medium heat until the curd is thick and bubbly.
4. Transfer mixture to a bowl. Stir in butter, cover surface with plastic wrap, and chill until ready to use.

# ICING

- 2 cups / 500 ml icing sugar
- ¼ cup / 60 ml butter, softened
- Milk, enough to make a spreadable icing

1. Combine icing sugar and soft butter in a medium bowl.
2. Stir in a few teaspoons of milk at a time until icing reaches spreadable consistency. Beat with a wooden spoon until smooth and creamy.

*—Lovella*

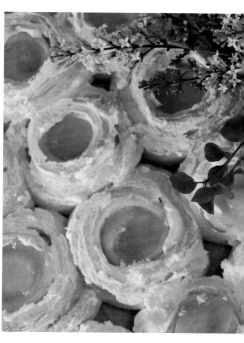

BREAD FOR THE JOURNEY

# KEEPING AN OPEN DOOR

*Therefore, as we have opportunity, let us do good to all.*

—GALATIANS 6:10 (NIV)

{ Over the forty years that we have lived in our home, we've seen a number of families move in and out of the neighborhood. Others have been here almost as long as we have and have become close friends. All of these neighbors have influenced our lives.

We've watched our families grow, helped with babysitting, brought baked goods, and shared meals and garden produce. We've moved each other's pianos, started each other's cars, mowed each other's lawns, collected each other's mail, and gone looking for each other's wandering children and pets. We've wept with those who have experienced loss and rejoiced with those who were celebrating. In more recent years, we've taken turns hosting neighborhood Christmas parties and summer barbecues.

None of this can happen, however, unless we acknowledge our part in community and are willing to interact with our neighbors. We can live in the same spot forever but never know a single neighbor—unless we are willing to knock on their doors or open ours in welcome when they come knocking on ours.

Jesus was a prime example of someone who was involved in his community. He showed his compassion to those who were sick and wept with those who had lost family members. He often went out of his way to lighten burdens. He showed hospitality, using what was available. He blessed children with love and attention. He invited friends and strangers to join him in his God-given tasks.

Jesus also made himself vulnerable by asking for and receiving help from friends and strangers alike. So often we as Christians think that we should be the strong ones who help others, and we do not allow our neighbors the opportunity to help us. I learned this lesson many years ago when we couldn't find our six-year-old son after school one day. We were frantic and called our neighbor, a single father, to help us look for him. He willingly came to our aid, and after a concentrated search, he was the one who found our son. He told me later that it blessed him so much to be asked to help. We had helped him on numerous occasions, but this experience told him that we trusted him and valued his help.

Let's encourage each other to be deliberate about opening our doors to friends, family, children's playmates, and strangers. Let's offer friendship and encouragement to those who enter and help to those in need. And we shouldn't hesitate to knock on our neighbors' doors when we need help. Sometimes our vulnerability is exactly what is needed to build community. ∾

—*Bev*

# CELEBRATING *Hospitality*

Hospitality is the opening of your heart and home to others, whether friends or strangers. It's about blessing others . . . not impressing them. Let us share with you a few easily prepared dishes that allow you to invite guests into your home without a lot of fuss.

## CELEBRATE WITH

*A generous person will prosper; whoever refreshes others will be refreshed.*
—PROVERBS 11:25 (NIV)

# CHARLOTTE REFLECTS *on* HOSPITALITY

This story is not so much about how I "do" hospitality. Rather, it's how I was the recipient of hospitality during a difficult time in my life.

It started about the time we began writing our first book, *Mennonite Girls Can Cook*. Without warning, life as I knew it changed, literally overnight. I developed a form of arthritis, and it felt like shards of glass were piercing my joints. Taking the stairs became a frightening task, and I couldn't open a jar or hold a book. My youngest daughter chose to tuck me into bed at night, like I had done for her when she was little, because simply lifting the blanket over myself had become painful for me. I lost my ability to work as a reflexologist, which required strong hands. I was no longer able to serve our local

*We are all called to be hospitable, and that means so much more than "entertaining" people.*

crisis pregnancy center as a crisis line counselor and coordinator, which I loved and had been doing for twenty years. It also became impossible to continue serving the Lord with my gift of hospitality, which had always been a joy. I needed the little energy I had to simply cope with everyday living. I could no longer give what I did not have.

The ways to be hospitable are as unique as the givers, as I learned from friends who were beside me during this time. Simple things filled me with joy and gratitude, and I learned that genuine hospitality requires nothing fancy. Being invited into the homes of friends for an evening of playing games and ordering takeout, sitting by a backyard fire, discovering cookies left on our doorstep or a gift card for pizza in the mailbox: these things were welcomed acts of kindness. One Saturday morning two friends came by with a bucket and cleaning supplies and blessed us with a deep-cleaned kitchen. Big or small, these gifts offered me hope. I knew that people cared about me and my family.

I began asking myself: *is there something that I can still offer to give others hope as well?* The Lord assured me that I did not have to be completely well to serve him again. Even when I felt I was at my worst, I desired to listen, encourage, and pray with those who needed it as much as I did, if not more. So I did what I could, on a much smaller scale than what I was used to. I would pack a basket for two, with pretty dishes and a thermos of tea, and then I would visit those who were dealing with even more difficult challenges than mine.

Chronic illness doesn't go away overnight, if ever. It takes courage to walk alongside someone with a long-term ailment. Sometimes, all that is needed is to *be there*, and be willing to listen. There are no words to make it better and no easy answers, but a listening heart and a word of encouragement are gifts. Journeying with someone is sometimes done quietly, through simple acts of love and kindness.

I am happy to say that, after two years, my health is slowly being restored. As my pain becomes more manageable, we are able to have guests in our home again, with a lot of help and unwavering support from my loving husband and children. They clean, I cook: we make a good team. I don't know what tomorrow will hold, but I know who holds my future. Even though I still struggle at times, I know that God hears my pleas, he knows my situation, and I see his great love for me in spite of the pain. I do what I can as I am able, and I rest in God's grace.

We are all called to be hospitable, and that means so much more than "entertaining" people in one's home or cooking a fancy meal. Being willing to enter the dark place with someone who is struggling is hospitality of the truest kind. The Lord has blessed me in unexpected ways, through unexpected people, and I will always be grateful. I was at the receiving end of hospitality, instead of the giving end, and my experience is a gift worth sharing with others. ✍

—*Charlotte*

183

# BISCUIT CINNAMON ROLLS

**YIELDS 12 ROLLS**

## BISCUIT DOUGH

- 2 cups / 500 ml flour
- 2 tablespoons / 30 ml sugar
- ½ teaspoon / 2 ml baking soda
- 2 teaspoons / 10 ml baking powder
- ½ cup / 125 ml butter, cold
- 1 cup / 250 ml half and half (light cream)

## FILLING

- ½ cup / 125 ml butter, room temperature
- ¼ cup / 60 ml sugar
- ¼ cup / 60 ml brown sugar
- 1½ tablespoon / 22 ml cinnamon

We have hosted many overnight guests in our home. On Sunday mornings, we serve these tender little biscuits with fruit and coffee. When our daughter was going to Bible college, she would often bring home students for weekends, and they would wake to the smell of these cinnamon rolls coming out of the oven. This dough is very easy to make and rolls up and bakes quickly.

1. Preheat oven to 400° F / 205° C.
2. Combine dry ingredients for dough in a medium mixing bowl.
3. Cut in cold butter until the mixture becomes fine crumbs.
4. Using a fork, stir in the half and half until the dough comes together.
5. Lightly dust a pastry mat or counter with flour. Gently knead the dough until smooth. Do not overwork it.
6. Roll out dough into an 8 x 12-inch / 20 x 30-cm rectangle.
7. Spread dough with room-temperature butter.
8. Mix together white and brown sugar and sprinkle over buttered dough. Sprinkle with cinnamon.
9. Roll up dough in a jelly-roll fashion. Slice into 12 equal pieces, and place in a lightly greased or parchment-lined 9 x 13-inch / 22 x 33-cm baking pan.
10. Bake for 12–14 minutes. Biscuits will be a light golden brown.
11. Remove from oven and transfer to a cooling rack.
12. While still warm, drizzle with icing (next page). Serve warm.

*TIP*

- When ready to drizzle with icing, place cooling rack with biscuits over sink so that the extra icing drips through into the sink, leaving you with no mess on the counter to clean up.

# ICING

- 1 tablespoon / 15 ml butter
- 1 cup / 250 ml icing sugar
- 5 tablespoons / 75 ml half and half (light cream)

- 1 teaspoon / 5 ml pure vanilla extract

1. Melt butter and pour over icing sugar. Stir in half and half and vanilla.
2. Using a fork, mix well until mixture is smooth and makes a thick drizzle. Add a few more drops half and half to icing as needed.

*—Kathy*

# CRAB *and* SHRIMP APPETIZERS

## SERVES 12 AS AN APPETIZER

- 1 long sandwich loaf (square slices)
- butter, room temperature
- 8 ounces / 250 g cream cheese
- ⅔ cup / 150 ml shrimp, cooked, peeled, and chopped
- ⅔ cup / 150 ml imitation crab, chopped
- ½ cup / 125 ml mayonnaise or salad dressing
- ⅓ cup / 75 ml green onions, finely chopped
- 1 4.5-oz / 125-g package freshly grated Parmesan cheese
- Fresh dill weed, finely chopped (optional)

1. Toast slices of bread. Spread butter on them and remove crusts.
2. Mix the remaining ingredients, except the dill and cheese, and spread on toast.
3. Sprinkle with Parmesan cheese.
4. Cut in half diagonally to form triangles.
5. Place on baking sheet to bake immediately, or package up in an airtight container to freeze and bake at a later date.
6. To serve, preheat oven to 350° F / 175° C. Bake the appetizers for 15 minutes or until cheese bubbles.
7. Garnish with fresh dill, if desired, prior to serving.

*—Marg*

This appetizer has been a favorite at our annual New Year's Eve party, and we always hope that our friend Elsie will bring this dish. She claims that it is simple because it can be easily prepared ahead of time. It is wonderful to have ready in the freezer for unexpected guests. It was fun pulling these out for an unexpected celebration with my *Mennonite Girls Can Cook* friends, who gave this appetizer a thumbs-up.

# EASY CHEESY TORTELLINI CASSEROLE

**SERVES 4–5**

- 1 12-ounce / 350-g package fresh cheese tortellini
- ¾ pound / 375 g smoked sausage, sliced diagonally
- 1 tablespoon / 15 ml vegetable oil
- About 2 cups / 500 ml red, green, or yellow bell peppers, cut in chunks
- 1 22–24-ounce / 650–700-ml jar red pasta sauce
- 2 cups / 500 ml grated cheddar, mozzarella, or Italian cheese mix

1. Preheat oven to 350° F / 175° C.
2. Spray a shallow oval casserole or 9 x 13-inch / 22 x 33-cm pan with cooking spray.
3. Cook tortellini according to package directions, being careful not to overcook. Drain and set aside.
4. Sauté smoked sausage in vegetable oil.
5. Stir-fry peppers lightly, just to heat through.
6. Combine tortellini, sausage, and peppers.
7. Add pasta sauce and stir to combine.
8. Pour tortellini mixture into prepared casserole dish. Top with grated cheese.
9. Bake uncovered for 30 minutes or until hot and bubbly.

*TIPS*
- If you prefer a vegetarian dish, omit the sausage.
- Use a spicy red pepper pasta sauce or use your favorite variety.

*—Judy*

If you keep a few basic ingredients on hand, you can always bring company home for dinner. Keep a supply of tortellini in the freezer and prepared pasta sauce in the pantry, add a few staples from the fridge, and you have the makings of a simple and delicious meal in short order. Serve with a green salad and enjoy the taste of home-cooked Italian food without a whole lot of home-cooking! This recipe is easily doubled for a larger dinner party.

# TOMATO RICE SOUP

## SERVES 8–12

- 2–4 tablespoons / 30–60 ml olive oil
- 1 medium onion, chopped
- 5 garlic cloves, minced
- 1 28-ounce / 796-g can petite diced tomatoes
- 6 cups / 1½ L chicken broth
- 1 6-ounce / 156-g can tomato paste
- 4–5 small bay leaves
- ½ teaspoon / 2 ml dried basil
- ¼ teaspoon / 1 ml dried thyme
- Pinch of saffron
- 1 teaspoon / 5 ml dried parsley
- ¼ teaspoon / 1 ml fennel seeds crushed in mortar and pestle
- ½ cup / 125 ml uncooked rice
- Salt and pepper to taste

1. Heat olive oil in heavy pot or Dutch oven and add chopped onion.
2. Cook until almost translucent and add garlic.
3. Cook the onion and garlic for 1–2 more minutes, and then add the diced tomatoes. Cook until bubbly.
4. Add broth, tomato paste, and spices. Add salt and pepper to taste.
5. When the soup comes to a boil, add rice and return to boil.
6. Lower heat and simmer, partially covered, until rice is cooked, approximately 45 minutes. Simmering longer simply enhances the overall flavor.
7. Remove bay leaves before serving.

*TIPS*

- Saffron adds a very nice dimension to this soup, but it is expensive. If you don't have it in your pantry, you can omit it.
- To make this recipe gluten free, use gluten-free chicken or vegetable broth. ⓖⒻ

*—Ellen*

My husband, Greg, made this soup for me on one of our first dates. These days, whenever guests travel to our home from afar, we have a pot of this soup on the stovetop, ready for their arrival. The inviting aroma greets our weary travelers. It's the perfect simple meal served with crusty bread.

# SEAFOOD CHOWDER

**SERVES 8–10**

- 3 cups / 725 ml water
- 2 envelopes or 2 cubes chicken bouillon
- 2 sprigs fresh parsley
- 1 bay leaf
- 6–10 peppercorns
- 1 medium onion, diced
- 2 stalks celery, diced
- 3 medium potatoes, diced
- 1 carrot, diced
- 1 red bell pepper, diced
- 1 12-ounce / 375-ml bottle clam juice
- ½ teaspoon / 2 ml celery salt
- ½ teaspoon / 2 ml seasoned salt
- ½ teaspoon / 2 ml seasoned pepper
- ½ teaspoon / 2 ml dried thyme
- Dash hot pepper sauce, if desired
- 1 teaspoon / 5 ml Worcestershire sauce
- ¼ cup / 60 ml butter
- ¼ cup / 60 ml flour
- 1 cup / 250 ml milk
- ½ cup / 125 ml heavy cream
- Salt and pepper to taste
- 2 cups / 500 ml seafood, cooked and chopped
- 3 slices bacon, fried and crumbled (optional)

1. Place water and chicken bouillon granules in large pot. Add parsley, bay leaf, and peppercorns.
2. Add diced vegetables and bring to a boil.
3. Simmer until vegetables are tender but not overcooked.
4. Remove bay leaf, parsley, and peppercorns.
5. Add clam juice and seasonings.
6. Make a white sauce from the butter, flour, and milk. (To make a white sauce, melt butter and then stir in flour. Add milk and cook, stirring constantly, until it comes to a boil.)
7. Stir white sauce and cream into the soup.
8. Add seafood and bacon, stirring until heated. Add salt and pepper to taste.
9. If desired, garnish with a fish shape made out of cut red pepper or oyster crackers and parsley.

*TIPS*

- Bay shrimp and imitation crabmeat can be used in this recipe.
- You can add any white-fleshed fish to the seafood mix. Poach the fish in a little salted water prior to making the soup and then add with the shrimp and crabmeat. Adding the seafood right before serving prevents it from getting overcooked and rubbery.
- Use a spice bag if you do not want to "fish" around for the seasonings later.

*—Bev*

Although the ingredient list is long, this soup can be made in about an hour. Paired with fresh biscuits, this makes a nice lunch.

# VEGETARIAN TACO SALADS

**SERVES 8–10**

## TACO BEAN SALAD

- 2 14-ounce / 398-ml cans baked beans in tomato sauce
- 1 16-ounce / 475-ml bottle French or Catalina dressing
- 2 cups / 500 ml corn, canned or thawed
- 1 medium green pepper, diced
- 1 small onion, diced
- 2 tomatoes, diced
- 1 cucumber, diced
- 1 large head Romaine lettuce, torn into bite-sized pieces
- 2 cups / 500 ml grated cheese
- 1 bag of corn chips or tortilla chips

1. Combine the beans, dressing, and vegetables in a salad bowl.
2. Place a layer of lettuce on serving platter.
3. Top with bean mixture.
4. Sprinkle cheese and chips on top.

## BLACK BEAN TACO SALAD

- 1 19-ounce / 540-ml can black beans, drained and rinsed
- 2 cups / 500 ml fresh salsa
- 2 cups / 500 ml corn, canned or thawed
- 1 head Romaine lettuce, torn into bite-sized pieces
- 1 medium green pepper, diced
- 1 small onion, diced
- 2 tomatoes, diced
- 1 cucumber, diced
- Guacamole
- Plain Greek yogurt
- Baked tortilla chips

1. Combine the beans, salsa, and corn.
2. In a large bowl, make a salad of greens and vegetables.
3. Top with black bean mixture.
4. Add guacamole, yogurt, and chips for a special touch and according to personal taste.

My aunt always receives requests to bring this taco bean salad to family gatherings. She makes a huge bowl of it, and it doesn't take long before the bowl is empty and people come back looking for more. I like to have all the ingredients on hand to make a quick meal for a spontaneous invitation or when unexpected guests arrive. This is definitely a crowd-pleaser. The black bean taco salad is a healthy alternative packed with flavor and protein. You can purchase the salsa and guacamole or use the recipes on pages 136 and 134.

**TIPS**

- Assemble the salad just prior to serving. The bean mixture can be prepared in advance and will remain good for several days if refrigerated.
- Mix only as much salad as is needed, because once the salad has been mixed, it does not keep well.
- Use your favorite kind of cheese. We like to use a Tex-Mex mix or sharp cheddar.
- Use either plain taco chips or your favorite flavor; the size of the bag you use depends on how many chips you and your guests prefer.

*—Charlotte*

# WHOLESOME FREEZER BISCUITS

## YIELDS 4 DOZEN

- 6 cups / 1.5 L unbleached flour
- 2 cups / 500 ml oatmeal, finely ground in food processor to make 1½ cup / 375 ml
- 1 cup / 250 ml whole wheat flour
- ½ cup / 125 ml rye flour
- 2 tablespoons / 30 ml instant yeast
- 1 tablespoon / 15 ml baking soda
- 4 tablespoons / 60 ml baking powder
- ½ cup / 125 ml sugar
- 1 tablespoon / 15 ml salt
- 1 pound / 454 g butter, chilled and cubed
- 1 quart / 1 L *minus* ¼ cup / 60 ml buttermilk
- 3 tablespoons / 45 ml fresh lemon juice

1. Stir the dry ingredients together in a large bowl.
2. Cut in butter with a pastry blender. Rub the flour and butter mixture together with your fingers to make sure that no large chunks of butter remain.
3. Add the buttermilk and lemon juice and stir with a large spoon until most of the dry ingredients have been moistened.
4. Turn out the dough onto a floured counter and press together, folding over several times. Pat the dough out into a rectangle. Sprinkle the counter and the top of the dough lightly with flour, and roll into a ½-inch / 1.5-cm thick rectangle about 12 x 20 inches / 30 x 50 cm.
5. Using a sharp-edged 2-inch / 5-cm biscuit cutter, cut straight down. Cut biscuits as close as possible and place them on a parchment-lined baking sheet, spacing them close together. Place them in the freezer. Once frozen, stack them in rows and store in freezer bags.
6. Since biscuit dough toughens when reworked, set aside leftover dough to make cinnamon maple biscuit bites (next page).
7. To bake biscuits before freezing, set biscuits 1-inch / 2.5-cm apart on a baking sheet and allow to rest, covered, for 1½–2 hours or until nearly doubled. Bake in the top third of a preheated 425° F / 220° C oven for 12–15 minutes or until evenly browned.
8. To bake frozen biscuits, remove from freezer bags and, as instructed above, place on baking sheets. Cover and thaw in a cool place until doubled—about 4 hours on the counter or up to 8 hours in a cool place. Bake as above.

### TIP

- It is important that the biscuit dough does not get too warm before baking, as the butter will start to melt and the biscuits will not keep their shape or be as flaky.

When your home is blessed with guests, it is wonderful to be able to bake these biscuits while your ham is baking or the soup is simmering on the stove. You won't need to ask twice for family and friends to gather at the table, because the aroma of freshly baked biscuits will have them coming into the kitchen. The biscuits may take some time and effort and space on the counter on the day you mix and roll them, but on the day that you open your freezer and pull out as many biscuits as you need for supper, it is only a baking sheet that will require washing. This keeps your kitchen tidy and allows you to spend more time with your guests.

# CINNAMON MAPLE BISCUIT BITES

**YIELDS 1 DOZEN**

- ¾ cup / 175 ml brown sugar
- 2 tablespoons / 30 ml butter, melted
- ½ teaspoon / 2 ml cinnamon
- 1 teaspoon / 5 ml maple flavoring
- ½ cup / 125 ml chopped walnuts (optional)
- ½ cup / 125 ml raisins (optional)
- Leftover pieces of biscuit dough

1. Combine all the ingredients except biscuit pieces in a freezer bag. Rub ingredients together to distribute. Add leftover pieces of biscuit dough and shake to distribute ingredients.
2. Spray a 12-cup muffin pan with cooking spray and divide ingredients into the pan. Cover and let rise several hours. Preheat oven to 375° F / 190° C and bake for 12–15 minutes. Drizzle with a simple glaze of 1 cup / 250 ml icing sugar and enough cream to make a consistency that can be drizzled.

*TIPS*

- It doesn't matter how large or small the leftover pieces of biscuit dough are; they will fill in the spaces as they rise in the muffin tins.
- If you do not wish to bake the biscuit bites on the same day, place pan in a plastic bag and freeze. The night before you plan to serve the bites, remove from freezer, keep covered, and allow to rise overnight.

*—Lovella*

# FREEZER-DOUGH PIZZAS

## STIR-AND-REST PIZZA DOUGH
### YIELDS 6 MEDIUM THIN-CRUST PIZZAS

- 2 cups / 500 ml lukewarm tap water
- 2 teaspoons / 10 ml sugar
- 2 tablespoons / 30 ml active dry yeast
- 2 cups / 500 ml semolina flour, plus ¼ cup / 60 ml for kneading

- 3 cups / 750 ml white flour
- 1½ teaspoons / 7 ml salt
- ⅓ cup / 75 ml olive oil
- 1 tablespoon / 15 ml cornmeal per pan

1. Measure water and sugar into a large glass bowl and sprinkle with yeast.
2. Allow yeast to proof until foamy; then stir down.
3. Add flours, salt, and oil. Stir well to combine.
4. Spray counter with cooking spray and turn dough out onto it.
5. Knead dough, working in extra semolina flour as needed to make a soft, non-sticky dough.
6. Divide into 6 equal portions and flatten into disks, wrapping each disk in parchment paper and store in freezer bags. At this point, the dough can be used after rising, placed in refrigerator for several days, or kept in freezer for several months.
7. To shape and use right away, roll out dough to fit pizza pan, grease pan, and sprinkle pan well with cornmeal. Lay rolled-out dough in pan, cover, and allow to rise for 30 minutes.
8. To use frozen dough, take out of freezer in the morning and place in refrigerator to thaw in time for supper. Or allow dough to thaw on counter, which would take approximately 2 hours. Roll out and fit onto pan as instructed above.
9. Add toppings and bake at 425° F / 220° C for 15–20 minutes or until crust is golden brown.

We decided to blend work on this cookbook with a much-anticipated girlfriend day together. While the dough was chilling and rising, Kathy chopped and prepped, and Lovella took photos of the pizza party in the making.

Why order pizzas? Keeping pizza dough on hand is the perfect solution to serving unexpected guests. With pantry items in stock and a list of pizza options, your pizzas can come together in short order. While pizza bakes, set the table and toss a green salad, and you will be able to relax with your guests in no time at all.

# BREAD-MAKER PIZZA DOUGH
## YIELDS 2 LARGE PIZZA SHELLS

- 1 cup / 250 ml water
- 2 tablespoons / 30 ml canola oil
- 1 large garlic clove, crushed
- 3 cups / 750 ml flour
- 1 teaspoon / 5 ml salt
- 2 teaspoons / 10 ml active dry yeast
- 1 tablespoon / 15 ml sugar
- ½ teaspoon / 2 ml Italian seasoning
- ¼ teaspoon / 1 ml ground dried oregano
- 1 tablespoon / 15 ml grated Parmesan cheese
- ¼ cup / 60 ml grated Parmesan cheese

1. Add all ingredients in order listed (except ¼ cup / 60 ml Parmesan cheese) to bread maker pan. Turn bread maker to dough setting.
2. When cycle is complete, turn dough onto a lightly greased counter, pull together, and divide into 2 equal pieces.
3. Roll out each piece to fit a 12-inch / 30-cm pizza pan. Press into greased pans.
4. Sprinkle with remaining ¼ cup / 60 ml Parmesan and let rise 30 minutes.
5. Bake at 450° F / 230° C for 8 minutes or until light brown.
6. To use immediately, add your favorite sauce and toppings to the pre-baked crust and bake again with toppings at 425° F / 220° C for 12–15 minutes.
7. To use later, place baked pizza shells between sheets of parchment paper, wrap in foil, place in freezer bags, and then freeze. When ready to make pizza, allow crust to thaw, add toppings, and bake as directed above.

*TIP*

- Do not bake this bread-maker dough on a pizza stone; it would bake at a temperature too high for this dough.

# MULTIGRAIN PIZZA DOUGH
## YIELDS 4 LARGE THIN CRUST PIZZAS

- 4½ cups / 1 L multigrain flour
- 2 teaspoons / 10 ml salt
- 2 teaspoons / 10 ml sugar
- 4 teaspoons / 20 ml instant yeast
- 2 cups / 500 ml warm water
- ¼ cup / 60 ml oil
- Olive oil

1. In a large bowl, combine dry ingredients. Add water and oil and stir until well combined. Cover with plastic wrap and allow to rise for 2 hours.
2. Punch down the dough and brush with olive oil. Place in a bowl large enough for the dough to double, and cover loosely with plastic wrap.
3. Refrigerate overnight or for 12 hours before using to allow the flavor and texture of the dough to develop. Divide into 4 disk-shaped pieces. Stack any disks meant for future use between parchment paper and place in freezer bag. Freezes well for several months.
4. To prepare pizza, place disk between 2 sheets of parchment paper along with 1 tablespoon / 15 ml olive oil. Use the heel of your hand, pushing from the center out, to press dough into a very thin crust. Peel off the top piece of parchment paper but let it sit on top of the dough as it rises. Allow to rise for 1 hour.
5. Preheat oven to 425° F / 220° C while you place toppings on the pizza. Bake in the center of oven for 20 minutes.

## USING A PIZZA STONE AND PEEL

A *pizza stone* can be used to bake your pizza in the oven or on the grill. In our opinion, it's the best way to bake pizza. The instant high heat from the stone when the crust is laid on it will ensure that the crust is baked to perfection. To use a pizza stone, place it in a cold oven or on a cold grill. Turn heat to 450° F / 230° C and allow the stone to slowly heat up for approximately 30 minutes. A *pizza peel* (a flat, shovel-like tool) should be used for transferring the pizza on and off the hot stone. Place the dough, with toppings, onto a piece of parchment paper, and then slide the peel under the parchment and transfer onto the hot stone. If using a grill, close the lid while pizza is baking. Remove baked pizza by sliding the peel under the pizza and transferring to a pizza pan or wooden board. Allow the stone to cool in oven or on grill before removing to clean.

## PANTRY ITEMS SUGGESTIONS

- Alfredo sauce
- Barbecue sauce
- Capers
- Olives
- Pesto
- Pineapple
- Pizza sauce
- Refried beans
- Salsa
- Sun-dried tomatoes

## FREEZER AND REFRIGERATOR ITEMS

- Bell peppers
- Brie
- Cheese sticks
- Cheddar cheese, refrigerated or frozen
- Cream cheese
- Feta cheese, refrigerated or frozen
- Figs
- Jalapeño peppers
- Mexican-blend cheese, refrigerated or frozen
- Mozzarella cheese, refrigerated or frozen
- Mushrooms
- Onions
- Parmesan cheese
- Spinach
- Tomatoes

## MEAT AND SEAFOOD

- Bacon
- Chicken
- Chorizo
- Deli ham
- Ground beef
- Italian sausage
- Pepperoni
- Prosciutto
- Salami
- Smoked salmon, thinly sliced

## HERBS AND SPICES

- Basil
- Cilantro
- Dill weed
- Garlic
- Hot chili pepper flakes
- Oregano

# KATHY *and* LOVELLA'S TOP PIZZA PICKS

Place toppings on the pizzas in the order in which they are listed.

## 1. LOADED STUFFED CRUST

Cheese sticks, pizza sauce, oregano, basil, Italian seasoning, Parmesan cheese, ground beef, hot Italian sausage, mushrooms, onion, black olives, mozzarella cheese.

Fry ground beef and Italian sausage until the meat begins to brown. Add thinly sliced mushrooms and chopped onions. Fry until vegetables are tender. Add 1 small can of sliced black olives. To stuff crust, roll out dough 2 inches / 5 cm wider than pan, tear cheese sticks into long, thin strands, and place them around the edges. Roll up to form a casing of dough around cheese. Allow dough to rise for 30 minutes before adding pizza sauce, toppings, and cheese.

## 2. SMOKED SALMON THIN CRUST

Cream cheese, thinly sliced smoked salmon, fresh dill, red onion rings, and capers.

Bake a pizza crust for 10 minutes before topping. Add toppings, and then bake just until toppings are heated through.

## 3. FRESH FIG AND BRIE APPETIZER

Use a partially baked thin crust, sliced Brie, freshly sliced figs, sliced pear, liquid honey.

Bake at 400° F / 205° C until Brie is melted. Drizzle reduced balsamic vinegar over pizza.

## 4. FAMILY FIESTA

Salsa, refried beans, fried and seasoned ground beef, cheddar or Mexican blend cheese, slivered head lettuce, chopped tomatoes, green onions, sliced olives, and freshly sliced jalapeños (optional).

Layer salsa, refried beans, seasoned ground beef, and cheese over prepared dough or pre-baked crust. Bake at 425° F / 220° C until cheese is bubbly and crust is browned. Remove from oven and top with remaining toppings to garnish.

## 5. CHICKEN ALFREDO

Purchased Alfredo sauce, sautéed chicken in olive oil, enough pesto to coat chicken, sun-dried tomatoes, feta cheese, red onion rings.

Spread Alfredo sauce over prepared dough and layer remaining ingredients on top. Bake on a preheated pizza stone at 425° F / 220° C for about 20 minutes.

## 6. HOUSE SPECIAL

Deli ham, shredded mozzarella, finely diced onion, diced bell peppers, sliced mushrooms, sliced olives, feta cheese, crushed chili peppers, and oregano.

Layer toppings over your favorite pizza sauce on pizza dough. Bake as instructed on the pizza dough of your choice.

## 7. PIZZA PEPPERONI REFRIGERATOR SAUCE

Grated pepperoni stick, grated onion, grated pepper, pizza sauce, grated mozzarella.

Use equal amounts of ingredients listed. This sauce is a great base for additional toppings of your choice. Use instead of regular pizza sauce and top with veggies and cheese. Bake on pre-baked crusts until the topping is heated through and the cheese is bubbling. Sauce freezes well. This sauce can also top ready-made crusts, flat-bread, or bagels.

## 8. CALZONES

To make serving-sized calzones, roll pizza dough into 6-inch / 15-cm rounds, place a large tablespoon of filling in the center, fold dough in half, and crimp edges. Brush with an egg wash and bake at 425° F / 220° C until golden brown.

*—Lovella and Kathy*

# MAKE-AHEAD CRUMBS
## *for* FRUIT CRISP

- 1 cup / 250 ml flour
- 1 cup / 250 ml brown sugar, packed
- 1 cup / 250 ml butter, room temperature
- 1 cup / 250 ml sliced almonds (optional)
- 4 cups / 1 L rolled oats

1. In a large bowl, mix all ingredients with a pastry cutter until butter is well incorporated and mixture has a uniform crumbly texture.
2. Work crumbs with your hands to form more crumbs as you transfer them to a storage container or freezer bag. Freeze to have ready when you need a no-fuss dessert.
3. To prepare a dessert for 4–5 people, spread about 1 cup / 250 ml of the crumbs into a pie pan or similar baking dish. Top with 4 cups / 1000 ml fresh or frozen fruit. Cover with about 1–1¼ cups / 250–310 ml of crumb mixture and bake at 350° F / 175° C for 40 minutes. Serve warm with ice cream.

*TIPS*
- If available, large-flake oats work very well in this recipe.
- This recipe will make about 4 desserts for 4–5 people each; if you use the whole batch, it will serve 16–20 at one time.

—*Anneliese*

I love having these crumbs ready at all times—so much so that when my container is empty, I know it's time to make another batch. In summertime I freeze a good amount of blackberries, blueberries, and raspberries so that they are always ready to go into a fruit crisp in a matter of minutes. Sliced apples, peaches, cherries, rhubarb, or a combination are also great. Since the crumbs are quite low in sugar, you may wish to sprinkle extra sugar on the fruit, depending on the tartness of fruit and personal preference. It's hard to believe that a dessert can be so delicious and still have some health benefits! One of the healthiest aspects of the recipe may just be that you can relax and enjoy your company.

# APPLE CAKE *with* CARAMEL SAUCE

**SERVES 10–12**

## CAKE

- ½ cup / 125 ml butter, softened
- 1½ cup / 375 ml sugar
- 2 eggs
- 1 teaspoon / 5 ml vanilla extract
- 2 cups / 500 ml flour
- 2 teaspoons / 10 ml cinnamon
- ½ teaspoon / 2 ml nutmeg
- ½ teaspoon / 2 ml baking soda
- ½ teaspoon / 2 ml salt
- 5 cups / 1.1 L apples, peeled and chopped

1. Preheat oven to 350° F / 175° C.
2. In a large bowl, cream butter and sugar until light and fluffy.
3. Add eggs, 1 at a time, beating well after each addition. Beat in vanilla.
4. Mix together flour, cinnamon, nutmeg, baking soda, and salt.
5. Add to creamed mixture and mix well; batter will be stiff.
6. Stir in apples.
7. Spread into a greased 9 x 13-inch / 22 x 33-cm baking pan.
8. Bake for 40–45 minutes or until top is lightly browned and a toothpick inserted into the center comes out clean.
9. Cool 30 minutes before serving.

## CARAMEL SAUCE

- 1 cup / 250 ml brown sugar
- ½ cup / 125 ml butter
- 1 cup / 250 ml whipping cream
- 1 teaspoon / 5 ml vanilla extract

1. Combine brown sugar and butter in a saucepan. Cook over medium heat until butter is melted.
2. Gradually add cream and bring to a boil, stirring constantly.
3. Remove from heat and stir in vanilla.
4. Serve cake warm with caramel sauce.

*—Betty*

This cake is wonderful served fresh with warm caramel sauce. It freezes well and thaws quickly, so it is the perfect cake to have on hand to serve when unexpected company arrives. The caramel sauce can be kept in the refrigerator for at least a week and can be warmed up in the microwave. Top with a scoop of ice cream or a dollop of whipped cream if you wish.

# ALMOND SWEET ROLLS

## YIELDS 24

- 1 teaspoon / 5 g sugar
- 1 teaspoon / 5 g unflavored gelatin
- ½ cup / 125 ml warm water
- 2 tablespoons / 16 g active dry yeast
- ¾ cup / 90 g millet flour
- ⅓ cup / 45 g white bean flour
- ⅓ cup / 45 g brown rice flour
- ½ cup / 65 g tapioca starch/flour
- ¼ cup / 35 g arrowroot powder/starch/flour
- ½ cup / 45 g almond flour
- ¼ teaspoon / 3 g salt
- 1 teaspoon / 10 g xanthan gum
- ⅓ cup / 75 g sugar
- ¼ cup / 60 g butter, softened
- ¼ cup / 60 ml milk, warmed
- 1 teaspoon / 5 ml almond extract
- ½ teaspoon / 2 ml vanilla extract
- 1 recipe almond paste (next page)
- 1 egg white
- 1 tablespoon / 15 ml warm water
- Sweet rice flour (for rolling)

1. Mix sugar and gelatin, add warm water, and stir well. Then add yeast and stir again. Allow to proof in a warm place or set in a dish of very warm water.
2. Blend together dry ingredients and set aside.
3. Beat sugar and butter until light; then add warm milk and extracts.
4. Add yeast mixture and mix.
5. Add the dry ingredients all at once, blend, and then beat on high for 2 minutes.
6. Turn dough out onto parchment paper that has been sprinkled liberally with sweet rice flour.
7. Dough will be very soft. Work in just enough sweet rice flour to make dough barely manageable.
8. Divide dough in half and pat out into 2 9-inch / 22-cm circles.
9. Divide the almond paste in half and roll out each portion into a 9-inch / 20-cm circle between plastic wrap that has been dusted with sweet rice flour. Peel off top layer of wrap, and then turn each almond-paste circle onto the top of each dough circle, plastic wrap face-up. Peel off plastic wrap.
10. Using a pizza wheel dipped in sweet rice flour, cut each circle into 12 equal wedges.
11. Starting at the wide end, roll up each slice, tucking in the end point.
12. Whisk egg white with the 1 tablespoon warm water. Using your index finger, smooth the egg-white mixture over the rolls.
13. Place rolls on parchment-lined baking sheet. Let rise, uncovered, for 40 minutes in a warm place.
14. Bake for 20 minutes or until golden brown at 375° F / 190° C.
15. Remove rolls from the oven and let cool before decorating as desired.

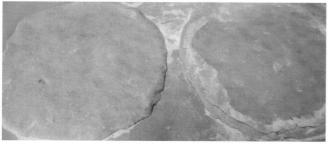
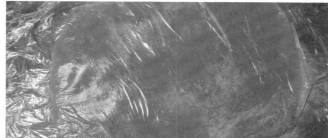

# ALMOND PASTE

- ➤ 1 cup / 100 g blanched almonds
- ➤ 1 cup / 125 g icing sugar
- ➤ 1 egg white
- ➤ ½ teaspoon / 2 ml almond extract

1. In a food processor, crush almonds. Add icing sugar and process until very fine.
2. In a bowl, mix the almond mixture with the egg white and the almond extract until it forms a ball. Use your hands if it is too stiff for a spoon.
3. Refrigerate until needed; this paste will keep for up to a week.

*TIPS*

- When baking with yeast, gluten-free dough will be sticky; sticky dough ensures a nicely risen, soft-baked product. Gluten-free dough stiff enough to knead, which is what many people are used to with regular gluten flours, will yield a hard brick.
- These rolls can also be made without the almond paste layer.
- Decorate the rolls with icing, crushed almonds, or chocolate drizzle, as desired.

*—Julie*

## BREAD FOR THE JOURNEY
# FELLOWSHIP, NOT PERFECTION, MATTERS

*Offer hospitality to one another without grumbling. Each of you should use whatever gift you have received to serve others, as faithful stewards of God's grace in its various forms. If anyone speaks, they should do so as one who speaks the very words of God. If anyone serves, they should do so with the strength God provides, so that in all things God may be praised through Jesus Christ. To him be the glory and the power forever and ever.*

—1 PETER 4:9-11 (NIV)

{ We can celebrate hospitality in various ways, showing generosity towards others and serving unselfishly from the heart. Being generous with what we have is one way to share with others what God has given to us.

Years ago, I attended a class in church about discerning the gifts that God has blessed us with, and we were encouraged to use what we enjoy doing to bless others. I enjoy spending time in my kitchen, baking and cooking, and I find much joy in sharing food with those who are too busy, who do not enjoy baking, or who are unable to do so. Those of us who love to cook and bake can bless someone at their place of work with a plate of freshly baked cookies, just in time for coffee break. We can invite people to our homes for a meal, which can be as simple as a bowl of soup and bread, or just for coffee and cookies. We should not worry about whether the furniture is dusted, or the dishes are in the sink, or the toys aren't put away. We want people to feel comfortable in our homes, and having a home that is warm and inviting will certainly do that. Overcoming the thought that we need a perfectly clean and beautifully decorated house allows us to open our hearts in fellowship with those we have invited into our home. The fellowship and sharing of God's love around the table is what really counts.

Volunteering to deliver meals to those in need is another way we enjoy serving, sharing words of encouragement those few moments we spend in their homes. We might be the only ones they see that day, and the joy on their faces is truly a blessing.

Jesus calls us to be hospitable whether in our homes or away from our homes. Hospitality is serving unselfishly from the heart. Whether it's a smile, a hug, a listening ear, or a shared meal, do it joyfully and without complaining.

*Jesus calls us to be hospitable whether in our homes or away from our homes.*

—*Betty*

208

# CELEBRATING *Milestones*

We love to rejoice with those who rejoice and celebrate the milestones of life. Whether it is a birthday, an anniversary, a graduation, or a promotion, let us help you with the dinner menu.

## CELEBRATE WITH

*For the Mighty One has done great things for me—holy is his name.*
—LUKE 1:49 (NIV)

# MARG REFLECTS *on* MILESTONES

The summer of 2012 was marked by three major milestones for our family. These events reminded me again that although we carefully schedule our calendars for milestone events, ultimately God orchestrates each day.

Last year my husband's father, John Henry Bartel, celebrated his one hundredth birthday. As time unfolded, it became apparent that there would be several parties for Papa (as we call him) in his church, community, and family. When we heard that family members from Europe would be arriving to join the celebration, our life went into full swing. Preparations, including cooking, baking, ironing pillow cases, and vacuuming furnace vents, began. While I concentrated on the inside of the house, my husband, John, managed outdoor projects that had not been attended to for years. We also spent time applying for and tracking down documentation of Papa's age, since formal birthday greetings from provincial and federal government officials in Canada are a significant part of one hundredth birthday celebrations. Having verified that all documents were authentic and that Papa had indeed reached this significant milestone, politicians and officials began sending their congratulations to him. I can still see Papa smiling when he read the Queen's letter and hear him saying, "Even the Queen sent her greetings!"

*Some milestones come in neatly timed packages, while other events are unexpected and appear as interruptions.*

While we prepared for these birthday celebrations, we were approached by a fine young man requesting permission for our daughter's hand in marriage. With the wedding date set for late summer, I immediately began to explore possible venues—until the bride said, "But Mom, I've always wanted to get married in our backyard." And so it was. Making lists began, as did shopping for the dress, ordering flowers, making gift registries, planning showers, hiring a string quartet and a photographer . . . And then came the day that my daughter gave me a questioning look and said, "Mom, you can make the wedding cake: your hazelnut roll!"

A milestone birthday celebrates the man who is our Papa, *Opa* (grandfather), and Great-*Opa*. This event gives recognition to one who has profoundly influenced all of us in one way or another. It is truly a time to reflect on the accomplishments, hard work, determination, and wisdom he has gained through his incredible challenges. When asked what his favorite motto is, my father-in-law replied, "*Gott kann,*" which means "God can."

A wedding commemorates the new love of two people choosing to join in union and celebrating with family and friends. All who attended our daughter's wedding experienced an emotional moment when Papa blessed the bride and groom in a benedictory prayer by placing his hands on them and prayerfully reciting the words from Numbers: "The LORD bless you and keep you; the LORD make his face shine on you and be gracious to you; the LORD turn his face toward you and give you peace" (Numbers 6:24-26, NIV). A blessing was handed down to the next generation.

After the busy summer, my husband and I booked a cabin for our thirty-ninth anniversary, intending to rest, ponder, and reflect on the events of the year. On our way, we planned a short visit to my brother, who had been ill, to deliver some authentic Mennonite food that he requested. A few hours prior to leaving, however, we received word that he was unexpectedly hospitalized again. Instead of going to the cabin, my husband and I spent the next few days standing by his children, supporting them and grieving together as we all said our last goodbyes. We carefully prepared the details that would celebrate and reflect his life.

Some milestones come in neatly timed packages, while other events are unexpected and appear as interruptions. Looking back, I can see now how these milestones allow us to celebrate our rich spiritual heritage. Celebrations give honor and praise to the God who gives and takes life, to the God who provides for us and who gives hope to future generations. *Gott kann!* ᴥ

*—Marg*

Patti Gerbrand / www.pattigerbrand.com

This is a classic appetizer, always popular and so simple to prepare.

You can use fresh shrimp or thawed, frozen shrimp, but be sure they are of top quality.

# SHRIMP COCKTAIL
## SERVES 6–8

## COCKTAIL SAUCE

- ½ cup / 125 ml bottled chili sauce
- 1 garlic clove, minced
- 1 tablespoon / 15 ml lemon juice
- 1 tablespoon / 15 ml Worcestershire sauce
- Hot pepper sauce to taste

1. Mix all ingredients an hour or more before serving.
2. Refrigerate.

## FOR EACH SHRIMP COCKTAIL, YOU WILL NEED

- ½ cup / 125 ml iceberg lettuce, chopped
- 5 large, cooked shrimp or prawns, tails off
- 3 large, cooked shrimp or prawns, tails on
- 1 tablespoon / 15 ml cocktail sauce
- Sliced lemon and fresh parsley for garnish

1. Place lettuce in a pretty stemmed glass or dessert bowl.
2. Top with 5 shrimp (tails off).
3. Add a dollop of cocktail sauce in the center of the shrimp.
4. Hang the 3 shrimp (tails on) on the sides of the dish.
5. Garnish with lemon and parsley.

### TIP
- To make this recipe gluten free, use gluten-free chili sauce and gluten-free Worcestershire sauce. 🇬🇫

*—Bev*

# RASPBERRY DRIZZLE SALAD DRESSING

## YIELDS 1 CUP

- 6 tablespoons / 90 ml raspberry jam
- 4 tablespoons / 60 ml red pepper jelly
- Juice from 2 limes
- 2 small garlic cloves, crushed
- 3 teaspoons / 15 ml olive oil
- ½ teaspoon / 2 ml dry mustard
- ½ teaspoon / 2 ml salt
- ¼ teaspoon / 1 ml pepper

1. Measure and add all ingredients into a glass jar. Seal jar and shake vigorously.
2. Refrigerate several hours to allow flavors to meld. Keeps well in refrigerator for up to 3 weeks.

*—Kathy*

This raspberry drizzle salad dressing is a combination of sweet and spicy with a twist of lime and a hint of garlic. This drizzle is a nice complement to a light, fresh salad of mixed greens and fresh fruit.

217

# ROASTED RED PEPPER SOUP

## SERVES 4 AS A MEAL, 8 AS AN APPETIZER

- 4 or 5 large red bell peppers
- 3 sweet potatoes or yams (2 pounds / 1 kg)
- 1 large onion
- 4 large garlic cloves

- 4 tablespoons / 60 ml olive oil
- 2 tablespoons / 30 ml Italian seasoning
- ¾ teaspoon / 3 ml salt
- ½ teaspoon / 2 ml pepper

- 2 cups / 500 ml cold water
- 2 cups / 500 ml chicken broth
- ⅛ teaspoon / 0.5 ml chili powder (optional)
- Sour cream (optional)

1. Preheat oven to 400° F / 205° C.
2. Hull and chop peppers into roughly 1-inch / 2-cm strips. Peel and slice yams into 1-inch / 2-cm slices. Peel, halve, and slice onion.
3. Toss vegetables, peeled garlic, oil, and seasonings in a large roasting pan. Cover with lid.
4. Roast vegetables for 45–60 minutes, until soft.
5. Stir cold water into roasted vegetables to cool. Blend in blender or food processor (in batches) to purée.
6. Pour into medium/large cooking pot. Add chicken broth. Bring to boil and simmer 5 minutes, adding more liquid or chili powder to taste, if needed. Serve with a dollop of sour cream or puff pastry top.

## OPTIONAL PUFF PASTRY TOP

1. Cool soup slightly and then refrigerate until ready to use. Ladle soup into 4–6 onion soup bowls or ramekin dishes, allowing 1 inch / 2 cm at top.
2. Roll out 1–2 14-ounce / 397-g packages thawed puff pastry to ⅛-inch / 0.25-cm thick.
3. Cut rounds, about 6 inches / 15 cm in diameter, slightly larger than tops of bowls. Cut a few slits to allow steam to vent.
4. Placing pastry rounds over individual bowls, press lightly to the outside of the bowl rim. Do not pinch to both inside and outside of rim. Chill 1 hour.
5. Bake in lower third of oven at 400° F / 205° C for 15–20 minutes, until golden brown in color.

### TIP

- For the puff pastry top, 1 package can be stretched to cover 6 bowls, but you will need to combine the scraps and re-roll them.

*—Anneliese*

218

One of the best things about this soup is the aroma that wafts out of the oven while you roast these flavorful vegetables. I enjoy serving this healthy, easy soup as an appetizer or as a quick soup, served with hearty rolls, to warm a cold day.

# BEEF WELLINGTON

## SERVES 6–8

- 2 pounds / 1 kg filet of beef, trimmed (filet mignon)
- Pepper, freshly ground
- 2 tablespoons / 30 ml extra virgin olive oil
- 1 tablespoon / 15 ml butter
- 1 shallot, minced

- ½ cup / 125 ml pancetta, cut into small pieces
- 1 pound / 500 g mushrooms, sliced
- ½ cup / 125 ml dry white wine
- ½ teaspoon / 2 ml kosher salt
- ¼ teaspoon / 1 ml pepper

- Fresh thyme, leaves from 3 sprigs
- ¼ cup / 60 ml fresh parsley, minced
- 1 package frozen puff pastry (2 sheets per package)
- 1 egg, beaten
- 1 tablespoon / 15 ml water

1. Place filet in a lightly greased roasting pan and season with freshly ground pepper.
2. Roast in an oven preheated to 425° degrees / 220° C for 30 minutes.
3. Remove from oven and put on a plate. Cool in refrigerator 1 hour.
4. While meat is cooling, thaw pastry sheets.
5. In a large sauté pan over medium-high heat, heat olive oil and butter until butter melts.
6. Add shallots and sauté for 2 minutes.
7. Add pancetta and cook 5 minutes longer.
8. Add all the mushrooms at once and mix well.
9. Stir in the white wine, salt, pepper, and thyme.
10. Cook until tender and liquid is evaporated. Remove from heat, add parsley, and let the mixture cool.
11. Roll out 1 sheet of puff pastry on lightly floured surface to approximately 14 x 16 inches / 35 x 40 cm.
12. Spread 2 cups / 500 ml mushroom mixture evenly over the dough, leaving a 1-inch / 2-cm border.
13. Place filet lengthwise on center of the mushroom mixture.
14. Carefully fold over the long ends of dough and press edges to seal.
15. Fold in the short ends and press to seal. If you have excess dough on the ends, cut the excess off before folding in and sealing.
16. Place carefully, seam-side down, on a lightly greased baking sheet.
17. Use excess dough or second sheet of dough to cut out decorative shapes, such as leaves or acorns, for the top.
18. Combine the beaten egg and water to make an egg wash. Brush the top, side, and ends of the pastry with the wash. Add the decorations and brush them with egg wash, as well.
19. Place in preheated 425° F / 220° C oven and bake for 25 minutes or until pastry is golden brown and beef registers at 145° F / 65° C with a meat thermometer.
20. Remove the filet from the oven and carefully transfer to a serving platter.
21. Just before serving, cut into evenly proportioned slices.

*—Ellen*

Beef Wellington is an elegant way to celebrate an important occasion. The filet mignon melts in your mouth. This cut of beef is expensive, but when you consider the final cost per serving, you may find that it's worth the price to share with loved ones you wish to honor for a great achievement.

Hosting a milestone celebration calls for something extra special. The blackberry sauce over the sweet and spicy chili-crusted tenderloin is not only an elegant presentation but a flavor combination that is sure to bring rave reviews.

# PORK TENDERLOIN *with* BLACKBERRY BALSAMIC SAUCE

## SERVES 6–8

- 2 1-pound / 500-g pork tenderloins
- 2 tablespoons / 30 ml olive oil
- 2 tablespoons / 30 ml chili powder
- 1 tablespoon / 15 ml brown sugar
- 1 teaspoon / 5 ml sea salt
- 1 teaspoon / 5 ml pepper, freshly ground
- ½ teaspoon / 2 ml chili powder
- ½ cup / 125 ml balsamic vinegar
- 1¼ cup / 300 ml blackberry jam
- ½ cup / 125 ml chicken or vegetable broth
- ½ cup / 125 ml sugar
- 2 tablespoons / 30 ml butter

1. Rub pork tenderloins with oil. Combine the first amount of chili powder with the brown sugar, salt, and pepper. Rub tenderloins with the spice-and-sugar mixture. Cover and refrigerate for 2–3 hours.
2. In a small saucepan, stir together ½ teaspoon / 2 ml chili powder, vinegar, jam, and broth. Heat together until it just begins to bubble. Remove from heat.
3. Place sugar in a nonstick or heavy pan over medium heat. Cook, stirring constantly, until sugar melts and becomes a rich caramel color.
4. Add the hot jam mixture to the sugar and continue to cook over medium heat, stirring constantly, until jam and sugar mixture is well blended. If the sugar mixture begins to harden, continue stirring and the sugar will melt as the mixture continues to cook.
5. Simmer uncovered for 10–15 minutes, stirring occasionally.
6. Remove from heat and stir in butter. Set aside until pork comes off the grill.
7. Heat a grill to 400° F / 205° C. Place seasoned tenderloins on grill and cook 4–5 minutes on each side, for a total of 16–20 minutes. Cook until a meat thermometer registers 145° F / 65° C.
8. Remove meat from the grill and allow to rest for 5 minutes.
9. Slice pork and arrange on a serving platter. Pour ½ cup / 125 ml warm sauce over sliced meat. Serve remaining sauce on the side.

*TIP*
- To make this recipe gluten free, use gluten-free broth. 🟢

*—Kathy*

# RICE PILAF

## SERVES 6–8

- ½ cup / 125 ml uncooked vermicelli, broken into small pieces
- 1½ cup / 375 ml white rice
- 1 tablespoon / 15 ml butter
- 3⅓ cups / 825 ml water or chicken broth or a combination of the two
- ½ teaspoon / 2 ml salt
- 2 tablespoons / 30 ml butter
- ½ cup / 125 ml raisins
- ½ cup / 125 ml pine nuts or blanched almond slivers
- ¼ cup / 60 ml fresh parsley, chopped

1. Preheat oven to 350° F / 175° C.
2. In a heavy pan with a tight-fitting lid, sauté the vermicelli and rice in 1 tablespoon / 15 ml butter for about 1 minute.
3. Add the liquid and salt and bring to a boil.
4. Lower heat, cover, and simmer for 20 minutes.
5. In a frying pan, sauté raisins and nuts in 2 tablespoons butter until the raisins plump and the nuts start to brown slightly.
6. Empty half of the cooked rice mixture into a 2-quart / 1.8 L oven-proof casserole dish. Add all the raisins and nuts (along with any melted butter) on top of this layer. Cover with the remaining rice and bake for 25 minutes.
7. Remove from oven and stir the rice mixture to distribute the nuts and raisins evenly.
8. Fold in parsley and serve hot.

*TIP*

- Angel hair pasta (broken into small pieces) can be used in place of the vermicelli.

*—Ellen*

The added ingredients in this rice give it great flavor and an extra crunch. Using chicken broth instead of water to cook the rice will also enhance the final product. This is a great side dish to add to a special meal or celebration.

223

# VEGETARIAN LASAGNA ROLL-UPS

## YIELDS 15 LASAGNA ROLLS

## NOODLES

- 15 lasagna noodles

1. Cook lasagna noodles according to instructions on the package.
2. Lay noodles on parchment-lined baking sheets that have been sprayed with cooking spray. Set aside.

## BÉCHAMEL SAUCE

- ⅓ cup / 75 ml butter
- ⅓ cup / 75 ml flour
- 3 cups / 750 ml milk
- 1 cup / 250 ml heavy cream
- 3 egg yolks
- 1 teaspoon / 5 ml salt
- ¼ cup / 60 ml Parmesan cheese

1. In a large saucepan, melt butter. Add flour and 1 cup / 250 ml milk and whisk together. Continue to add the milk, whisking over medium heat.
2. Combine heavy cream and egg yolks in a small bowl. Add cream-and-egg mixture, along with remaining milk, to the pan, whisking until the sauce becomes a thick cream.
3. Add salt and Parmesan cheese. Pour sauce into 11 x 15-inch / 28 x 38-cm rectangular baking dish that has been sprayed with cooking spray.

## CHEESE MIXTURE

- 2 cups / 500 ml ricotta cheese
- 1 cup / 250 ml herb-flavored feta cheese, crumbled
- ½ cup / 125 ml Parmesan cheese
- 2 cups / 500 ml mozzarella/cheddar blend cheese
- 1 egg
- 1 teaspoon / 5 ml salt

1. Combine cheeses, egg, and salt in a large bowl and set aside.

## VEGETABLE MIXTURE

- 1 cup / 250 ml onion, minced
- 1 cup / 250 ml mushrooms, minced
- 1 cup / 250 ml zucchini, minced
- 1 cup / 250 ml bell peppers, minced
- 1 cup / 250 ml asparagus stalks, finely chopped
- 2 garlic cloves, minced
- 1 cup / 250 ml marinara sauce

1. Spray a large frying pan with cooking spray and add all the vegetables. Stir-fry over medium-high heat for about 5 minutes or until tender.
2. Stir in the marinara sauce and the cheese mixture.

## ASSEMBLING THE LASAGNA ROLLS

> 1 cup / 250 ml marinara sauce  > 1 cup / 250 ml Parmesan cheese  > 1 cup / 250 ml mozzarella cheese (optional)

1. At one end of each lasagna strip, put about ⅓ cup / 75 ml of the vegetable-cheese mixture. Spread the vegetable mixture about ⅓ of the way down the noodle, and then roll up.
2. Repeat with all the lasagna noodles, dividing the mixture evenly.
3. Lay the lasagna rolls over the Béchamel sauce. Spoon marinara sauce over each roll and sprinkle with Parmesan cheese and mozzarella cheese.
4. Cover with plastic wrap and refrigerate for up to 1 day, or bake immediately in a 350° F / 175° C oven for 35 minutes or until edges bubble. Allow additional time to bake when chilled.

### TIPS
- Using various colors of bell peppers makes this an even more attractive dish.
- Store-bought marinara sauce works fine in this recipe.

*—Lovella*

My favorite way to serve these roll-ups is in individual ovenproof baking dishes. Place a pretty napkin underneath the hot dish before placing on a serving plate, and remind your guests that the little dish is piping hot. For a buffet table, I bake them in a pretty ovenproof dish that can be placed right onto the buffet table; that way the heat from the dish helps to keep the roll-ups warm until all the guests have walked through the buffet line.

# ROULADEN

## SERVES 4

- 8 slices beef, cut thinly for *Rouladen*
- Mustard
- 1 onion, cut into thin slices
- 8 dill pickle halves
- 4 slices bacon, cut in half
- 16 toothpicks
- 1 tablespoon / 15 ml butter
- 1 tablespoon / 15 ml oil

- 2 cups / 500 ml mushrooms, sliced
- 2 cups / 500 ml beef broth
- 2 tablespoons / 30 ml cornstarch
- ¼ cup / 60 ml cold water
- ½ cup / 125 ml cream (sweet or sour cream)
- Salt and pepper to taste
- Additional bacon (optional)

1. Preheat oven to 350° F / 175° C.
2. Lay slices of meat flat on a clean surface.
3. Thinly spread each slice with your favorite mustard.
4. On 1 end of each slice, lay several onion slices, a pickle half, and half a slice of bacon.
5. Tightly roll up each piece of meat, securing with 2 toothpicks.
6. In a large ovenproof, stainless-steel frying pan, heat oil and butter.
7. Brown the meat on all sides. Remove from pan.
8. To the pan, add mushrooms and any remaining onion that wasn't used in the filling. Cook until soft.
9. Add the beef broth and deglaze all the brown bits from the frying pan.
10. Lay the beef back into the broth.
11. Cover each piece of beef with additional bacon, if desired.
12. Cover the frying pan with a lid and bake for 1½ hours.
13. Remove the beef and place on a platter.
14. Mix cornstarch with cold water. Add this to the gravy; cook on the stovetop over medium heat until thickened.
15. Add cream and heat through, but do not boil.
16. Add salt and pepper to taste.

This is my husband's request for his birthday meal. Serve it with *Spaetzle* (German dumplings) or mashed potatoes. Green beans or red cabbage make a good side dish.

## TIPS

- Ask your butcher to slice the meat for you if you cannot find beef cut for *Rouladen* in your local grocery store.
- Make sure to use toothpicks that are not flavored. Flavored toothpicks can adversely affect the taste of a dish.
- If you do not have a stainless steel frying pan large enough to hold all the *Rouladen*, transfer everything into a large casserole dish. When you make the gravy later, just keep the *Rouladen* warm on the platter and make the gravy in a saucepan.
- If you use bacon on the top of the *Rouladen*, take off the cover for the last 5 minutes of baking. This will make the top brown and crispy.
- This recipe is easily adjusted to make as many as you need. I usually serve 2 *Rouladen* per person.
- To make this recipe gluten free, use gluten-free broth. ⓖ

*—Charlotte*

# BUTTERMILK-DRESSED POTATOES

## SERVES 4 AS A SIDE DISH

### POTATOES

- 4–5 medium potatoes
- Buttermilk dressing
- ¼ pound / 125 g bacon, diced
- 2 cups / 500 ml cheese, grated
- ¼ cup / 60 ml green onions, finely chopped

### BUTTERMILK DRESSING

- ⅔ cup / 150 ml mayonnaise
- ⅓ cup / 75 ml buttermilk
- 2 garlic cloves, minced
- 1 tablespoon / 15 ml fresh parsley, chopped
- 1 tablespoon / 15 ml fresh chives, chopped
- 1 teaspoon / 5 ml seasoned salt, or to taste
- ½ teaspoon / 2 ml pepper

> These potatoes have become a family favorite. The buttermilk dressing does double duty as a tasty salad dressing. If you substitute the parsley with fresh dill, it is delicious drizzled over a shrimp or salmon salad.

1. Bake or boil potatoes in their skins, just until done. This can be done ahead of time. Potato skins can be left on or removed.
2. Fry bacon until crisp and drain on a paper towel.
3. Meanwhile, mix buttermilk dressing by placing ingredients in a jar or gravy shaker and blending until thoroughly combined. The dressing can also be made ahead and refrigerated.
4. Cut cooked potatoes into 1-inch / 2.5-cm cubes and place in a 9-inch / 22-cm buttered glass tart pan or baking dish.
5. Drizzle buttermilk dressing over potatoes. Sprinkle with cheese and bacon.
6. Bake in a 350° F / 175° C oven for 30–40 minutes or until potatoes are thoroughly heated and dressing is bubbly.
7. Sprinkle with green onions and serve.

### TIPS

- I use cheddar, mozzarella, and Parmesan cheeses tossed together.
- Don't drench the potatoes in the dressing, but be sure all the potatoes have some dressing. Leftover dressing can be used on salads.
- All of the ingredients can be prepared the day before and then assembled just before you place them in the oven.
- This recipe can easily be doubled to serve 10.
- To make this recipe gluten free, use gluten-free mayonnaise. ⒼⒻ

*—Bev*

# CREAMY CHEESECAKE

## YIELDS 12–16 SLICES

### CRUST

- 2 cups / 500 ml graham cracker crumbs, finely ground
- ½ teaspoon / 2 ml ground cinnamon
- ¼ cup / 60 ml walnuts, finely chopped
- ½ cup / 125 ml butter, melted

1. In a mixing bowl, combine crust ingredients together with a fork until evenly moistened.
2. Lightly coat the bottom and sides of a 10-inch / 25-cm springform pan with cooking spray.
3. Firmly press the mixture over the bottom of the pan and ½ inch / 1.5 cm up the sides. Using your fingers or the bottom of a glass, smooth out the crust.
4. Refrigerate the crust while preparing the filling.
5. Preheat oven to 350° F / 175° C.

### FILLING

- 2 8-ounce / 250-g blocks cream cheese, room temperature
- 1 cup / 250 ml sugar
- ¼ teaspoon / 1 ml salt
- 3 eggs
- 2 teaspoons / 10 ml vanilla extract
- ½ teaspoon / 2 ml almond extract
- 3 cups / 750 ml sour cream

1. In the large bowl of a mixer, beat the cream cheese on low speed for 1 minute, just until smooth and free of any lumps.
2. Gradually add the sugar and salt and beat until creamy, 1–2 minutes. Scrape down the sides of the bowl and beaters during the process.
3. Add the eggs, 1 at a time, and continue to beat until combined.
4. Stir in vanilla and almond extracts. Blend in the sour cream.
5. The batter should be well mixed but not overbeaten.
6. Pour filling into the crust-lined springform pan and smooth with a spatula.

# WATER-BATH BAKING METHOD

Using this method gives you a better chance of a crack-free cheesecake than the traditional method.

1. Set the springform pan on a large piece of aluminum foil and fold up the sides. This will prevent water from seeping into the pan.
2. Carefully set the cake pan in a larger roasting pan. Pour boiling water into the roasting pan until the water is about halfway up the side of the springform pan.
3. Bake in a preheated 350° F / 175° C oven for 45–50 minutes.
4. The cheesecake should still jiggle when you pull it out of the oven; it will firm up after chilling. Be careful not to overbake! Do not insert toothpick or anything in cake's center—this will cause a crack.
5. Loosen the cheesecake from the sides of the pan by running a thin metal spatula around the edge of the cheesecake. Let cake cool in the pan for 30 minutes. Chill in refrigerator, loosely covered, for at least 4 hours to set up.
6. Remove from springform pan and transfer to cake plate. Cut and serve.

This is the go-to cheesecake recipe at our house and for our friends. It has graced the table at many special occasions over the years. The hint of almond flavor and nutty crust are a nice surprise.

**TIP**

- Be sure not to overbeat the filling mixture. Overbeating incorporates too much air and will cause the cake to puff up when baking and then fall and crack when cooling.

*—Ellen*

# RASPBERRY-LEMON LAYERED TORTE

## SERVES 16

## CAKE

- 1½ cup / 375 ml sugar
- ½ cup / 125 ml butter, softened
- 4 large eggs
- 2 tablespoons / 30 ml lemon zest
- 2 tablespoons / 30 ml fresh lemon juice
- 2 cups / 500 ml flour
- 1½ teaspoon / 7 ml baking powder
- ½ teaspoon / 2 ml baking soda
- ½ teaspoon / 2 ml salt
- 1 cup / 250 ml buttermilk

1. Preheat oven to 350° F / 175°C. Line 8 9-inch / 22-cm round foil pans with parchment paper and spray with cooking spray.
2. In a large mixing bowl, beat sugar and butter until fluffy.
3. Beat in eggs 1 at a time, and then stir in lemon zest and juice.
4. In a separate bowl combine flour, baking powder, baking soda, and salt.
5. Alternately beat flour mixture and buttermilk into the egg mixture.
6. Divide batter equally into prepared pans. Spread with spatula to cover bottom.
7. Bake for 10 minutes or until beginning to brown around the edges. (Bake 3 cake layers at a time or bake them all at once in a convection oven.)
8. Cool in pans on a wire rack. Remove from pans, leaving parchment between layers if not using right away. The layers can be stacked, wrapped, and frozen at this stage.

## RASPBERRY CURD FILLING

- 2 cups / 500 ml raspberries, fresh or frozen and thawed
- ¾ cup / 175 ml sugar
- 1½ tablespoon / 22 ml fresh lemon juice
- 2 large eggs
- 2 tablespoons / 30 ml butter
- ⅛ teaspoon / 0.5 ml salt
- 3 cups / 750 ml whipping cream, chilled
- ½ cup / 125 ml sugar
- 1 tablespoon / 15 ml instant vanilla pudding powder
- Extra raspberries to decorate cake

1. Purée raspberries in a blender. Then force through a strainer to remove the seeds.
2. In a medium saucepan, combine strained raspberry purée, sugar, eggs, lemon juice, butter, and salt.
3. Cook slowly over low heat, stirring constantly until thickened and smooth (about 10 minutes).
4. Remove from heat and put through the strainer once more to ensure a completely smooth consistency.
5. Refrigerate until cold, at least 2 hours or overnight.
6. Whip cream and ½ cup / 125 ml sugar until frothy.
7. Add instant pudding powder. Continue to beat until stiff.
8. Fold 1½ cup / 375 ml whipped cream into raspberry curd.
9. Reserve remaining whipped cream to frost and decorate the cake.

# ASSEMBLING THE CAKE

1. Place the first cake layer on a serving plate.
2. Top with a scoop of raspberry filling (about ⅓ cup / 75 ml) and spread evenly.
3. Carefully set the next cake layer on top and add another layer of raspberry filling.
4. Repeat until all cake layers are used, ending with cake.
5. Spread whipped cream over top and sides of cake. Place remaining whipped cream in a pastry bag fitted with a star tip to decorate cake, if desired.
6. Arrange fresh berries on top of cake.
7. Chill until cold, about 2 hours.

## TIP

- If you want a cake with the same flavor but a little less effort, bake the cake in 2 9-inch / 22-cm layer pans at 350° F / 175° C for 30 minutes. Split each layer horizontally, and assemble in the same way but with a more generous amount of raspberry filling between each layer.

This cake has served as a summertime birthday cake in our family on many occasions, featuring raspberries picked fresh from the garden and usually having only four layers. When a dear friend had a milestone birthday not so long ago, I decided to try making the multi-layered version. It went over well, and I have made it for special occasions several times since then. Frozen raspberries can be used for the curd filling, but a few fresh raspberries add that special touch to the decorated cake.

*—Judy*

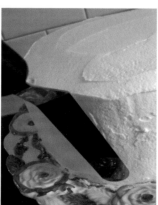

# BREAD FOR THE JOURNEY
## STONES *of* REMEMBRANCE

*Then Samuel took a stone and set it up between Mizpah and Shen and called its name Ebenezer; for he said, "Till now the LORD has helped us."*

—1 SAMUEL 7:12 (ESV)

The milestones of life are meant to be marked and celebrated. We gather friends and family together and cement a particular moment with an event or a celebration that becomes a "stone of remembrance." We celebrate the birth of each child in our family and then mark every year by throwing a party. Each step along the way is a milestone to be marked: baptism, graduation, engagement, marriage, and anniversaries. And when the journey comes to an end, despite our tears, we can celebrate the lives of our dear ones. Life is meant to be celebrated, and in doing that, we are honoring the Giver of Life.

*We can go forward, knowing that God will complete what he has begun in us.*

We have celebrated several milestone occasions in our family recently. My husband and I had our fortieth wedding anniversary not long ago, and we marked that milestone by taking our family on a vacation. I turned sixty. That called for many celebrations, big and small. My father had his ninetieth birthday recently. The family came together and we celebrated this man who is our dad, granddad, and great-grandad.

Each milestone is a reason to celebrate! Though our journey in life is mostly about pressing forward, milestone occasions are the perfect time to stop and reflect. Like Samuel did so long ago, we can erect a marker on that spot and acknowledge that it is God who has helped us to reach it. And we can go forward, knowing that God will complete what he has begun in us. The apostle Paul wrote, "And I am sure of this, that he who began a good work in you will bring it to completion at the day of Jesus Christ" (Philippians 1:6 ESV). He who has been faithful to every milestone marker along the way will be faithful to the end.

*—Judy*

Till now the Lord has helped us. I Sam. 7:12

# CELEBRATING *Holidays*

There are certain dishes that we associate with the holiday table, be it Thanksgiving, Christmas, or Easter. Here are a few that have taken on meaning for us over the years.

## CELEBRATE WITH

*O come, let us adore him, Christ the Lord.*
—JOHN F. WADE, "O COME, ALL YE FAITHFUL"

# ELLEN REFLECTS *on* HOLIDAYS

What stands out to me the most about holidays when I was growing up is the music, especially songs associated with Christmas and Easter. Russian was the first language used in the churches we attended. By the time I was in high school, our Russian Baptist church was bilingual. Our Christmas and Easter services rang out with carols and hymns sung in Russian and English. Our youth choir would practice for weeks before each of these holidays in order to prepare a cantata for the Sunday evening service. Our cantatas were in English.

On Christmas Eve, the youth would always go caroling. We would start at the apartment building a couple doors down from the church, where my maternal grandmother (*Babushka*) lived, along with a few other widows from our congregation. We would then travel around the Los Angeles area to carol at senior homes where church members were being cared for. We'd sing in English and Russian at these homes. Arriving home late on Christmas Eve, my sisters and I would

*When God calls me home, I hope to go out singing.*

find our mom still sitting at the sewing machine, finishing our new Christmas dresses.

Christmas morning and Easter morning we would have an early breakfast at our maternal *Babushka*'s apartment and then walk to our church. On Easter, the greeting of "*Hristos voskrese!*" ("Christ is risen!") would be on everyone's lips, along with the response "*Voistinu voskress!*" ("He is risen indeed!"). I miss these days at my church. It was guaranteed that we'd sing "Low in the Grave He Lay" on Easter morning, with no one holding back. To this day I expect to be able to sing that hymn on Easter.

Music played a big part in my history, even apart from holidays. My husband, Greg, and I met in a Christian singing group, and we fell in love while practicing and singing in concerts in the United States and in Great Britain. Our group sang songs about the Lord, and we gave our testimonies between songs. During this time, Greg and I also worked with our Russian youth choir in Los Angeles

to record hymns in Russian to broadcast into the Soviet Union. Greg is not Russian, but he took Russian in a college course and was able to read and sing the words of the songs we practiced.

God has used music to speak to me in a personal way and to prompt me in my growth with him. When I wake up in the middle of the night, a hymn or worship song is often going through my mind. I like waking up that way. I loved singing songs about Jesus to our children when they were young. Music adds a special joy in my life, and I'm happy to sing all year long. To this day, whenever my extended family gets together, we end up singing a few songs together in Russian and English. As a popular worship song states, I want to start my day with a song of worship and I want to still "be singing when the evening comes." When God calls me home, I hope to go out singing! "I will sing to the LORD as long as I live; I will sing praise to my God while I have being. May my meditation be pleasing to him, for I rejoice in the LORD" (Psalm 104:33-34, ESV). ❧

*—Ellen*

# PEAR AND GOAT CHEESE SALAD *with* MAPLE BALSAMIC VINAIGRETTE

**YIELDS 10 STARTER SALADS**

## SALAD

- Your choice of greens
- Pear slices (about ¼ pear for each serving)
- Celery, chopped
- Red onion, thinly sliced
- Goat cheese or feta cheese, crumbled
- Candied pecans or almonds (below)
- Maple balsamic vinaigrette (below)
- Dried cranberries or fresh raspberries

1. Arrange salad ingredients on individual serving plates.

## MAPLE BALSAMIC VINAIGRETTE
**YIELDS 1½ CUP DRESSING**

- 2 tablespoons / 30 ml balsamic vinegar
- 1 tablespoon / 15 ml red wine vinegar
- 1 tablespoon / 15 ml fresh lemon juice
- ¼ cup / 60 ml olive oil or vegetable oil
- ¼ cup / 60 ml pure maple syrup
- 1 teaspoon / 5 ml Dijon mustard
- 1 tablespoon / 15 ml fresh parsley, minced
- Freshly cracked pepper to taste

1. Combine ingredients and whisk together. Make this dressing early in the day or the day before to let the flavors blend.

## CANDIED PECANS

- ¼ cup / 60 ml sugar
- ¼–½ teaspoon / 1–2 ml cayenne pepper
- 1 cup / 250 ml pecan halves or sliced almonds

1. In a nonstick pan over medium heat, combine the sugar and the cayenne pepper.
2. Add the nuts.
3. Stir until sugar is dissolved; this may take some time. Stir often to prevent the sugar from burning.
4. Remove nuts to a parchment-lined baking sheet to cool. Cool completely, then break apart and sprinkle over salads.

*TIP*

- To make this recipe gluten free, choose a brand of Dijon mustard that is gluten free. ⒢

*—Charlotte*

At Christmas, we still have the privilege of having large extended gatherings of both my father's and mother's sides of the family. Salads of all kinds are always in abundance, served in large bowls. However, if I am making this salad for a smaller meal or gathering, I like to use this as a starter salad, served individually on small plates.

# ROASTED BUTTERNUT SQUASH SOUP

## SERVES 8

- 1 large butternut squash
- 2 carrots
- 3 tablespoons / 45 ml butter
- 1 medium yellow onion, finely chopped

- 1 leek, chopped (white portion only)
- 1 Granny Smith apple
- 1 small pear
- 8 cups / 2 L chicken stock

- ¼ teaspoon / 1 ml ground nutmeg
- 1 teaspoon / 5 ml brown sugar
- 1 small bay leaf
- Brie cheese or sour cream for garnish (optional)

1. Preheat oven to 350° F / 180° C.
2. Cut butternut squash in half lengthwise. Scoop out seeds and discard.
3. Place squash, flesh-side down, on a baking pan with a rim. Pour ½ cup / 125 ml water into pan around squash.
4. Roast squash for 15 minutes.
5. Peel carrots and cut into large chunks. Add to the pan of squash and continue to roast squash, along with the carrots, for another 30 minutes.
6. In a frying pan, melt butter. Add onion and leek, and sauté until onion becomes translucent.
7. Peel and grate apple and pear and add to the onion-leek mixture. Sauté another 3–4 minutes.
8. Pour chicken stock into a large pot and place over medium heat until stock comes to a slow boil.
9. While stock is heating, remove roasted squash and carrots from oven. Scoop out roasted squash flesh and add squash and carrot chunks to the chicken stock.
10. Add the mixture of onion, leek, apple, and pear to soup pot.
11. Stir in nutmeg, brown sugar, and bay leaf.
12. Simmer uncovered for 1 hour. Using a potato masher, stir and mash vegetables every 15 minutes. Remove from heat and discard bay leaf.
13. Allow soup to cool slightly, and then purée soup in small batches in blender.
14. Return puréed soup to pot and reheat soup over low heat until steaming hot. Serve with a small slice of Brie cheese or a dollop of sour cream.

*TIP*
- To make this recipe gluten free, use gluten-free chicken stock. ⒼⒻ

*—Kathy*

Autumn's bounty is roasted and then simmered together, making a delicious soup starter for your next holiday dinner party. Add some whimsy to your table by serving this steaming hot soup in teacups. Billowy high savory popovers fresh from the oven are a perfect choice to serve with this soup.

245

# SAVORY POPOVERS

## YIELDS 6 LARGE POPOVERS

- 1½ cup / 375 ml milk
- ¼ cup / 60 ml water
- 3 large eggs, room temperature
- 2 cups / 500 ml flour
- ¾ teaspoon / 3 ml salt
- ¾ teaspoon / 3 ml baking powder
- ½ cup / 125 ml Parmesan cheese
- ½ tablespoon / 7 ml dried parsley
- ½ tablespoon / 7 ml dried thyme
- 2 tablespoons / 30 ml butter

1. In a small saucepan, heat milk and water until just warm.
2. Add room-temperature eggs to large bowl of mixer and beat for 2 minutes.
3. Continue to beat eggs while slowly pouring warm milk-water mixture into eggs. Beat another 3 minutes.
4. Into a small bowl sift flour, salt, and baking powder.
5. Slowly add flour mixture to egg-milk mixture. Beat well for 2–3 more minutes until all ingredients are well incorporated and batter is smooth.
6. Allow to sit at room temperature for 1 hour.
7. Into a small bowl, grate fresh Parmesan cheese using the fine side of a grater.
8. Stir together herbs and crush slightly in the palm of your hand. Stir into cheese.
9. Generously grease a popover pan with real butter, making sure you grease the insides and the top rim of each cup.
10. Take the batter that has been sitting for 1 hour and beat it for 2 minutes in order to add air. Divide batter equally between the 6 cups of the pan.
11. Sprinkle the tops with the cheese and herb mixture.
12. Divide the butter into small pieces and place a piece on the top of each filled cup.
13. Bake in oven preheated to 450° F / 230° C for 15 minutes. Do not open the oven door during any of the baking time.
14. Turn oven temperature down to 375° F / 190° C and continue to bake for 30 minutes.
15. Remove popovers from oven. Using a sharp knife, make a small slit in the top of each popover. This will release the steam, helping popovers not to become soggy in the middle.
16. Serve while still warm. Alternatively, popovers can be frozen, thawed, and reheated in a 350° F / 175° C oven until warmed through and crispy on the outside.

*—Kathy*

There are three secrets to achieving beautifully high, airy popovers. The first is allowing the batter to rest for one full hour to ensure it is at room temperature. The second is using a popover pan; you can use a regular muffin tin, but you won't get the same inflation. Third, and most important, is not opening the oven door while they are baking! Turn on your oven light and watch them rise through the window, but do not open the door for a peek.

Savory popovers are halfway between a bun and a Yorkshire pudding. Serve these alongside roasted butternut squash soup.

# CROWN ROAST OF PORK

**SERVES 14**

## CROWN ROAST

> Crown roast of pork

> Salt and pepper

Traditionally, a crown roast is made from the rib section and formed into a circle or crown. The tips of the rib bones are "frenched," or stripped of meat, and the center is left hollow so that it can be filled with stuffing. It is recommended that there be 1 rib (or chop) per person. To serve, a cut is made between each bone, and each guest receives a chop with rib attached.

My local butcher introduced me to a new way of preparing the crown roast. I told him I was serving 14 people. He took a rib section and cut the baby back ribs away from the meat, leaving a long boneless roast (photo A). This he divided into 3 roasts, each about 6 inches long. He cut a slit into the center of each roast and filled it with the stuffing I had brought (photo B).

He then set the roasts on end and tied them together tightly (photo C). He stripped the meat away from the top 2 inches of each rib (photo D) and then tied the ribs around the 3 roasts, forming a crown (photo E). I added more stuffing to the center of the roast, covering it loosely with foil partway through the roasting time to keep it from over browning.

## CRANBERRY APPLE STUFFING

> 16 cups / 3.8 L cups bread, cubed

> 1 cup / 250 ml butter, divided

> 1 large onion, diced

> 6 celery ribs, diced

> 2 large unpeeled apples, cored and diced

> ½ –¾ cup / 125–175 ml apple juice, divided

> 1½ tablespoon / 22 ml poultry seasoning

> ½ teaspoon / 2 ml salt, or to taste

> Pepper, to taste

> 2 cups / 500 ml dried cranberries

> Zest of 1 orange

> ¼ cup / 60 ml brandy (optional)

1. Cut bread into cubes 2 days before preparing this roast; let the cubes sit, loosely covered, to dry.
2. On the day that you serve the roast, place bread cubes in a large bowl.
3. Melt ¾ cup / 175 ml butter in a large frying pan.
4. Add onion and celery. Sauté over medium to low heat until soft but not brown, about 10 minutes.
5. Pour over bread in bowl and toss.
6. Melt remaining ¼ cup / 60 ml butter in pan and sauté apples until they start to soften slightly. Add ¼ cup / 60 ml apple juice and cook for 1 minute longer.
7. Add to mixture in bowl.
8. Add remaining ingredients and toss until well mixed, adding brandy or apple juice to moisten if necessary. Stuffing should be slightly moist but not wet. Set aside.

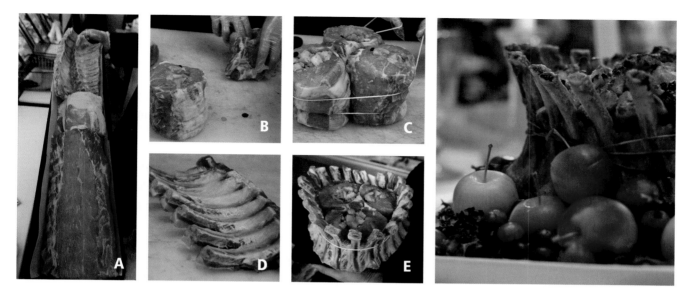

# ROASTING INSTRUCTIONS

1. Preheat oven to 425° F / 220° C.
2. Salt roast on all sides.
3. If using a traditional crown roast, sear un-stuffed roast in preheated oven for about 10 minutes. If following the instructions above, sear assembled crown roast for 10 minutes.
4. Turn oven down to 325° F / 160° C.
5. For traditional crown roast, fill center of roast with stuffing. For the method described above, top the center of the roast with stuffing.
6. Wrap remaining stuffing in 2 layers of foil, forming a package. Leave a small vent at the top. Place this extra stuffing in oven about 1 hour before roast is done.
7. Place roast in oven and roast until meat thermometer reads 160° F / 70° C when inserted in several places in the roast. About halfway through the cooking, cover ribs and stuffing loosely with foil to prevent overbrowning.
8. Remove roast from oven, tent loosely with foil, and let rest for 20 minutes before carving.
9. To serve traditional crown roast, cut string around roast and cut between the ribs, serving one chop to each guest. To serve this alternate roast, as shown, cut string around roast to release ribs. Cut ribs into 2-rib serving pieces. Take one of the boneless roasts in the center and turn it on its side to cut into slices, revealing the "eye" of stuffing.

## TIPS

- Order a crown roast several days ahead from your local butcher.
- How many people this dish serves depends upon the size of the crown pork roast. The roast pictured was about 12 pounds and served 14 people with some left over.
- Plan on approximately 15 minutes cooking time per pound / 500 g of roast.

Although a crown roast looks impressive and complicated, it is one of the easiest roasts to cook. It is beautiful to serve and the meat is tender and delicious.

*—Bev*

# SPECIAL CHICKEN

## SERVES 8

- 3 pounds / 1.25–1.5 kg boneless skinless chicken breasts
- 6 cups / 1.5 L vegetables such as broccoli, cauliflower, carrots, and Brussels sprouts, cut into bite-size pieces
- Aromat seasoning (optional)
- ¾ cup / 175 ml mayonnaise
- 2 10-ounce / 284-ml cans low-fat cream of chicken soup
- ¼ –½ teaspoon / 1–2 ml curry powder
- 2 cups / 500 ml cheese (cheddar/ mozzarella mix), grated
- ¾ cup / 175 ml dried bread crumbs

1. Preheat oven to 375° F / 190° C.
2. Cut chicken breasts into serving-size pieces, slicing through at an angle or horizontally so that they are not more than ¾-inch / 2-cm thick. This amount should make about 10–12 pieces.
3. Grease a 9 x 13-inch / 22 x 33-cm glass or stoneware baking dish with butter.
4. Cover bottom with vegetables that have been cut into small pieces. Season lightly.
5. In a small bowl, mix soup with mayonnaise and curry. Use half to spread over the vegetables and set the rest aside.
6. Lay out chicken pieces over the vegetables, overlapping thinner sides, to cover the whole pan evenly.
7. Spread remaining soup-mayonnaise mix over the chicken.
8. Top with shredded cheese and sprinkle with bread crumbs. Can be refrigerated for several hours at this time.
9. Bake for 1 hour until golden and bubbly around the edges.

*TIP*

- Aromat is a seasoning mix made by Knorr and available in many delis. If you can't find it in a store near you, you can order it online.

—*Anneliese*

This simple recipe takes me back many years to a meal our friends Harv and Bonnie prepared for us. Since then, it has become one of our family favorites, served with cranberry jelly and stuffing on the side. Sometimes it is a nice alternative when we've already had turkey over the holidays; other times it makes for a special birthday meal. Served with basmati rice or mashed potatoes and a salad, this dish comes with its own vegetables and gravy.

251

# PRIME RIB *with* YORKSHIRE PUDDING

## YIELDS 8–10 SLICES

- 1 6-pound / 3-kg bone-in prime rib roast
- 3 large garlic cloves, crushed
- Leaves from 2 fresh rosemary sprigs
- Leaves from 4 fresh thyme sprigs
- ¼ cup / 60 ml kosher salt
- ⅛ cup / 30 ml pepper
- ⅓ cup / 75 ml olive oil

1. Preheat oven to 350° F / 175° C approximately 3 hours before you intend to eat.
2. Place beef, bone-side down, in a roasting pan slightly larger than the roast.
3. Make a paste with the next 6 ingredients.
4. Rub paste onto the roast generously, from the top down the sides, but very sparingly on the exposed ends of the roast.
5. Put roast in the oven, uncovered, and cook until internal temperature reaches 125° F / 50° C (rare).
6. Remove meat to a cutting board and allow to rest for 20 minutes before slicing.

## YORKSHIRE PUDDING
### YIELDS 10–12 WEDGES

- 1½ cup / 375 ml flour
- ¾ cup / 175 ml whole milk
- ¾ cup / 175 ml water
- 3 large eggs
- ¾ teaspoon / 3 ml salt
- 2 tablespoons / 30 ml butter

## STEP ONE

1. Blend all ingredients except the butter in a blender until smooth, stopping occasionally to scrape down sides, about 1 minute.
2. Cover and refrigerate at least 1 hour and up to 3 hours.

## STEP TWO

1. An hour before the meal, preheat second oven to 400° F / 205° C.
2. Take batter out of refrigerator.
3. Heat butter in a 12 inch / 30 cm ovenproof pan over high heat until the butter browns.
4. Whisk the batter and pour into pan all at once.
5. Put the pan in the preheated oven.
6. Immediately reduce heat to 375° F / 190° C and bake until top is golden brown and edges have puffed, approximately 25–40 minutes.
7. Cut into wedges and serve while hot.

**TIPS**

- It's important that the Yorkshire pudding batter has time to rest before you bake it, so plan ahead. If you don't have a second oven, as soon as you take your roast out of the oven, increase the temperature and follow the same steps for the Yorkshire pudding.
- A beef *au jus* or beef gravy would complement this meal very nicely.

*—Ellen*

This meal has become our traditional Christmas Eve dinner. We look forward to it every year. Our middle son makes sure to remind me to make his favorite creamed corn recipe to serve along with it. After our meal, we enjoy attending a candle-light Christmas Eve service.

We have been enjoying this yam dish for many years. With just a touch of sweetness and a light texture, the puffs go perfectly with many different holiday entrées. These pretty little puffs are perfect to make ahead for family gatherings since you prepare them early and then pull them out of the freezer to bake. Place the hot ramekins on a serving tray with pretty little pot holders and remind the guests they are piping hot from the oven.

# MAPLE YAM SOUFFLÉ PUFFS

## YIELDS 6 SMALL SOUFFLÉS

- 1½ pound / 750 g yams (about 3 medium)
- 1 cup / 250 ml Japanese-style bread crumbs
- 1 tablespoon / 15 ml brown sugar
- 2 tablespoons / 30 ml butter, melted
- 2 tablespoons / 30 ml butter
- 3 tablespoons / 45 ml flour
- ½ cup / 125 ml milk
- ¼ cup / 60 ml cream cheese, softened
- ¼ cup / 60 ml maple syrup
- 5 eggs, separated
- 1 teaspoon / 5 ml baking powder
- 1 teaspoon / 5 ml salt
- ¼ teaspoon / 1 ml pepper

1. Wrap yams in foil and bake in a 400° F / 205° C oven for 1 hour or until tender and soft.
2. Cool yams enough to handle, and then peel and discard the skin. Mash yams with potato masher, measure 2 cups / 500 ml, and place in a large bowl.
3. Prepare crumbs for topping by combining bread crumbs, brown sugar, and melted butter. Set aside.
4. Grease 6 7-ounce / 225-ml ramekins. To keep the crumbs from falling off and to encourage soufflé puffs to rise up, wrap parchment paper around each ramekin and tie on with kitchen string.
5. In a medium saucepan, melt 2 tablespoons/ 30 ml butter, add flour, and stir over medium heat until it thickens. Add milk a little bit at a time to make a smooth, thickened sauce. Add to mashed yams.
6. Add cream cheese, maple syrup, egg yolks, baking powder, salt, and pepper. Beat with hand mixer until smooth.
7. Beat the egg whites with a mixer until stiff peaks form. Do not overbeat, as this will result in curdled-looking egg whites and prevent your soufflé from rising as it should.
8. Gently fold the egg whites into the yam mixture, a small amount at a time.
9. Spoon gently into individual ramekins, filling to the top. Sprinkle with crumbs.
10. Freeze on a baking sheet or bake immediately. Once frozen, store in freezer bags or an airtight container.
11. Place on a baking sheet and bake at 350° F / 175° C for 30 minutes (if thawed) or 45 minutes (if frozen) until puffed and golden brown.

*TIP*

- This can be made in a greased, shallow casserole dish instead of individual ramekins. Freeze and bake as instructed, allowing additional time to bake.

*—Lovella*

This vegetable casserole has been a favorite side dish at family turkey dinners over the years. It is easy to prepare the day ahead so that you can simply bake it right before the guests arrive.

# VEGETABLE MEDLEY

## SERVES 8

- 1 small head cauliflower, broken into florets
- 1 bunch broccoli, cut into florets
- 3–4 cups / 750–1000 ml baby carrots
- ¼ cup / 60 ml onions, chopped
- ¼ cup / 60 ml butter

- ¼ cup / 60 ml flour
- 1 teaspoon / 5 ml salt
- ⅛ teaspoon / 0.5 ml pepper
- ½ teaspoon / 2 ml dry mustard
- 2 cups / 500 ml milk
- 1 cup / 250 ml cheddar cheese, shredded

## TOPPING

- 2 cups / 500 ml buttery crackers, crushed
- ¼ cup / 60 ml butter, melted
- ¼ cup / 60 ml Parmesan cheese

1. Preheat oven to 350° F / 175° C.
2. Steam vegetables until tender crisp (cauliflower for about 5 minutes, broccoli for about 4 minutes, and carrots for about 7 minutes). Rinse with cold water to cool.
3. Spread vegetables in a greased 9 x 13-inch / 22 x 33-cm casserole dish.
4. In a saucepan over medium heat, cook onions in butter until tender.
5. Stir in flour and seasonings.
6. Add milk slowly, stirring with a wire whisk, and cook over medium heat until thickened.
7. Add shredded cheese and stir until melted.
8. Pour sauce over vegetables and stir gently. The casserole can be covered at this stage and refrigerated until later.
9. To make topping, mix crackers, butter, and Parmesan cheese until well combined. When ready to bake casserole, sprinkle with topping.
10. Bake until heated through and bubbly (about 30 minutes). If casserole has been refrigerated, it will need to cook longer.

*TIP*

- Do not overbake this casserole or vegetables will be mushy.

*—Judy*

256

# CHRISTMAS CAKE

## YIELDS 3 LOAVES

- ¾ cup / 180 ml butter, room temperature
- 1 cup / 200 g sugar
- 5 eggs
- ¼ cup / 60 ml pineapple juice
- 1 teaspoon / 5 ml vanilla extract
- 2 cups / 450 g candied mixed fruit, diced
- 1 cup / 225 g candied citrus peel, diced
- 1 cup / 225 g sweetened dried cranberries
- 1 cup / 225 g crushed pineapple, drained
- ½ cup / 50 g almonds, blanched
- ½ cup / 80 g maraschino cherries, quartered
- ¾ cup / 95 g millet flour
- ½ cup / 75 g brown rice flour
- ⅓ cup / 50 g white bean flour
- ⅓ cup / 40 g arrowroot powder/starch/flour
- 2 teaspoons / 20 g baking powder
- 1 teaspoon / 6 g xanthan gum
- Candied pineapple rings for decorating

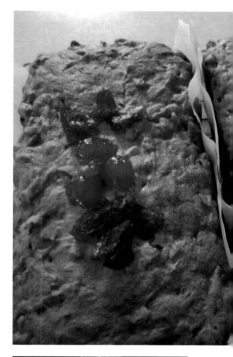

1. Preheat oven to 300° F / 150° C.
2. Cream butter and sugar until light and fluffy.
3. Add eggs one at a time and beat until smooth and thick.
4. Add pineapple juice and vanilla.
5. Mix together the fruits, citrus peel, and nuts.
6. Mix together the dry ingredients, making sure the flours are well blended.
7. Stir ½ cup / 50 g of the flour mixture into the fruit mixture.
8. Beat remaining flour into the egg batter.
9. Mix fruit mixture into the flour-egg batter and stir until well blended.
10. Line 3 medium (8½ x 4½-inch / 21½ x 11-cm) loaf pans with parchment paper.
11. Spoon batter evenly divided into the three pans. Since the loaves will not rise very much, you may fill the loaf pans up to ¾ full.
12. Bake for 2 hours. After 1 hour of baking, carefully place candied pineapple pieces on the top of each loaf, as desired, for decoration.
13. Remove from pans and cool. When completely cooled, package and freeze until needed.

I love Christmas cake and can't tell that this one is gluten free! This cake freezes and keeps well.

—*Julie*

# CHRISTMAS FRUIT *and* NUT WREATH

**SERVES 10–12**

Although I have not learned to listen to his advice, my husband has informed me year after year that the only Christmas baking I need to do is this sweet bread—many times over. A few months after Christmas, we always still have cookies in the freezer but no more "wreath," as he calls it. For my immediate family it would not quite be Christmas without it, decorated for the season. I usually double the recipe, mixing it in a stand mixer with a dough hook, and divide by three to make smaller rings. Some years I have multiplied this procedure a number of times so that we could deliver edible wreaths to teachers, neighbors, and family.

I altered the filling slightly for this book, a tweak inspired by my sister-in-law, who does not care for the traditional cherry candied fruit. Try the recipe with either candied citrus peel or candied mixed fruit, and with either raisins or dried cranberries. But don't miss out on the pure almond flavoring in the icing at the end!

## DOUGH

- ½ cup / 125 ml butter
- ½ cup / 125 ml milk
- ½ cup / 125 ml cold water
- 3–3½ cups / 750–875 ml flour, divided
- ¼ cup / 60 ml sugar
- 1½ tablespoon / 22 ml instant yeast
- 1 teaspoon / 5 ml salt
- 1 egg

## FILLING

- 2 tablespoons / 30 ml butter, melted
- ½ cup / 125 ml brown sugar, packed
- ⅓ cup / 75 ml sliced almonds
- ⅓ cup / 75 ml dried cranberries
- ⅓ cup / 75 ml dried apricots, finely chopped
- ¼ cup / 60 ml diced candied citrus peel
- 1 tablespoon / 15 ml orange rind
- ½ teaspoon / 2 ml cinnamon

## FROSTING DRIZZLE AND TOPPING

- 1 cup / 250 ml icing sugar
- 1½–2 tablespoons / 22–30 ml milk
- ½ teaspoon / 2 ml pure almond extract
- Sliced almonds, toasted

1. Prepare a pizza pan by greasing or lining with parchment paper.
2. Melt butter, then add milk and continue to heat.
3. Meanwhile, in a mixing bowl, stir together 1½ cup / 375 ml flour, sugar, yeast, and salt.
4. Add cold water to cool down butter and milk to just very warm—make sure it's not hot—and stir into dry ingredients.
5. Beat in egg and stir in the remaining flour, ½ cup / 125 ml at a time and not more than 2 cups / 500 ml total. Knead in the final amount of flour, using just enough to make a soft, manageable dough that can be shaped into a ball.
6. Cover loosely with plastic wrap or wax paper and then a tea towel. Let rise until doubled, about 30 minutes.
7. On a floured surface, roll out dough to about 16 x 9 inches / 40 x 22 cm.

8. Brush the dough with melted butter. Combine the rest of the filling ingredients and then spread the filling on the dough.
9. Starting with the long side, roll up jelly-roll fashion. Place seam-side down onto prepared pizza pan, shaping the roll into a donut. Tuck 1 end inside the other.
10. Using a serrated knife, cut about ⅔ of the way into the ring at 1-inch / 2.5-cm intervals.
11. Turn each slice slightly outward on its side.
12. Cover and let rise about 30–45 minutes.
13. Bake in oven preheated to 350° F / 175° C for 20 minutes or until golden.
14. Slide wreath off pan and onto cooling rack.
15. Mix frosting ingredients, using just enough milk to make a thin icing. After the wreath has cooled, drizzle with icing and sprinkle with toasted, sliced almonds.

*—Anneliese*

# COCONUT CREAM TART *or* PIE

## COCONUT CREAM FILLING
**YIELDS FILLING FOR 1 11-INCH / 28-CM TART
OR 1 DEEP-DISH 9-INCH / 22-CM PIE**

- ⅔ cup / 150 ml sugar
- 1⅔ cup / 400 ml unsweetened light coconut milk
- ¼ cup / 60 ml cornstarch
- 1 cup / 250 ml milk
- ⅓ cup / 75 ml cream
- 6 egg yolks
- ½ teaspoon / 2 ml salt
- 2 teaspoons / 10 ml vanilla extract
- 1 cup / 250 ml flaked sweetened coconut, divided
- 2 tablespoons / 30 ml butter
- Whipped cream

1. In an 8-cup / 2-L measuring cup or other large glass microwave-safe bowl, combine the sugar and the coconut milk. Alternatively, place sugar and coconut milk in a medium saucepan.
2. In a small bowl, whisk the cornstarch with the milk and cream until no lumps remain. Add to the coconut milk-sugar mixture.
3. Place in microwave and heat for 2 minutes. Remove, stir, and heat again for 2 minutes, repeating the process until the mixture is bubbly. Or stir over medium heat until it comes to a light boil.
4. Put egg yolks into a small bowl and add several tablespoons of the hot milk mixture to temper the eggs. Whisk and continue to add a small amount of hot milk until you have added about half the hot milk. Pour egg yolk-milk mixture back into hot milk.
5. Heat again in the microwave until thickened and bubbly. Alternatively, return to heat and continue to stir until thickened and beginning to bubble.
6. Add vanilla, ½ cup / 125 ml coconut, and butter, and stir to combine.
7. Pour the hot filling into a baked tart shell or pie shell (see recipes following) and place plastic wrap on surface of filling.
8. Toast remaining coconut for garnish in a frying pan over medium heat, stirring until lightly browned.
9. Refrigerate until chilled through. Garnish with whipped cream "trees," if desired, and toasted coconut.

*TIPS*

- The pie or tart is delicious with or without coconut in the filling. If you prefer a smooth cream pie, omit the coconut from the filling and top with ½ cup / 125 ml toasted coconut.
- This filling can be used for tarts, pies, and cake fillings.
- To make whipped cream "trees," fill a pastry bag fitted with a large star tip. Pipe out whipped cream, swirling around to make a tree shape. To keep the whipped cream trees firm, add whipped cream stabilizer while you are whipping. Sprinkle with edible sparkle glitter.

# ALMOND CRUMB BASE FOR TART
## YIELDS 1 11-INCH / 28-CM TART SHELL

- 1 cup / 250 ml flour
- 1 cup / 250 ml sliced almonds
- 2 tablespoons / 30 ml sugar
- ½ cup / 125 ml flaked sweetened coconut
- 2 egg yolks
- 3 tablespoons / 45 ml cream
- 3 tablespoons / 45 ml butter, softened

1. Preheat oven to 350° F / 175° C.
2. Combine flour, almonds, and sugar in a food processor, and pulse until it resembles a fine meal.
3. Add coconut and pulse again to combine ingredients.
4. Add egg yolks, cream, and butter, and pulse to combine. Pinch together crumbs and, if needed, add another tablespoon of cream to the food processor. Pulse again to make a crumb that sticks together.
5. Turn into an 11-inch / 28-cm tart pan with a removable bottom. Using your fingers, press mixture to the sides and back firmly.
6. Bake for about 20 minutes or until lightly browned.

## PIE PASTRY
### YIELDS 2 LARGE DOUBLE-CRUST PIES
### PLUS 1 PIE SHELL, OR 5 PIE SHELLS

- 5 cups / 1.25 L flour
- 4 teaspoons / 20 ml brown sugar
- 2 teaspoons / 10 ml salt
- 1 teaspoon / 5 ml baking powder
- 1 pound / 454 g lard, cubed
- 1 egg
- 1 tablespoon / 15 ml white vinegar
- Cold water

I have often seen pie crust on my friend Dorothy Friesen's counter, and her friends and family will agree with me that she makes fantastic pies. Her recipe for pastry uses slightly less flour than most recipes, which enables you to use flour for rolling out without the worry of adding too much. This pastry freezes well and bakes up flaky every time.

1. Measure flour, brown sugar, salt, and baking powder into a large, wide bowl. Stir with a fork to distribute the dry ingredients.
2. Cut in lard with a pastry blender, while turning the bowl around with your other hand.
3. Put the egg into a 1-cup / 250-ml measuring cup and whisk it slightly. Add the vinegar and fill with water to the 1-cup / 250-ml line.
4. Slowly stir the egg mixture into the flour mixture. Using 2 forks, toss the pastry as you would a salad until the flour is uniformly moistened. Depending on the moisture in the flour, you may not need all the liquid.
5. Turn out onto a floured counter, press together, and shape into a loaf shape. Then, using a sharp knife, divide into 5 equal pieces. Flatten balls into disks, wrap separately in plastic wrap, and freeze any disks that you are not using.
6. To bake pastry shells, preheat oven to 400° F / 205° C.
7. Set disk of pastry on floured surface and use a rolling pin to tap from the center out a few times. Give the pastry a quarter turn and tap again to flatten and enlarge the disk slightly before beginning to roll. Gently roll the pastry from the center out, lifting, turning, and dusting with flour, until you have a round slightly larger than your pie plate.
8. Roll pastry over your rolling pin and then unroll over the pie plate, gently easing it in. Trim excess, leaving a ½-inch / 1.5-cm rim to fold under. Crimp edges and prick pastry all over with a fork.
9. Press aluminum foil firmly onto the bottom and sides of the pastry and bake for 10 minutes. Remove foil and continue to bake until golden brown, about another 10 minutes.

*TIPS*

- This dough can be frozen in disks to use later. Thaw the pastry in the refrigerator.
- Baking time will vary based on the kind of pie plate used. Glass, dark metal, shiny metal, and foil pans all bake differently, so turn on your oven light and watch carefully.

*—Lovella*

# BERRY RIPPLE CHEESECAKE

**SERVES 16**

## CRUST

- ¾ cup / 175 ml graham cracker crumbs
- 2 tablespoons / 30 ml sugar
- ¾ cup / 175 ml almonds, finely ground
- ¼ cup / 60 ml butter, melted

1. Preheat oven to 350° F / 175° C.
2. Combine crumbs, almonds, sugar, and melted butter. Press into a 9-inch / 22-cm square or round springform pan.
3. Bake for 8 minutes or until fragrant and lightly browned. Set aside to cool.

## MERINGUE

- 1 cup plus 2 tablespoons / 280 ml sugar
- ½ cup / 125 ml water
- 4 egg whites

1. Combine sugar and water in a small saucepan and bring to boil. Once the sugar and water come to a boil, begin beating egg whites with a mixer until they form stiff peaks.
2. Boil sugar and water at medium-high heat, creating a syrup, until a candy thermometer reaches 240° F / 115° C or a thread forms when you drop some from a teaspoon. This will take about 10 minutes.
3. Turn the mixer to medium and slowly pour the syrup into the egg whites. Do your best to avoid pouring the syrup onto the beaters or the side of the bowl.
4. Continue whipping at high speed about 10 minutes or until cooled. Set aside.

## CREAM CHEESE FILLING

- 2 8-ounce / 250-g packages cream cheese, softened
- ½ cup / 125 ml sour cream
- ½ cup / 125 ml whipping cream
- 2 teaspoons / 10 ml vanilla extract
- Meringue

1. In a large mixing bowl, use a mixer to beat the cream cheese. Add sour cream, whipping cream, and vanilla, and whip until smooth.
2. Gently fold in the meringue with a spatula until no white streaks remain.

On a warm summer evening, this no-bake cheesecake is a cool, refreshing treat, especially when served semi-frozen. We live in the Fraser Valley, surrounded by berry fields. The ditch along the back of our acreage has a blackberry patch that we visit nearly every day during the last weeks of August. I freeze the berries on a baking sheet and then store them in freezer bags. If time is short during the summer to make jams and jellies, I use frozen berries to make small batches of jam during the winter. I've been whipping up this cheesecake for over two decades. During the holidays, I find it satisfying to know that I have this dessert tucked away and ready to serve.

# BERRY RIPPLE

> ½ cup / 125 ml soft blueberry or blackberry jam or jelly

1. On top of the cooled crumbs, place half of the cream cheese mixture. Top with dollops of jam and then with remaining cream cheese mixture. Draw a knife down into the filling and swirl. Cover well with plastic wrap and freeze overnight.
2. Slice the cheesecake while semi-frozen. Serve it semi-frozen or thawed with blackberry or blueberry sauce.

# BERRY SAUCE

> 6 cups / 1⅓ L blackberries
> or blueberries
> ½–¾ cup / 125–175 ml sugar

> 2 tablespoons / 30 ml cornstarch
> 1 cup / 250 ml water

1. Combine sugar and cornstarch (start with the smaller amount of sugar and add more after the sauce has cooked, if necessary). Slowly whisk in water. Pour mixture over the berries.
2. Cover and microwave on high, stirring every 5 minutes, until the filling begins to boil and becomes clear.
3. Store covered in refrigerator. Leftover sauce is perfect over shortcake, ice cream, yogurt, or waffles.

*—Lovella*

# *HIMMELS* TORTE

**SERVES 8–10**

## CAKE

I love the rustic beauty of this cake, with the dense texture of the cake and creamy tart filling in the center. My great-aunt Agnes would make it and bring it to our family gatherings, an anticipated dessert by many of us. The gooseberry filling is our family favorite. Gooseberries are hard to find unless you have your own bush, however, so I have included alternate filling options. Rhubarb is a good substitute for gooseberries to give the sweet cake a tart balance in flavor. My second favorite filling is canned peaches that have been diced and folded into the whipped cream. The options to fill the cake are endless! Tante Agnes would double the recipe and bake it in 2 baking sheets to make sure there was always enough to go around. She would take home an empty platter every time. One recipe makes enough to bake in a 10 x 15-inch / 25 x 38-cm pan. Just double the recipe to bake in two sheet pans to feed a crowd.

- ½ cup / 125 ml butter or hard margarine, room temperature
- ½ cup / 125 ml sugar
- 4 egg yolks
- 1 teaspoon / 5 ml vanilla extract
- 1 cup / 250 ml flour
- 1½ teaspoon / 7 ml baking powder
- ¼ cup / 60 ml milk
- 4 egg whites, beaten
- ¾ cup / 175 ml sugar
- ½ cup / 125 ml sliced almonds, blanched

1. Preheat oven to 350° F / 175° C.
2. Cream butter and sugar until light and creamy.
3. Add egg yolks, one at a time, and mix thoroughly. Add vanilla.
4. Sift the dry ingredients together and add to creamed mixture, mixing alternately with the milk.
5. Pour into 2 9-inch / 22-cm round greased cake pans lined with greased parchment paper.
6. Beat the egg whites separately until soft peaks form, adding sugar a little at a time until sugar is dissolved.
7. Spread the egg whites over the cake batter.
8. Sprinkle the top with sliced almonds.
9. Bake for 25–30 minutes. Cakes should be golden brown and pull away slightly from the sides.
10. Remove cakes from the pans and cool completely.
11. Make your favorite filling and the whipped cream (see below).
12. Layer in the following order: 1 cake with meringue-side up, cooked filling, whipped cream, 1 cake with meringue-side up. If using fresh fruit instead of cooked fruit, fold it into the whipped cream.

## WHIPPED CREAM

- 2 cups / 500 ml whipping cream
- ¼ cup / 60 ml sugar
- 2 0.35-ounce / 10-g packages of whipping cream stabilizer

## OPTIONS 1 AND 2: GOOSEBERRY FILLING AND RHUBARB FILLING

- 3 cups / 750 ml frozen gooseberries or rhubarb, chopped
- 1 cup / 250 ml sugar
- 1 tablespoon / 15 ml cornstarch

1. Cook the frozen gooseberries in a medium saucepan until some pop open slightly. Add the combined sugar and cornstarch and cook for another 3–4 minutes, until mixture is thick and clear.
2. If using rhubarb, cook until soft, about 5 minutes. Then add combined sugar and cornstarch and cook as above.
3. Do not add water to either option. When cool, spread on cake and top with whipped cream.

### OPTION 3: FROZEN BERRY FILLING

➤ 3 cups / 750 ml frozen berries (blueberries, strawberries, or raspberries)

➤ ½ cup / 125 ml sugar

➤ 1 tablespoon / 15 ml cornstarch

1. Cook the frozen berries in a medium saucepan for about 5 minutes. Do not add water.
2. Combine the sugar and cornstarch.
3. Mix into the berries and cook for 3–4 minutes, until mixture is thick and clear.
4. When cool, spread filling on cake and top with the whipped cream.

### OPTIONS 4 AND 5: FRESH FRUIT

➤ 2 cups / 500 ml fresh fruit, or

➤ 1 28-ounce / 796-ml can of peaches, drained and diced

1. Fold either fresh fruit or canned fruit into whipped cream and spread on cake.

### OPTION 6: PASTRY CREAM

➤ 1 cup / 250 ml milk

➤ ¼ cup / 60 ml sugar

➤ 1 tablespoon / 15 ml cornstarch

➤ 1 egg

➤ ½ teaspoon / 2 ml vanilla extract

1. Heat milk until simmering, stirring constantly.
2. Mix together sugar, cornstarch, and egg.
3. Slowly pour a little of the hot milk into the sugar-egg mixture.
4. Pour egg-milk mixture back into the remaining milk and bring to simmer until slightly thickened.
5. Cool completely.
6. Mix in 1 cup / 250 ml cream, whipped with sugar and cream stabilizer.

*—Charlotte*

# GLUTEN-FREE *PASKA*

- 1 teaspoon / 8 g sugar
- 1 teaspoon / 5 g unflavored gelatin
- 2 tablespoons / 20 g regular yeast
- ¾ cup / 175 ml milk
- 3 eggs
- ½ cup / 110 g sugar
- ¼ cup / 60 ml oil
- 1 teaspoon / 5 ml vanilla extract
- ½ lemon, zest and juice

- ½ cup / 90 g millet flour
- ½ cup / 70 g tapioca starch/flour
- ¼ cup / 35 g white bean flour
- ¼ cup / 40 g brown rice flour
- ¼ cup / 30 g arrowroot powder/starch/flour
- ¼ cup / 30 g sweet rice flour
- 1 teaspoon / 5 g xanthan gum
- ½ teaspoon / 2 g baking powder
- ¼ teaspoon / 2 g salt

1. Mix together 1 teaspoon / 8 g sugar and gelatin and then stir into milk that has been warmed in the microwave. Stir in yeast and allow it to proof.
2. Beat eggs, sugar, and oil until fluffy.
3. Add vanilla and lemon zest and juice.
4. Add yeast mixture.
5. Blend together dry ingredients.
6. Add dry ingredients all at once to liquids, blend together, and then beat on high for 2 minutes.
7. Grease the sides of baking containers and line bottoms with parchment paper for easy removal. Spoon into prepared baking containers, not more than half full.
8. Let rise, uncovered, in a warm place until doubled in bulk, about ¾–1 hour. The *Paska* will rise more in the oven.
9. Bake at 350° F / 180° C for about 20 minutes or until quite brown. Do not underbake.
10. Let cool for a few minutes before removing from tins or pans.
11. Decorate with icing and sprinkles.
12. If not serving the same day, package and freeze.

### TIPS

- With gluten-free yeast baking, it is best to avoid doubling recipes. It is much better to make the recipe twice.
- It is best to freeze *Paska* not eaten within a day, but do not freeze longer than 1–2 weeks. Refresh by warming in the microwave.

*—Julie*

The traditional way to bake *Paska* was in food tins that were saved during the year. I used clean aluminum tins, muffin pans, and mini-loaf pans to bake the *Paska* in the photographs. You can also bake it in a medium loaf pan. If using tins, make sure they are BPA-free.

This *Paska* is very light, with good texture and excellent flavor. For my granddaughters, I always serve more icing on the side.

# *PASKA*

## YIELDS 5 LOAVES

- 2 tablespoons / 30 ml active dry yeast
- 1 teaspoon / 5 ml sugar
- 1 cup / 250 ml warm water
- 1 medium lemon
- 1 medium orange
- 1¼ cup / 310 ml milk
- ½ cup / 125 ml butter
- 2 large eggs
- ¾ cup / 175 ml sugar
- 1 teaspoon / 5 ml salt
- 7½–8 cups / 1.7–1.8 L flour

1. Mix yeast, sugar, and warm water in a large mixing bowl. Let stand for 10 minutes or until the yeast has formed a foamy top.
2. While the yeast is proofing, peel lemon and orange with a vegetable peeler. Place peels in a blender jar. Remove and discard the white parts of the lemon and the orange. Chop the lemon and the orange into quarters, discard the seeds, and add the chopped orange and lemon to the blender.
3. Heat milk and butter in a small saucepan over medium heat until the butter has melted. Add the warm milk and butter to the blender.
4. Blend on high speed for 2–3 minutes. The mixture will be frothy and light. Do not try to save time here; it is important that the citrus is puréed with only flecks of citrus showing when finished.
5. Add the eggs, sugar, and salt to the mixture. Blend for another minute or until very smooth.
6. Measure this mixture; it should be close to 4½ cups / 1.1 L. If you have a bit more or less, adjust the amount of flour used.
7. Add the liquid to the yeast mixture. Add the flour, 1 cup / 250 ml at a time. Do not add more than 8 cups of flour. It will be soft but the longer you knead it, the more manageable it becomes. Knead for 8–10 minutes either by hand or by machine with a dough hook until it forms a ball and the sides come clean in the bowl.
8. Transfer dough to a large bowl and cover with plastic wrap and a tea towel. Let rise until doubled, 1–1½ hours. Punch down and let rest at least 10 minutes or up to 1 hour.
9. During this time, prepare baking pans using cooking spray, shortening, or parchment paper. Make round, rectangle, or braided loaves and let rise until doubled in bulk, 1–1½ hours.
10. Preheat oven to 350° F / 175° C. Bake the loaves until golden brown. Check loaves after about 25 minutes. Each sized pan will take a different length of time to bake.
11. Cool on wire racks. Serve with *Paska* spread (recipe follows).

..................................................................................................

While this recipe was in our first cookbook, *Mennonite Girls Can Cook*, this continues to be our most-requested recipe—and it's the recipe that brought us all together. This recipe for *Paska* is light, soft, and moist, with the addition of a whole lemon and orange. Bake it in loaf pans or fill muffin tins, make into buns or form into a braid, ice and sprinkle to decorate . . . and be prepared to do it all over again before Easter is over! My beloved's Grandma Fast gave me this recipe, using these ingredients, and I modernized it using a blender and kitchen machine with a dough hook.

## PASKA SPREAD

- ➤ 1 cup / 250 ml butter, room temperature
- ➤ 2 teaspoons / 10 ml vanilla extract
- ➤ 4 pasteurized egg whites or the equivalent in pasteurized egg-white powder and water
- ➤ Icing sugar, enough to make a soft spreadable icing

1. Beat all ingredients together until light and smooth.
2. Spread on each slice of *Paska*. Sprinkle with colored sugar.
3. Store *Paska* spread in refrigerator.

*TIP*

- Store loaves in the freezer unless you are eating them the same day.

—*Lovella*

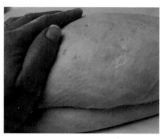

BREAD FOR THE JOURNEY

# WHAT MAKES A HOLY DAY A CELEBRATION?

*You prepare a table before me.*

—PSALM 23:5 (ESV)

{ *H*oliday. The word is so familiar on our tongues that our brains often make no cognitive connection between holiday and its root: *holy day*. Since *holy* means "set apart," a *holiday* is a day that is set apart from the other days in a calendar year. But set apart for what? By whom? For what purpose?

*Fully entering the spirit of the holy day requires love, joy, and thankfulness.*

Holidays are yearly memorials of something too important to forget. We celebrate to honor a person or an event that in some way touched us. Millennia ago, when he established his nation, Israel, God decreed holidays: days throughout the year that were to be set apart and celebrated, reminding the people of what God had done and what he promised. God called them "feast days," because what is a holiday without food?

As I was thinking about holidays and how they are celebrated, and about how traditions are built and memories are treasured, I realized that three key ingredients are necessary to make a holy day a celebration. Fully entering the spirit of the holy day requires love, joy, and thankfulness.

*Love.* When we think of holidays like Christmas, Valentine's Day, Easter, Mother's Day, and Father's Day, we see how love defines their expression. We plan our celebrations with others in mind— those we love and also those outside our family circle who are less fortunate or lonely. Celebrating love warms us from the inside out and satisfies a desire to make our world a better place.

*Joy.* Our own childhood memories and the children in our lives now embody the joy of celebration. Celebration without joy is

no celebration at all. As we plan the details that will make a celebration special, anticipation builds our joy. We think of bringing pleasure to those we love. No matter how old we are, celebrating brings out childlike joy.

*Thankfulness.* So much about a holiday stirs *thankfulness*! It is a time when we focus on the reasons we have to celebrate. We are thankful for family and loved ones to celebrate with. We are thankful that we have the ability to celebrate. We are thankful for freedom to celebrate!

Love, joy, and thankfulness are most meaningful when we recognize that all good things come from God: his love toward us, our joy in knowing him, and thankfulness to him for life itself! God's purpose for feast days—for *holidays*—is that we would remember the many ways that we are blessed and that God himself is the one who blesses.

Let us celebrate! Come . . . the food is ready. ✇

*God's purpose for feast days—for holidays—is that we would remember the many ways that we are blessed.*

**—Julie**

# CELEBRATING *Life*

From birth to the end of life, every day is a gift from God to be celebrated. At certain points on this journey, having others walk alongside us becomes critical. When we face illness in the family, find ourselves housebound, or lose a loved one, there's nothing more appreciated than a meal prepared with love and delivered to our door. Here are a few ideas for sharing a gift of love from your kitchen.

## CELEBRATE WITH

*Even to your old age I am he, and to gray hairs I will carry you. I have made, and I will bear; I will carry and will save.*

—ISAIAH 46:4 (ESV)

# BEV REFLECTS *on* LIFE

*O Joy that seekest me through pain,*
*I cannot close my heart to thee;*
*I trace the rainbow through the rain,*
*And feel the promise is not vain,*
*That morn shall tearless be.*

—GEORGE MATHESON, FROM "O LOVE THAT WILT NOT LET ME GO"

My life, like everyone else's, has been influenced by the passing of loved ones. My birth was interwoven with the death of my maternal grandfather. I was four months old when my parents received an urgent call to come to the hospital where Grandpa lay dying. They left home immediately, forgetting that I was asleep in my crib. After several miles they remembered that I was at home and frantically returned to get me. But by then they were too late to say their final goodbyes.

Growing up, I was never shielded from death. As part of a close church community, I often accompanied my parents to funerals. Over the years I have grieved the sudden and premature passing of family members and friends, and I have experienced the painful, long, drawn-out suffering deaths of others. When first my mother-in-law and then my mother passed away, however, I experienced the deep pain and sorrow of losing people who were very close to me.

*When I remember them and the many others who have gone ahead, I think of them as still living— just more fully and more joyfully than they ever did on earth.*

When I married and moved to British Columbia from Ontario, my mother-in-law, Ella, welcomed me as her own daughter. She unreservedly loved and mentored me. Ella died in 1996 at the age of seventy-five, after a year-long fight with cancer. I distinctly remember the heart-wrenching pain I felt when I realized she would not live. As I sobbed beside the door to her room, God reminded me that she was only going to a place I hadn't been yet. This brought me hope and assurance in the days and years following her death. I still miss her nurturing heart.

My parents had moved to British Columbia a few years earlier, and having my mom and dad close by helped to fill the void left by my mother-in-law's death. Then in 2008, my mother died. Her death came without warning. One day she and Dad celebrated their sixtieth anniversary; the next day, she walked with her friends, baked a rhubarb pie, and then slipped from vibrant life to death in the twinkling of an eye. I will never forget that day. My brother-in-law called with the news that Mom was gone. I was struck numb. My husband was away on

278

business, and I felt so alone. As I drove the few miles to Dad's house, I couldn't put my thoughts together enough to know what to do next. Reality disappeared, and denial and disbelief took its place.

After the funeral, my family had a decision to make. We as a family had planned to take Dad and Mom on an Alaskan cruise to celebrate their anniversary. The tickets were bought, and Mom's suitcase was half packed. After prayerful deliberation, we decided to go, and found it to be the perfect venue for being with Dad and remembering Mom. We left an empty chair at our dinner table each evening in her honor, and together we celebrated her life and legacy.

For a good part of the following year, I found myself distracted, unable to concentrate, and subject to sudden tears. My sister and I hovered over Dad, trying to lessen the shock for him. We got through that year, but as I remember, it was like we were in a fog, not seeing the way ahead.

I still think of my mom and Mom Klassen every day. I am sad that they have missed meeting several great-grandchildren and I wish I could call to invite them to lunch or to ask advice about a recipe. I cherish each memory and am so grateful to God for them. Today when I remember them and the many others who have gone ahead, I think of them as still living—just more fully and more joyfully than they ever did on earth. And I find, in surprise, that I can celebrate through my tears. ✎

*—Bev*

# CHICKEN POT PIES

## SERVES 8

## FILLING

- 6 tablespoons / 90 ml butter
- ½ cup / 125 ml flour
- 2½ cups / 625 ml chicken broth
- 1 cup / 250 ml milk
- ¼ cup / 60 ml sherry
- 3 carrots, diced
- 3 celery stalks, diced
- 1 teaspoon / 5 ml dried thyme, chopped
- 1 cup / 250 ml bell peppers, diced
- ¾ cup / 175 ml peas, fresh or frozen
- 2 tablespoons / 30 ml fresh parsley, chopped
- 2 teaspoons / 10 ml salt
- ½ teaspoon / 2 ml pepper
- 3 cups / 750 ml chicken, cooked and cubed

1. Melt butter in a saucepan and stir in flour until smooth. Add broth, milk, and sherry. Cook over medium heat until the mixture thickens.
2. Add carrots, celery, peppers, and thyme and cook until tender.
3. Add peas, parsley, salt, pepper, and chicken.
4. Set aside to cool.

## PIE CRUST

- 1½ cup / 375 ml flour
- ½ teaspoon / 2 ml salt
- ⅛ teaspoon / 0.5 ml pepper
- ½ cup / 125 ml butter, chilled and cubed
- ¼ cup / 60 ml shortening, chilled and cubed
- 4 tablespoons / 60 ml ice water
- 1 egg
- 1 tablespoon / 15 ml water

1. Preheat oven to 400° F / 205° C.
2. Combine flour, salt, and pepper in food processor.
3. Add butter, pulse 5 times to combine. Add shortening and pulse a few more times.
4. Slowly add ice water, 1 tablespoon / 15 ml at a time, pulsing after each addition, until dough sticks together.
5. Remove dough and shape into a ball.
6. Roll out dough and using one of the foil pans as a pattern, cut 8 circles to fit 8 5½-inch / 14-cm foil pans.
7. Fill foil pans with chicken filling and cover with cut circles of dough.

Chicken pot pies are great to pop in the freezer and thaw as needed. I freeze them baked, but you can freeze them unbaked and bake when needed; just remember to allow thawing time. This is a perfect meal to deliver to someone who needs a little encouragement or who is having a busy day. It will surely be appreciated.

8. Tuck in the edges and press down with a fork.
9. Brush with egg wash, made from egg whisked with 1 tablespoon / 15 ml water.
10. Bake for 30 minutes until crust is golden and filling is bubbly.
11. Cool 5 minutes before serving.

TIP

- New parents and those who are sick often receive numerous meals and can't always use them immediately. If you package up your meal for the freezer, labeling the package with the date and reheating instructions, the recipient can store it in the freezer until needed.

*—Betty*

# CHICKEN LASAGNA

## SERVES 8

- 8 lasagna noodles, cooked
- 4 cups / 1 L chicken, cooked and cubed
- ½ cup / 125 ml Parmesan cheese, grated
- 1 cup / 250 ml cottage cheese, creamed
- 2 cups / 500 ml white sauce (recipe below)
- ½ teaspoon / 2 ml salt
- ½ teaspoon / 2 ml pepper
- 1 cup / 250 ml spinach, finely chopped
- 1 cup / 250 ml cheddar cheese, grated
- 1½ cup / 375 ml mozzarella cheese, grated

1. Preheat oven to 375° F / 190° C.
2. Combine chicken, Parmesan cheese, cottage cheese, white sauce, salt, and pepper.
3. Spread half of the chicken mixture in a 9 x 13-inch / 22 x 33-cm baking dish.
4. Place half of the cooked lasagna noodles over the chicken mixture.
5. Cover with spinach and cheddar cheese.
6. Spread the other half of the chicken mixture over the spinach and cheddar cheese.
7. Top with the remaining lasagna noodles.
8. Sprinkle mozzarella cheese on top.
9. Bake for 40 minutes.

This is a nice change from the usual tomato-based lasagna. Wrap the dish in a basket with a fancy bow and bless someone with a ready-made meal.

## WHITE SAUCE

- ½ cup / 125 ml mayonnaise
- ½ cup / 125 ml plain yogurt
- 1½ cup / 375 ml evaporated milk
- ½ cup / 125 ml chicken broth
- 2 teaspoons / 10 ml dry mustard
- 2 teaspoons / 10 ml lemon juice

1. Combine all ingredients in a saucepan and cook on low heat for 5 minutes or until thickened, stirring constantly.

*—Betty*

# MEXICAN MEATBALLS

## SERVES 8

- 2 pounds / 1 kg ground beef
- 2 cups / 500 ml cornflakes, gently crushed
- 1 medium onion, minced
- 2 tablespoons / 30 ml ketchup
- ⅓ cup / 75 ml nonfat dry milk powder
- 1 garlic clove, minced
- Small handful fresh parsley, chopped
- 1 package taco seasoning
- 1 egg
- 2 tablespoons / 30 ml water

1. Preheat oven to 400° F / 205° C.
2. Mix together all the meatball ingredients in a large mixing bowl.
3. Line a baking sheet with parchment paper for easy cleanup.
4. Using a small, spring-loaded ice cream scoop, make meatballs and place them on the cookie sheet.
5. Bake for 15 minutes.

## SAUCE

- 1 tablespoon / 15 ml oil
- 10 large button mushrooms, sliced
- 2 10-ounce / 284-ml cans tomato soup
- 2 10-ounce / 284-ml cans mushroom soup
- 1 16-ounce / 500-ml jar salsa
- 2 cups / 500 ml cheddar or Mexican-blend cheese, shredded

This recipe has been a family favorite for years and has become a favorite in the homes of the next generation. Using common pantry ingredients, it is a tasty meal that is welcomed and easily rewarmed by those who need tender loving care.

1. Lower oven to 350° F / 175° C.
2. Fry mushrooms in oil in a medium skillet over medium heat until the mushrooms have released their liquid and begun to brown.
3. Add soups and salsa and bring to a simmer.
4. Add the cheese and stir to melt.
5. Pour the sauce into a large casserole dish, and add cooked meatballs. Cover and bake for 1 hour.
6. Serve over rice. Also serve with a bowl of tortilla chips to dip into the extra sauce.

*—Lovella*

283

# SZECHUAN CHICKEN BOWL

## SERVES 4

- 2 boneless, skinless chicken breasts
- 1 red bell pepper, cut into thin strips
- ½ cup / 125 ml carrots, cut into thin matchsticks
- ½ cup / 125 ml mushrooms, thinly sliced
- ¼ cup / 60 ml water chestnuts, sliced
- 1 cup / 250 ml snow peas
- 1 cup / 250 ml bean sprouts
- 1 cup / 250 ml chicken stock
- 2 tablespoons / 30 ml cornstarch
- 1 tablespoon / 15 ml fresh ginger, finely grated
- 1 garlic clove, crushed
- 2 teaspoons / 10 ml Asian hot chili sauce (optional)
- 2 tablespoons / 30 ml liquid honey
- 1 tablespoon / 15 ml rice vinegar
- 1 tablespoon / 15 ml sesame oil
- 3 tablespoons / 45 ml soy sauce
- 1 tablespoon / 15 ml black bean sauce
- 1 12-ounce / 340-g bag steam-fried noodles
- 2 tablespoons / 30 ml olive oil
- ½ teaspoon / 2 ml salt
- ½ teaspoon / 2 ml pepper
- 1 tablespoon / 15 ml fresh lime juice
- 2 green onions, white and green parts, thinly sliced
- 2 tablespoons / 30 ml sesame seeds, toasted (optional)
- Cashews or peanuts (optional)
- Chow mein noodles (optional)

1. Cut chicken breasts into thin strips and place in a bowl.
2. Wash, cut, and measure into separate bowls the red pepper, carrots, mushrooms, water chestnuts, snow peas, and bean sprouts.
3. In a glass jar, combine the chicken stock, cornstarch, ginger, garlic, Asian hot chili sauce, honey, rice vinegar, sesame oil, soy sauce, and black bean sauce. Shake vigorously until mixture is well combined and set aside.
4. Cook noodles according to package directions.
5. While noodles are cooking, heat olive oil in a frying pan or wok. Add cut-up chicken and stir-fry for 3–4 minutes.
6. Add salt, pepper, and lime juice.
7. Add red pepper, carrots, mushrooms, and water chestnuts, and continue to stir-fry for another 3 minutes.
8. Pour liquid mixture into the stir-fry, stirring well. Reduce heat to low. When mixture begins to thicken, add snow peas and bean sprouts and continue to stir-fry for 2–3 minutes.
9. Drain noodles and place in serving bowl.
10. Pour Szechuan chicken and vegetable mixture over noodles.
11. Top with sliced green onions. Pass around the optional toppings of toasted sesame seeds, cashews, peanuts, and chow mein noodles.

*—Kathy*

When we were going through a time of loss, our family was on the receiving end of meals arriving at the door and invitations to friends' homes for supper. These meals were such a help and encouragement during a difficult and busy time, and I have been able to pass the blessing forward to others in their times of need.

Sometimes guests may not be sure when they will be arriving, and this recipe will come in handy for those times. Earlier in the day, cut up and refrigerate the chicken and vegetables, and make the sauce. When your guests arrive, begin boiling the noodles and stir-frying the chicken. You'll be serving supper within fifteen minutes. For dessert, serve bowls of ice cream and freshly baked cookies. Package up some of the cookies and send them home with your friends.

This soup became a family favorite as turkey vegetable chowder, but it has evolved into a soup that uses store-bought rotisserie chicken and can be cooked quite quickly. If you make it along with French bread (page 291), it is the perfect meal to take to a family in need. Deliver one large jar of soup and a loaf of French bread to someone else, and have plenty of soup and another loaf of bread left for dinner at home.

# CHICKEN VEGETABLE CHOWDER

## SERVES 8

- 1 rotisserie chicken
- 8 cups / 2 L chicken broth
- 2–4 carrots, sliced
- 3 stalks celery, including tops, chopped
- 4–5 medium potatoes, cubed
- 1 large onion, chopped
- 1 teaspoon / 5 ml fresh basil, chopped
- 1 teaspoon / 5 ml fresh oregano, chopped
- 1 teaspoon / 5 ml fresh thyme, chopped

- 2 teaspoons / 10 ml salt
- ¼ teaspoon / 1 ml pepper
- 1 14-ounce / 398-ml can cream-style corn
- 1 12-ounce / 341-ml can whole kernel corn
- 1 14-ounce / 398-ml can sliced green beans
- ¼ cup / 60 ml flour
- 2 cups / 500 ml milk
- 1 cup / 250 ml cheddar cheese, grated
- Fresh parsley, chopped

1. Remove meat from bones of chicken and cut into bite-sized pieces.
2. Bring chicken broth to a boil.
3. Add carrots, celery, potatoes, onion, basil, oregano, thyme, salt, and pepper. Simmer for about 20 minutes or until vegetables are tender.
4. Add corn, beans, and chicken pieces.
5. Using a wire whisk, combine flour and milk. Stir mixture into soup.
6. Add grated cheese and cook, stirring constantly, until soup returns to a boil.
7. Cook several minutes longer to melt cheese and thicken slightly.
8. Sprinkle with parsley.

*TIP*

- Use dried herbs if fresh are not available.

*—Judy*

# HONEY BRAN BUNS

## YIELDS ABOUT 3 DOZEN

- 1 cup / 250 ml wheat or oat bran
- ⅓ cup / 75 ml honey
- ½ cup / 125 ml oil
- 2 cups / 500 ml boiling water
- 1 teaspoon / 5 ml salt
- 2 eggs, beaten with fork
- 6 cups / 1.4 L flour (can use half whole wheat)
- 1 tablespoon / 15 ml instant yeast

1. Combine bran, honey, oil, boiling water, and salt.
2. Cool until lukewarm.
3. Add beaten eggs to lukewarm bran mixture.
4. Add 3 cups / 750 ml flour along with dry yeast, stirring and adding more flour until it becomes difficult to stir. Knead in remaining flour until dough is soft but no longer sticky.
5. Place in a large greased bowl, turning once to grease all the dough.
6. Cover with a tea towel and put in oven with the oven light on for about 40 minutes or until doubled in size.
7. Punch down dough and shape into buns. Cover and let them rise on a greased or parchment-lined baking sheet for another 30–40 minutes.
8. Bake at 375° F / 190° C for about 15–18 minutes, until golden.

*—Charlotte*

These are light, slightly sweet buns that make a nice addition to any meal that you are delivering to someone. I usually bring extra buns so that the recipient can use them with another meal or for sandwiches the next day.

Before making a meal to bring to a friend, take a trip to your local thrift store and buy a couple of inexpensive casserole dishes. I have found several very pretty ones with lids for under five dollars. Use one of these instead of a foil pan and let your meal recipients know that they do not need to return the dish. At a thrift store I have also found wire baskets, which are perfect for carrying meals.

This creamy casserole is real comfort food. It could be accompanied by a bag of salad, a jar of pickles, or a loaf of bread and a simple dessert.

# ROSEMARY POTATO SAUSAGE CASSEROLE

## SERVES 8–10

- 2 tablespoons / 30 ml butter, divided
- 1 medium onion, thinly sliced
- 2 cups / 500 ml fresh mushrooms, sliced
- ¼ cup / 60 ml butter
- ¼ cup / 60 ml flour
- 1½ cup / 375 ml milk
- 1 tablespoon / 15 ml fresh rosemary, finely chopped
- Salt and pepper to taste
- 5 medium potatoes, peeled and thinly sliced
- 1 link smoked sausage (approximately 1½ pound / 675 g)
- 1½ cup / 375 ml cheese, grated

1. Preheat oven to 350° F / 175° C. Butter a 9 x 13-inch / 22 x 33-cm glass or ceramic baking dish or 2 6-cup / 1.35-L round casseroles.
2. In a frying pan, sauté onion in 1 tablespoon / 15 ml butter over medium heat until caramelized. Set aside.
3. In the same pan, add another tablespoon / 15 ml butter and sauté mushrooms. Set aside.
4. Make a white sauce by melting ¼ cup / 60 ml butter in microwavable bowl or in a saucepan on the stove. Add flour and blend well. Add milk a little at a time, mixing until smooth. Microwave 1 minute at a time, stirring after each interval until it thickens. Or stir constantly on stove until thickened.
5. Add rosemary and salt and pepper to taste. Stir well and set aside.
6. Layer half the sliced potatoes in the baking dish.
7. Top the potatoes with all of the onions and mushrooms.
8. To prepare sausage, remove skin and slice into ¼-inch / .5-cm slices.
9. Cover the casserole with a layer of sausage slices and ladle half of the sauce over it all.
10. Top with the rest of the potatoes and arrange the remaining sausage slices on top.
11. Cover with the rest of the sauce and top with grated cheese.
12. Bake for 1 hour or until potatoes are done.

*TIPS*

- A mixture of cheddar and mozzarella cheeses works well in this recipe.
- Use farmer sausage or garlic sausage for a nice flavor.

*—Bev*

# HAMBURGER SOUP

## YIELDS 14 CUPS / 3 L

### HAMBURGER

- 1 tablespoon / 15 ml olive oil
- ½ cup / 125 ml onion, chopped
- 1½ pound / 750 g ground beef
- ½ teaspoon / 2 ml salt
- ¼ teaspoon / 1 ml pepper

### SOUP

- 1 tablespoon / 15 ml olive oil
- ½ medium onion, chopped
- 2 cups / 500 ml carrots, sliced
- 2 cups / 500 ml new potatoes, diced
- 1 jalapeño pepper, diced (optional)
- 4 cups / 1 L beef stock
- 1 28-ounce / 796-g can crushed tomatoes
- 1 15-ounce / 398-g can black beans, drained and rinsed
- 1 garlic clove, crushed
- ½ teaspoon / 2 ml dried thyme
- ½ teaspoon / 2 ml dried oregano
- ½ cup / 125 ml fresh parsley, chopped
- Salt and pepper to taste

1. In a stock pot, heat 1 tablespoon / 15 ml olive oil on medium heat and add chopped onion. Sauté until onion is soft.
2. Add ground beef, salt, and pepper to the onion and cook until ground beef is no longer pink.
3. Drain the hamburger, remove to a bowl, and set aside.
4. In the same stock pot, add olive oil and heat over medium heat.
5. Add onion, carrots, potatoes, and jalapeño pepper. Cook until softened, about 3–5 minutes.
6. Return cooked ground beef to the stock pot.
7. Add remaining ingredients and bring to boil.
8. Lower the heat and simmer for 30–60 minutes.
9. Taste and add more salt and pepper if needed.

*TIP*

- To make this recipe gluten free, use gluten-free beef stock. ⓖ

*—Ellen*

This soup is hearty and, with the added vegetables, could be a main dish served with crusty bread. Enjoyed by young and old alike, this soup freezes well and travels well. A salad can be added but is not necessary.

# CHEESE-STUFFED BREADSTICKS

## YIELDS 20–24 BREADSTICKS

### BREAD

- 2 tablespoons / 30 ml sugar
- 2 tablespoons / 30 ml oil
- 2 teaspoons / 10 ml salt
- 2 cups / 500 ml hot water
- 4–4½ cups / 1 L flour (can be a mix of white and whole wheat)
- 2 tablespoons / 30 ml instant (quick-rise) yeast

### CHEESE FILLING AND TOPPING

- 3 cups / 750 ml cheese, shredded
- 1 egg
- 2 tablespoons / 30 ml milk
- 2 tablespoons / 30 ml Parmesan cheese, finely grated
- 1 teaspoon / 5 ml dried oregano or basil
- 1 garlic clove, crushed (optional)

1. Line an 11 x 17-inch / 28 x 43-cm baking sheet with parchment paper.
2. Put first 4 bread ingredients into a mixing bowl or a stand-mixer bowl. Stir in 2 cups / 500 ml flour mixed with the yeast.
3. Mix until well combined and then add remaining flour, ½ cup / 125 ml at a time, until dough can easily be shaped into a ball. If using a stand mixer, use a dough hook.
4. Divide in half. Roll first half out on a floured surface, to the approximate size of the baking sheet. Dust with flour and roll up on a rolling pin; then unroll onto baking sheet. Stretch into shape as needed. Sprinkle with shredded cheese.
5. Roll out second half a bit larger than the first half, and dust with flour. Roll onto rolling pin and unroll on top of cheese. Fold sides under the bottom layer. Cut through the dough with a pizza cutter to create 20–24 pieces. Cover with a tea towel and let rise 20–30 minutes.
6. In a small bowl, whisk together the egg, milk, Parmesan cheese, oregano, and garlic. Brush evenly over dough.
7. Bake in a preheated 425° F / 220° C oven for about 15 minutes, until breadsticks are light golden in color. If a bubble pops up while baking, break it with a fork or knife.
8. Cut along original lines to separate. Serve warm with soup. Can also be frozen and used for packed lunches.

*TIP*

- Mozzarella, cheddar, or a mix of cheeses works well for these breadsticks.

A good friend gave me this French bread recipe many years ago. Over the years, I have found it to be the easiest and most versatile bread recipe. I have used it for pizza crust, pizza buns, focaccia bread, cinnamon buns, and, most recently, these cheese-stuffed breadsticks. My favorite meal to take to someone needing a meal is a fresh-baked loaf of French bread or cheese-stuffed breadsticks with a large jar of soup.

## FRENCH BREAD
**YIELDS 2 LOAVES**

Follow instructions for breadsticks to step 3, and allow bread dough to rise for about 30 minutes. Divide in half. Roll out each half to a 12 x 15-inch / 30 x 38-cm rectangle. Roll up jelly-roll style and place on greased or parchment-lined baking sheet. Cut diagonal slits on top. Cover loosely with plastic wrap and a tea towel. Let rise 30 minutes. Brush with plain egg wash, if desired, and bake at 400° F / 205° C for 20 minutes.

## PIZZA BUNS
**YIELDS ABOUT 2 DOZEN BUNS**

Follow instructions for breadsticks to step 3, and allow dough to rise for about 30 minutes. Divide in half and roll out each half to a 12 x 15-inch / 30 x 38-cm rectangle. Spread with a thin amount of spaghetti sauce and a good sprinkling of shredded cheese, along with some dried oregano and basil. Roll up, cut as for cinnamon rolls, and place about 1 inch / 2.5 cm apart on a parchment-lined baking sheet. Let buns rise for 45 minutes; then bake at 400° F / 205° C for 15–20 minutes. Pizza buns are great for lunches.

*—Anneliese*

# OLD-FASHIONED CRUMB CAKE

### YIELDS 9 PIECES

- 1 cup / 250 ml sugar
- ¾ cup / 175 ml butter, softened
- 2 cups / 500 ml flour
- 1 teaspoon / 5 ml baking soda
- ¼ teaspoon / 1 ml ground cloves
- ¼ teaspoon / 1 ml nutmeg
- ½ teaspoon / 2 ml cinnamon
- 1 egg
- 1 cup / 250 ml buttermilk

1. Preheat oven to 350° F / 175° C.
2. In a medium bowl, cream the butter and sugar with a mixer on medium speed.
3. Add the flour and continue to mix until fine, even crumbs form.
4. Set aside 1 cup / 250 ml of mixture for the cake topping.
5. Stir baking soda and spices into the remaining crumbs.
6. In a small bowl, beat the egg until foamy, add buttermilk, and stir to combine.
7. Add the liquid ingredients to the dry ingredients, stirring gently to combine.
8. Spread the batter into a greased 8 x 8-inch / 20 x 20-cm baking pan. Sprinkle the set-aside crumbs evenly on top of the batter.
9. Bake for 50 minutes or until a toothpick inserted into the center of the cake comes out clean.

*—Lovella*

This moist, simple spice cake is one that my mother-in-law, Pauline, often made over the years. It is perfect for serving with a cup of tea but also makes a wonderful small cake to pack and share, especially with the re-usable foil baking pans with lids that are now available.

# BAKED RICE PUDDING

**SERVES 6–8**

- 3 large eggs
- ½ cup / 125 ml sugar
- ¼ teaspoon / 1 ml salt
- 1 teaspoon / 5 ml vanilla extract
- 2 cups / 500 ml milk
- 1¾ cup / 425 ml cooked rice
- ¾ cups / 175 ml raisins
- Dash cinnamon

1. Preheat oven to 325° F / 160° C.
2. Whisk eggs, sugar, salt, and vanilla together in a bowl.
3. Add milk, cooked rice, and raisins. Mix well.
4. Pour into a greased 9 x 9-inch / 22 x 22-cm pan.
5. Place the dish into a larger pan that contains 1 inch / 2.5 cm hot water.
6. Bake for 30 minutes. Stir rice pudding and bake for another 40 minutes. A knife inserted in the middle should come out clean. Do not overbake.
7. Sprinkle with cinnamon and serve warm.

*—Betty*

This rice pudding is a classic comfort food. Curl up in a blanket in front of the fireplace with a good book and a bowl of rice pudding. Truly comforting! Or fill up a pretty jar and you have a perfect gift to give a friend. Freshly baked biscuits pair wonderfully with this rice dish.

# PIES-*in*-JARS

## SERVES 15

This recipe makes 15 pies-in-jars in 3 different flavors: 5 pumpkin-gingersnap, 5 lemon-graham, and 5 vanilla-ladyfinger. The cream layer goes on the pumpkin and lemon "pies," and the whipped cream topping goes on all 15.

## CREAM LAYER
## (FOR PUMPKIN-GINGERSNAP AND LEMON-GRAHAM)

- 2 cups / 500 ml whipping cream
- 1½ cup / 375 ml icing sugar
- 8 ounces / 250 g cream cheese, room temperature
- 2 teaspoons / 10 ml vanilla extract

1. Whip cream until stiff, add icing sugar, and beat just until combined.
2. In another bowl, beat cream cheese until creamy and then blend in vanilla.
3. Gently whisk half of the sweetened whipped cream into the cream-cheese mixture. Set aside the other half to use as a topping for the 15 jars before serving.
4. Divide cream-cheese mixture in half: one half for the 5 pumpkin-gingersnap jars, and the other half for the 5 lemon-graham jars.

## PUMPKIN-GINGERSNAP

- ¾ cup / 175 ml gingersnap cookie crumbs, processed until fine
- 1 tablespoon / 15 ml butter, melted
- ½ cup / 125 ml milk
- 1 cup / 250 ml pumpkin purée
- 1 4-serving / 102-g box instant vanilla pudding
- 1 teaspoon / 5 ml cinnamon
- ¼ teaspoon / 1 ml ground ginger
- Toasted pecans for garnish

1. Pour melted butter over gingersnap cookie crumbs and mix until crumbly.
2. Spoon evenly into 5 jam jars. Set aside.
3. Put all remaining ingredients (except pecans) into a medium bowl. Whisk for 2 minutes. The mixture will be quite thick.
4. Spoon half of the cream layer on top of the gingersnap cookie base in the 5 prepared jam jars.
5. Cover with a layer of pumpkin mixture.
6. If serving right away, pipe some of the whipped cream on top and garnish with toasted pecans.
7. Screw lids on jars and store in refrigerator.

I loved serving dessert in these delightful little jam jars. Mini-jars are just the right size to serve to small children. Take the time to make extra and deliver a few of these pies to bring a bit of cheer to someone.

## LEMON-GRAHAM

> 2 cups / 500 ml prepared lemon pie filling
> Graham cracker crumbs

1. Spoon half of the cream layer into 5 jam jars.
2. Add a layer of lemon pie filling, followed by a layer of graham cracker crumbs.
3. Top with reserved whipped cream.
4. Screw lids on jars and store in refrigerator.

## VANILLA-LADYFINGER

> 2 cups / 500 ml prepared vanilla pudding
> Ladyfingers

1. Crumble pieces of ladyfingers in the bottom of 5 jam jars. Cover with a layer of vanilla pudding.
2. Top with reserved whipped cream and fresh berries.
3. Screw lids on jars and store in refrigerator.

*TIP*

- These "pies" can be prepared the day before serving. If you do so, omit the whipped cream until ready to serve.

*—Betty*

295

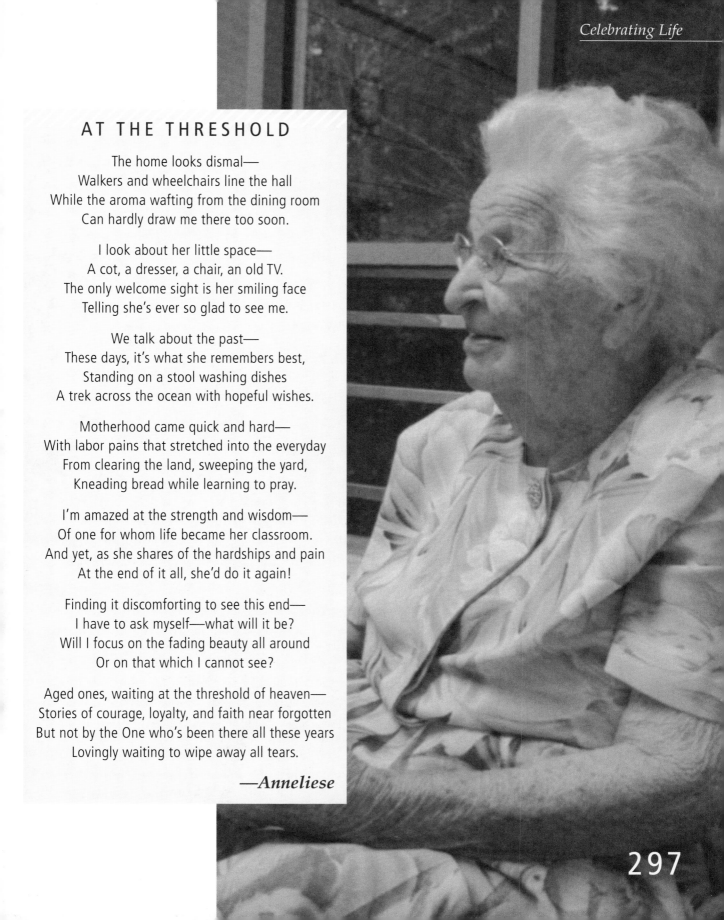

## AT THE THRESHOLD

The home looks dismal—
Walkers and wheelchairs line the hall
While the aroma wafting from the dining room
Can hardly draw me there too soon.

I look about her little space—
A cot, a dresser, a chair, an old TV.
The only welcome sight is her smiling face
Telling she's ever so glad to see me.

We talk about the past—
These days, it's what she remembers best,
Standing on a stool washing dishes
A trek across the ocean with hopeful wishes.

Motherhood came quick and hard—
With labor pains that stretched into the everyday
From clearing the land, sweeping the yard,
Kneading bread while learning to pray.

I'm amazed at the strength and wisdom—
Of one for whom life became her classroom.
And yet, as she shares of the hardships and pain
At the end of it all, she'd do it again!

Finding it discomforting to see this end—
I have to ask myself—what will it be?
Will I focus on the fading beauty all around
Or on that which I cannot see?

Aged ones, waiting at the threshold of heaven—
Stories of courage, loyalty, and faith near forgotten
But not by the One who's been there all these years
Lovingly waiting to wipe away all tears.

—*Anneliese*

# *the* MARRIAGE SUPPER *of the* LAMB

*But when the goodness and loving kindness of God our Savior appeared, he saved us, not because of works done by us in righteousness, but according to his own mercy, by the washing of regeneration and renewal of the Holy Spirit, whom he poured out on us richly through Jesus Christ our Savior, so that being justified by his grace we might become heirs according to the hope of eternal life.*

—TITUS 3:4-7 (ESV)

{One moment on July 8, 1965, holds a memory so clear that even though no video camera captured the event, my mind's eye recalls the scene perfectly. My older brother, Gerry, had just returned from summer Bible camp, where he had accepted Christ as his Savior. As a six-year-old, I had been attending Sunday school for four years and knew the many Bible stories taught there. Flannelgraph characters designed for little ones like me captivated my mind and brought the stories to life. Vivid depictions of Moses crossing the Red Sea; Abraham preparing to sacrifice his son, Isaac; Noah finding dry land after the flood; and King David seeking God's own heart: all these stories had a common thread. Out of thankfulness or in need of forgiveness, the people in them built altars to God. They often sacrificed a lamb to atone for their sins.

The love and holiness of God were woven through each lesson, and celebrations in church and our home reinforced all that I had been taught. Each evening in the weeks leading up to Christmas Day, we sat around the Advent candles and sang carols as a family. These songs reminded me of how the world waited for a Savior to be born. Then on Christmas Day, we celebrated the birth of Jesus, the perfect Lamb of God who would become the ultimate and final sacrifice. At Easter we remembered how Jesus Christ, fully God and fully human, lived a sinless life, died on the cross, and rose from the grave to give people eternal life.

Although I did not understand the fullness of the gospel on that July day, I realized that I wanted to follow Christ and accept his gift of forgiveness. Finding the only room in the house with a door to lock, I knelt alone beside the bathtub and simply prayed that Jesus would forgive all my sins and come into my heart. That day, my name was written in the Lamb's book of life, and my destiny was sealed. Joyfully, I shared my newfound faith with my family and began a relationship with my Lord and Savior.

*There is nothing I can add to what Christ endured on the cross for my sins. All that I do comes from a thankful heart.*

The years have flown by, and the more I understand God's love for me, the more I am motivated to live a life that honors him. Without God's grace and mercy, I would be eternally lost. I've learned difficult lessons from poor choices along the way, and I continue even now to struggle in some areas. As a little girl, I would sometimes feel sick to my stomach because I needed to say I was sorry for being naughty. Mom would crouch down and, with tears in her eyes, tell me I was forgiven. That example stays with me. Since then, I have sometimes had sleepless nights because I have needed the forgiveness of family and friends. How, then, could I possibly hold a grudge against someone needing *my* mercy and forgiveness?

There is nothing I can add to what Christ endured on the cross for my sins. All that I do comes from a thankful heart. Dad often prayed that our family circle would not be broken in heaven. As a parent and grandparent, I now understand how nothing on earth compares to that desire for our family and friends to have the assurance of eternity in heaven. Revelation 19 describes the marriage supper of the Lamb, a feast to which we are all invited.

As one who is naturally sentimental about precious items and special memories, I know that none of those things will matter in that moment when God calls me home and I see my Savior face to face. While my life on earth will be celebrated by the loved ones I leave behind, I will be fully alive with those who have gone on before me, in a celebration of life and of the Lamb for all eternity. ❧

—*Lovella*

## HOW GREAT THOU ART

And when I think that God his son not sparing,
Sent him to die—I scarce can take it in,
That on the cross my burden gladly bearing,
He bled and died to take away my sin:

Then sings my soul, my Savior God, to Thee,
How great Thou art, how great Thou art!
Then sings my soul, my Savior God to Thee,
How great Thou art, how great Thou art!

When Christ shall come with shout of acclamation
And take me home—what joy shall fill my heart!
Then I shall bow in humble adoration
And there proclaim, my God how great thou art!

Taken from "How Great Thou Art" by Stuart K. Hine. © 1949 and 1953 The Stuart Hine Trust. All rights in the U.S.A. except print rights administered by EMI CMG. U.S.A. print rights administered by Hope Publishing Company, Carol Stream, IL 60188. All rights reserved. Used by permission.

# GLUTEN-FREE COOKING

$A$ s recently as five years ago, a puzzled expression was the immediate response of most people hearing the words *celiac* or *gluten*. Today that is changing as the awareness of this disease is growing. In Canada, for example, it is estimated that 1 in 133 people have celiac disease.

Celiac is an auto-immune medical condition that prevents the small intestine from absorbing nutrients. Gluten's irritation of the small intestinal wall allows food toxins that would otherwise be eliminated as waste to escape into the body and cause severe damage. Cancer or other medical conditions can result.

There is no cure, but the disease can be totally controlled by a life-long avoidance of gluten. Gluten is the protein found in wheat, rye, and barley. It is this protein that triggers the body's immune system to turn on itself.

Gluten-free recipes for main dishes, desserts, and breads in this cookbook are indicated with ⓖ. (Please note that all of the beverage recipes in this book are also gluten free.) Because the success of gluten-free baking depends on consistent and accurate measurements, this book includes the weight (in grams) conversions for dry ingredients in many of the gluten-free recipes. Additionally, many more recipes in the book can be adapted for people with celiac disease by carefully reading labels and choosing gluten-free ingredients. For example, make the Nanaimo Bars with gluten-free graham-like crackers and use gluten-free mayonnaise for the West Coast Chicken Salad Sandwiches and Egg-Filled Spirals (listed under Tea Sandwiches).

## SEARCHING FOR GLUTEN

Simply avoiding gluten-containing flours is not enough. A person with celiac disease must read every single label because of "hidden" gluten. For example, there is gluten in malt, soy sauce, and many packaged foods. Chewing gums can be dusted with gluten, too.

Restaurants, while much more celiac-friendly and knowledgeable than they used to be, are still a challenge for those on a gluten-free diet. French fries may or may not be coated with gluten. Some chefs coat plain rice and potatoes with gluten. Sauces and gravies and soups are often thickened with flour.

Oats, while they do not contain the offensive gluten protein, are cross-contaminated because oats are grown as alternate crops in wheat fields. There are, however, gluten-free oats available, which have been grown in virgin fields.

There is a huge list of alternate gluten-free flours that can be substituted for wheat, rye, and barley—and the wonderful advantage is that these flours are full of rich vitamins, protein, and minerals that have been processed out of wheat flour. The disadvantage is that without the gluten, which is what gives us that wonderful elastic quality in breads, baking with gluten-free flours requires a completely new way of doing things.

*It may seem overwhelming to invite people with celiac for dinner, but following a few simple rules makes it quite doable.*

Terminology for gluten-free flours can also be confusing for cooks. Ground tapioca can be referred to as *tapioca starch* or *tapioca flour*; both refer to the same product. Ground arrowroot can be referred to as *arrowroot powder*, *arrowroot starch*, or *arrowroot flour*; again, all these terms refer to the same product. We have chosen to use the terms *tapioca starch/flour* and *arrowroot powder/starch/flour* to signal that, although manufacturers don't agree on terminology, these words refer to the same ingredients. But be careful: potato flour and potato starch are two different products. Learning to cook gluten-free recipes takes some time, but it's worth it.

## GLUTEN-FREE ENTERTAINING

It may seem overwhelming to invite people with celiac for dinner, but following a few simple rules makes it quite doable. Serving food that is naturally free of gluten is the easiest way to go—homemade soups, meat dishes, casseroles, vegetables, and fruit are always great. Also, there are many pre-prepared gluten-free foods or mixes available now in grocery or health-food stores. ✍

*—Julie*

# HOSTING TIPS

*A*s people who love to extend hospitality, we often compare notes on how to make hosting gatherings less stressful for us and more relaxing for our guests. The list of ideas below is not at all exhaustive; rather, it includes simple, common things that have become our way of blessing those who enter our homes.

When possible, plan your menu in advance and make a grocery list that is as complete as possible.

If you are not familiar with your guests' dietary needs, ask them in advance to be sure they can eat what you put on the table. Gluten, nuts, and dairy are common allergies.

If you are hosting a large group, allow others to bring dishes to share. Keep the menu simple for larger groups. Salads are especially good for others to bring, since they don't require last-minute cooking.

Hosting guests for meals several days in a row is easier when you consider that the house only needs to be given touch-ups in between guests. Many recipes can be kept several days without any deterioration in quality or flavor. A large freezer dessert can be made early in the week. A pot of soup keeps well for several days for a soup course. Wash all the vegetables at one time and put them in separate bags for each meal.

Set your table early in the day. Prayerfully consider where to seat your guests, and then pray for each person who will be seated in that chair.

Do as much as possible early in the day. Wash salad greens and chop vegetables early and keep them refrigerated separately. Toss and dress just before serving.

307

Use ovenproof dishes for serving the meal. Most foods keep well in a warm oven while you wash cooking pots. Having your counters tidy when guests arrive will help you to feel relaxed.

Slow cookers are not only good for cooking main courses but are also useful for keeping food hot, allowing roasters to be cleaned up ahead of time.

Check your bathroom to be sure there is enough toilet tissue. Put out clean hand towels and ensure there is adequate soap, bathroom spray, and hand lotion.

Empty the dishwasher and the garbage cans in the kitchen and bathroom.

Toss used tea towels and dishcloths in the clothes hamper, and place a fresh dishcloth and tea towel beside the sink.

If young children are coming over, create a relaxed atmosphere around the table by putting a paper runner under the plates and have crayons available for coloring. Allow children to run and play once they have all finished their meals. Remember what it was like to be a child!

When your guests arrive, give them a warm welcome at the door. Encourage all your guests to join the conversation by asking questions about their interests and family life. If they are interested, be willing to share about your own.

If you want to give your guests an opportunity to cook with you, be organized and have food prepped and neatly stored.

Unless there are activities planned after the meal is finished, there is no need to rush. Take time between courses to change conversation topics.

Remove dinner plates and cutlery and place them directly into the dishwasher while you prepare coffee and tea and plate the dessert. It gives guests a chance to find room for their dessert.

Prepare as best as you can in advance, but when things go wrong, remember not to take yourself too seriously. If you find yourself running late, offer your guests something to drink or a simple appetizer, and give yourself the time you need without a lot of explaining. They may be grateful for some time to relax and visit before rushing to the table.

Hospitality can be very simple and last minute. Soup and sandwiches are a great combination to serve for those spur-of-the-moment invitees!

If you don't have time to tidy as much as you hoped, put a few fresh flowers on the table. Every effort, no matter how small, will make your guests feel special.

Treat your guests like family and treat your family like guests.

Thank God for those around your table and pray for blessings on them and their families.

# INDEX

# THE AUTHORS

## LOVELLA SCHELLENBERG

Lovella Schellenberg enjoys farm life together with her husband, Terry, near the west coast of British Columbia. Having been married thirty-five years, they are enjoying this season of their life with both sons married and the blessing of daughters-in-law and five delightful grands.

Lovella and Terry's passion for seeing marriages thrive has filtered down to their involvement together in a pre-marriage mentoring capacity at Northview Community Church.

They love camping near the beautiful coastal beaches and in the mountains. Picking ripe produce from her vegetable garden, taking in the fragrance of fresh roses, and watching storm clouds reminds her that she is surrounded by God's beautiful creations and blessings.

## ANNELIESE FRIESEN

Anneliese Friesen and her husband, Herb, have made their home in the beautiful Fraser Valley of British Columbia, where they have raised three children. They are the proud grandparents of eight sweet grandchildren.

Together they have been involved in various ministries related to care and hospitality for over thirty years. She is now in what she calls the fall season of her life, enjoying the vibrant colors of the changes this season has brought with it. Her desire is to encourage younger women in their roles as wives and mothers, being grateful to her Lord and Savior for his wonderful provision for such a time as this.

## JUDY WIEBE

Judy Wiebe lives with her husband, Elmer, in the Fraser Valley of British Columbia, where she is involved in the family dairy farm operation. Her three grown children, their spouses, and her delightful grandchildren live nearby.

Judy enjoys spending time in the great outdoors, creating things in her kitchen or sewing room, and traveling whenever possible. But her favorite times are those spent with friends and family. She attends Central Community Church in Chilliwack.

## BETTY REIMER

Betty Reimer and her husband, John, live in Steinbach, Manitoba. She and her husband owned and operated a farm and garden equipment business for twenty-eight years and are now retired. They are blessed with two daughters, one son, one son-in-law, and four grandchildren.

Betty attends Evangelical Fellowship Church. She loves spending time with her family and friends and enjoys baking, reading, gardening, and traveling.

## BEV KLASSEN

Bev Klassen works with her husband, Harv, in a home-based business in Rosedale, British Columbia. They have three married children and seven grandchildren who bless their lives daily. Bev enjoys cooking and entertaining, and she and Harv often host family and friends in their home.

Bev's favorite activities are taking pictures, reading, gardening, and making cards. She and Harv do a lot of traveling for business and pleasure— either by car or on the back of a motorcycle. Greendale Mennonite Brethren Church has been her church home for forty years.

## CHARLOTTE PENNER

Charlotte Penner lives in Winnipeg, Manitoba, with her husband, Tony. She is the mother of two daughters, one son, and one son-in-law. They attend Douglas Mennonite Church and are involved in a variety of ways. She enjoys being with family and friends, attending Bible study, ministering to those who are hurting, and demonstrating spontaneous hospitality. "Come as you are" is Charlotte and Tony's motto.

Charlotte likes to cook and bake, and there is always room for more around her table. She has a special gift with her hands and uses them to serve others.

## ELLEN BAYLES

Ellen Bayles lives in the Seattle area with her husband, Greg. She was born and raised in the Los Angeles area and completed her education there with a bachelor of arts degree in home economics and a fifth year to earn her elementary teaching credential. She was an elementary school teacher until her first child was born.

Ellen and Greg raised two sons and a daughter, and they have a daughter-in-law and son-in-law. Ellen enjoys homemaking, traveling, and photography. She and Greg are members of Northshore Baptist Church in Kirkland, Washington.

## JULIE KLASSEN

Julie Klassen was born and raised in the Fraser Valley of British Columbia where she married, lived, and worked—never far from a sewing machine—until health challenges demanded life changes. Several years ago, Julie and Vic, her husband of forty-seven years, moved to Chilliwack and are now both enjoying retirement.

They live within walking distance of their daughter, son-in-law, and two beautiful granddaughters. Julie enjoys spending time with family and friends as well as reading, writing, baking, sewing, and leading a weekly Bible study group with her husband.

## KATHY MCLELLAN

Kathy McLellan grew up on Vancouver Island, British Columbia, where she met her husband, Scot. They have been married for thirty-five years and they have two married daughters and five grandchildren aged two to seven years old.

Kathy and Scot can often be found camping in some of British Columbia's most beautiful spots. If you ever happen to find them at their campsite where family and friends gather, you will see their unique way of cooking, taking the ordinary to the extraordinary. Their joy in serving is through random acts of kindness in unexpected places. Scot and Kathy are members of Promontory Community Church in Chilliwack.

## MARG BARTEL

Marg Bartel was born and raised in the Fraser Valley of British Columbia. She met her husband, John, at a farm sale, and together they continued a farming career. Later in life, when farming no longer demanded her strong support, Marg decided to continue her education and completed her baccalaureate degree, thus giving her new opportunities to work outside the home.

Marg is a sports enthusiast and enjoys traveling. She also enjoys the opportunity to be actively involved in the life of her family, friends, community, and church (Central Community Church in Chilliwack).

# Praise God from Whom All Blessings Flow

Rev. 5: 13

**OLD HUNDRED L. M.**

Thomas Ken, 1695

Guillaume Franc, 1543
Genevan Psalter, 1551

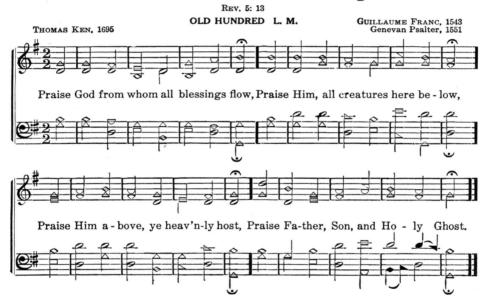

Praise God from whom all blessings flow, Praise Him, all creatures here be - low,

Praise Him a - bove, ye heav'n-ly host, Praise Fa-ther, Son, and Ho - ly Ghost.